Praise for *Lifting as They Climb*

"*Lifting as They Climb* is a beautiful tribute and testimony to the labor and care of Black Buddhist women who, in the very spirit of the Buddha, continue to show us how to get free."

—Lama Rod Owens, author of *The New Saints: From Broken Hearts to Spiritual Warriors*

"Toni spotlights the transformative stories of remarkable black women who have embraced Buddhism, weaving together spirituality and collective liberation. A compelling exploration of their journeys, this book celebrates the intersection of personal growth and societal change. Toni's work is an inspiring tribute to the resilience and profound impact of these women."

—Devin Berry, Dharma teacher and cofounder of Deep Time Liberation

"Toni Pressley-Sanon has written a unique and poignant account of Black Buddhist women stewarding a subtle yet fierce movement of liberation, not only for herself but for a multitude of Black women embarking on their meditative journeys. As a seeker, Toni graciously allows us to witness her personal voyage of spiritual growth by elevating the voices of contemporary scholars, practitioners, and Dharma teachers. Honoring the intricate intersections of race, gender, and Buddhism, this book assures readers they are welcomed, embraced, and valued in their individual and collective path of practice, just as they are."

—Noliwe Alexander, Dharma teacher and founder of Peace At Any Pace

LIFTING AS THEY CLIMB

BLACK WOMEN BUDDHISTS AND COLLECTIVE LIBERATION

Toni Pressley-Sanon

SHAMBHALA

Shambhala Publications, Inc.
2129 13th Street
Boulder, Colorado 80302
www.shambhala.com

Cover art and design: Katrina Noble
Interior design: Katrina Noble
Photo of Osho Zenju Earthlyn Manuel courtesy of Vaschelle Andrè.

9 8 7 6 5 4 3 2 1

First Edition
Printed in the United States of America

Shambhala Publications makes every effort to print on acid-free, recycled paper. Shambhala Publications is distributed worldwide by Penguin Random House, Inc., and its subsidiaries.

Library of Congress Cataloging-in-Publication Data
Names: Pressley-Sanon, Toni, author.
Title: Lifting as they climb: Black women Buddhists and collective liberation / Toni Pressley-Sanon.
Description: Boulder: Shambhala, 2024. | Includes index.
Identifiers: LCCN 2023011357 | ISBN 9781645470762 (trade paperback)
Subjects: LCSH: Women in Buddhism. | Women—Religious aspects—Buddhism. | Buddhist women—Biography.
Classification: LCC BQ4570.W6 P74 2024 | DDC 294.3092/52 —dc23/eng/20230505
LC record available at https://lccn.loc.gov/2023011357

I had crossed the line. I was free; but there was no one to welcome me to the land of freedom. I was a stranger in a strange land.

—Harriet Tubman

Are you sure, sweetheart, that you want to be well? . . . Just so's you're sure, sweetheart, and ready to be healed, cause wholeness is no trifling matter. A lot of weight when you're well.

—Toni Cade Bambara, *The Salt Eaters*

Contents

Acknowledgments

There is a Haitian proverb that says *Men anpil, chay pa lou,* "When the hands are many, the load is light." I have certainly found this to be true. Although it is my name on this book, bringing it forth to the world has taken the care and support of many souls.

There are, of course, the women who are the subjects and, equally important, the inspiration for this work: Dr. Jan Willis, Dr. bell hooks, Osho Dr. Zenju Earthlyn Marselean Manuel, Rev. angel Kyodo williams, Spring Washam, and Faith Adiele.

I thank Osho Zenju for taking me on as a student. My deepest bows. My dharma siblings of Still Breathing sangha hold a huge place in my heart. Thank you for holding space for me to bring all of myself.

When COVID-19 drove all of us indoors, many meditation centers began offering sangha online; some providing sanctuary for BIPOC folks to come together in community. Spirit Rock Meditation Center was one that began the lifeline tradition of offering BIPOC sangha every Sunday morning. Through that sangha I have found many brilliant teachers, including Dr. Margarita Loinaz with whom I was able to enter into life-transforming deeper study. I am profoundly blessed to be her student.

The Spirit Rock sangha has been facilitated by, first, Maria Cristina Tavera and then emiko yoshikami, holding the space so beautifully for all of us. Alongside Spirit Rock, Insight Meditation Society's Monday night BIPOC sangha has been a source of incredible soul healing. I can never thank enough the teachers and visionaries who fought hard for these refuges to be created. May they continue and grow well into the future so that others may benefit from the balm that they are.

Before COVID-19 hit, I signed up to participate in a Deep Time Liberation retreat with Noliwe Alexander, Devin Berry, Rosetta Saunders, and DaRa Williams. Doing what we have always done, these four extraordinary people and their team pivoted to make it happen on Zoom. They created sacred space and a sense of belonging even as we sheltered in place. Beyond that, remembering a different way of doing things from a place of love and community-building, they continue to offer periodic gatherings for those of us who have been part of the retreat. I am deeply grateful.

I thank the women who have paved the way for this work: Pamela Ayo Yetunde, Cheryl Giles, and Valerie Vimalasara Mason-John, whose edited books have broken new ground. I also thank Rima Vesely-Flad, whose brilliant exploration of Black Buddhists and the Black radical tradition engages and opens up many important conversations. Thank you for inviting me to read and comment on your work. It was an honor and a privilege.

I thank Peace Twesigye at Union Theological Seminary for being such a lovely host, and Claudine Michel for showing up to support me and drop a note in the chat. It means the world. I also thank dear Claudine, my tonton Patrick Bellegarde-Smith in his ready adoption of me, and LeGrace Benson and Gina Ulysse for modeling the way this kind of work can be done.

Thank you to the University of Mexico, Vera Cruz and the Women and Gender Studies Program under the leadership of Maria-Jose Garcia, a powerhouse, who invited me to share this work when it was still in its infancy.

Thank you to Raoul Peck who encouraged me to take a different approach to my work. My editor, Matt Zepelin, gently and tirelessly helped me mold this work into what you hold in your hands. His calls for "more Toni" and insightful questions and suggestions helped me dig deeper than I knew was possible. There is no one else I would've wanted to work with on this.

Almost finally, I am deeply grateful to my December 2022 Lotus Vine Journeys family!! From Yugo, who told me that I would find a way to make it to Costa Rica after Spirit Airlines canceled my flight; to Rodney, who reminded me to remember myself; to Darryl, who watched over me and covered me in blankets; to Spring and Fito, who sang for me. Tone for your wisdom teachings and for holding me up when I couldn't even. Thank you, Darsheel Kaur, for modeling a different way of being in the world. Thank you to my cushion sisters, whose voices let me know I was doing it right. Much love to Montez Freewoman, whose declaration of freedom helped me declare my own. Deep gratitude to Tyger Oshumaré and all ya'll who laid those healing hands on me when it was time for me to let it all go. Thank you to brother R. Earl Harris for your wonderful stories. Thank you to Ramses Amun, whose Kemetic yoga and music supported my moving the energy through. Matan and his wonderful partner kept our bodies nourished. There are no words to express my deep, deep gratitude to Spring for your vision, your teachings, your sense of humor, and your hugs. Harriet was definitely there with us.

Thank you, Amani Will, for the music that greeted us on the other side and the beauty you bring to the world.

There are people who were there with me from the beginning, like my sister, Lisa. And there are those who feel like they've been there from the beginning: my amazing son, Ruby; my sister-friends Ama, Nazalima, Glennie, and M-J—without you there would be no me. Thank you to Sharonda Purnell, the owner of Cocoa Healing Collective, for giving me a place to lay my weary body and spirit down.

Thank you to my beloved, David. I'm so grateful to have finally found you.

Finally, I'm grateful for my wonderful EMU students, who make me want to be and do better, and to my dedicated colleagues.

Finally, finally deep gratitude to Spirit, who continues to speak to and through me; and to Mother Earth for her unconditional Love.

Preface

Seeking Sanctuary—A Personal Journey

I came to meditation over a decade ago during a difficult time in my life. I had been through eight years of grueling graduate work and was rewarded with my doctorate degree, the first in my family. After a year of postdoctoral work in a competitive program at a prestigious university, I was one of the lucky ones who landed a tenure track position at a research university. Life was supposed to be good. But it wasn't. One year after starting my new job, my only child left for university many miles away. I had nothing much going on in my personal life except working on several book and article manuscripts simultaneously and teaching. And while both writing and teaching were sources of great joy, as intrinsic parts of the publish-or-perish culture of research universities they were also sources of huge stress. Though surrounded by people, I felt deeply isolated. I drank a potful of coffee in the morning and, more times than I can count, a bottle of wine at night. I often fell asleep in my living room because every time I closed my eyes, anxious thoughts would send my heart racing. I was deeply unhappy. I was lonely. I felt lost, adrift.

As someone who had adopted the mantra "There's always another way" several years before, I went looking for a solution. My search for relief led me to one of the many meditation apps that have proliferated in recent years, and there I began my journey toward ease from my suffering. After several months, what started out as a challenge—to sit with the app for just thirty seconds without jumping out of my skin—became a welcome respite from my racing mind and heart. Gradually I fell in love with the practice, extending the following of my breath in and out until I was soothed by the simpleness of it; until there was no longer *doing* but rather *being*. The noises that threatened to swallow me would sometimes actually quiet, and I have maintained a pretty consistent practice since I first hit play, back in 2011.

After several years of practicing alone, I began to want to dive deeper and be in community with other seekers. When in 2015 I moved to a new city that hosts several Buddhist meditation centers, including one based in the Zen tradition, I joined a sangha, a Sanskrit term for spiritual community or beloved community. I entered the meditation hall excited, eager to continue my journey within but now in community with other like-minded and, more importantly, like-hearted beings. But as I took my seat and looked around at the other meditators, I began to experience an uneasiness in the midst of what, on the surface, seemed like calm. The nature of the disquiet I experienced is easily guessed, as similar sentiments have been voiced by many other people: I did not see myself reflected in those around me.[1] I still felt very much alone. What was missing was a feeling of community. The leadership and the overwhelming majority of the practitioners were white. And even though there were a few other practitioners of color, I didn't connect with them. As such, I did not feel like I could bring my whole self to that environment.[2] This is where the "like-heartedness" came in.

Indeed, the whole time I attended Sunday morning services I felt like a "brown spill on a white carpet," as Katie Loncke, the former director of the Buddhist Peace Fellowship, so aptly describes it.[3] I remember one particular morning when, as usual, following our thirty minutes of silent meditation, we all arranged ourselves before the dais on which sat the teacher-in-training, a young white woman. Within a few minutes of settling onto my cushion, I found myself already frozen on the outside—and experiencing full fight-or-flight mode internally—as she stood and read a passage from the Bhagavad Gita, a seven-hundred-verse scripture considered to be one of the holy scriptures of Hinduism, about dreadlocked hair and its relationship to wisdom.[4] I became deaf to the message, overshadowed as it was by the burning in my ears and the heat working its way up my face. Even though I don't recall anyone turning to look at me, as the lone Black woman in the room with long flowing locks, I sensed a shift in the surrounding energy as I tried to appear "normal." I couldn't help but wonder if that passage had been chosen just for me. Was it the teacher's attempt to make me feel acknowledged and welcomed? Or had she not even considered who might be in the room? Had she thought about the passage's potential to cause harm when she chose it? (After all, the text is ancient.) Was it possible that because I was born and have lived in the United States for most of my life, a good part of it among majority white people, that I read something into what was simply coincidence? The thing is, I will never have answers to any of my questions because there was no one in the sangha with whom I felt like I could talk about what I was thinking and feeling.

After a couple more incidents—pregnant silences and awkward conversations—one morning, having had enough of feeling like I was integrating a space of kind, well-meaning people who just didn't know what to do with me, I unceremoniously got up from my cushion and made my way out of the meditation hall, never to return.

That was when the true journey began—to see and be seen, to witness and be witnessed, and to testify as a Black woman to feeling deeply connected to the teachings of the Buddha in a way that respectfully acknowledges and accounts for my embodiment. This is all because I understand that it is through *this* body that I experience this life. And it is through this body that I experience my awakening. This book is my offering to those who, like me, know in their bones that they deserve freedom and have wanted desperately to see themselves reflected in those who have found it.

LIFTING AS THEY CLIMB

INTRODUCTION

How We Do

IN HER 2018 tongue-in-cheek-titled article "Why Are There So Many Black Buddhists?" the gender and environmental studies scholar J. Sunara Sasser writes, "As numerous writers have noted, many Buddhist sanghas in the United States are largely white. Practicing in these spaces is often an isolating experience where people of color feel erased and invisible, or at times so hypervisible that simply being in the room invites assumptions that they will educate others about race."[1] Before walking into a meeting of the Nichiren Buddhist organization Soka Gakkai—the Buddhist lay tradition from Japan that boasts the largest number of members of color in the United States—Sasser had been to many meditation centers, most practicing Zen, Shambhala, or Vipassana traditions. Nine times out of ten, she was the only Black person in the room. And although the experience was common for her, she never became comfortable with it. She writes, "From the stares of other practitioners to the frustratingly obtuse mindfulness teachings that ignored the reality of the racialized body and attendant social injustices—I'd had enough."[2]

Following my first sangha experience, in a midwestern college town Zen temple, where I felt all of the things that Sasser describes—erased and invisible, yet at times hypervisible—I too had had enough. But because the nearest Soka Gakkai group was forty-five minutes away from where I lived, it did not really feel like an option. So, as I had been doing since 2011, when I began my meditation practice, I kept up my solitary sitting and read voraciously on the Buddha's teachings. I thought it was enough. But then I read Zenju Earthlyn Manuel's *Tell Me Something about Buddhism: Questions and Answers for the Curious Beginner* in which Zenju (Osho to her students), a Sōtō Zen priest, explores in a question-and-answer format many of the issues around embodiment with which I had been grappling. Early in the text, she explains the importance of the sangha in such a clear way that, upon reading it, I felt compelled to take a momentary break from the page; I needed to close my eyes and reflect on her words.

After informing the curious beginner that sangha members have "come together with an expressed willingness to deal with their suffering and its impact on others," she tackles the "stuff," the baggage that people bring with them into the meditation hall—first and foremost, "an expectation that all will be good in the land of meditation." She continues, "We expect the ground beneath Sangha to be stable and strong when, in truth, we are together in the confusion and challenge of living awake." As is true in any situation in which people have come together, conflicts and misunderstandings arise. Blame for one's discomfort is sometimes placed on the practice forms, other sangha members, the teachers, or even oneself. Osho Zenju counsels the importance of acknowledging that one's feelings are valid, but she holds that it is equally important to investigate those feelings. Rather than run away, one can stay and carry out the investigation "in the midst of the troubled souls, the Sangha, that one has chosen to commune with." She then asks the first of three all-important questions: "You could leave and find another community, but what happens for you when the earth begins to shake beneath the new Sangha in the same way as it did underneath the Sangha you left?"[3]

Osho Zenju invokes the original meaning of the word *sangha* as "beloved community," a term also used by the Reverend Dr. Martin Luther King Jr. to highlight our interconnectedness—that we are joined together in a single garment of destiny. What touches us individually impacts us collectively. Osho Zenju states, "In Sangha based on the teachings, you are reminded that you are not alone on the journey."[4] She also reminds us that we are mirrors for each other's suffering and awakening. Our sangha siblings "assist us by reflecting back to us the ways in which we respond to the events of life."[5] Following her explication of the ways that our sangha friends aid in our growth, she finishes with the second and third all-important questions, which I find even more pointed. In response to those who have told her that they do not need sangha, she asks, "Then where will you go when you begin to experience liberation?" and "Who will know the journey you have taken and your vow to be awake?"[6]

Her words emphasize for the curious beginner the importance of belonging to a community of like-minded *and* like-hearted people in a society in which the vast majority do not wish to wake up to our individual and collective suffering. She also teaches that the path to liberation is so much sweeter when undertaken in community. Finally, she alludes to the *body's* role in one's awakening—something that she explores in several of her other writings. The questions Osho Zenju poses and the declarations she makes are particularly prescient to people of African descent who attend majority white sanghas.

I open this book with my experience reading Osho Zenju because she points so directly and compassionately to the issue of embodiment on the spiritual path. The importance of the body to Black women Buddhists as a tool and vehicle of liberation is our starting point because all too often, instead of seeing ourselves reflected in our fellow seekers, we experience the sangha as a microcosm of the alienation and isolation that we endure in a nation founded on white male supremacy. Unfortunately our exclusion as true and equal members of the beloved community of the "United States" is mirrored in majority white sang-has of which they are part and parcel. In such spaces, instead of experiencing an alleviation of suffering—our reason for seeking refuge—we experience an intensification of it.

It would seem that those of us who opt out of majority white sanghas have not yet spiritually matured to a place where we can "get over" our bodily preoccupations as we strive for enlightenment. However, a close reading of and deep listening to Osho Zenju and the other women whose work I explore in this project reveal that they are not saying that at all. Rather, unlike many white convert Buddhist communities, they, as the mindfulness teacher and social justice advocate Konda Mason reminds us, insist that those of us who were born into these bodies in this country bring *all* of ourselves to our practice. This "all in" position is necessary if we are to experience full and whole liberation in the present moment.

It is true that many of us—people of color broadly and Black people in particular—seek respite and refuge from white supremacy in spaces where we are affirmed. The relief found in sangha (beloved community) where we see ourselves reflected in our fellow practitioners and in our leaders, where we hear music that stirs our souls and listen to dharma talks that tell our stories, fortifies us to continue the work of individual and collective liberation.

When we do not have to navigate and negotiate the Buddha's teachings through the lens of the dominant culture, we are able to look inward and remember to remember our innate Buddha nature. We have access to a more direct line to our individual awakening as inextricable from those in the meditation hall with us. There is then a natural, inevitable movement outward to wish those on the other side of the meditation hall wall access to that awakening. And, borrowing from the wisdom of preflight airplane announcements, only after we have seen to our own freedom do we begin in earnest the work of attending to the liberation of others.

The women whose work I discuss in this project take us on their journeys to show us the path to our own awakening. Clearly they are guided by the Buddha's teachings. Equally, for some, they are guided by their Christian upbringing, their blood ancestors and spiritual ancestors, the African American autobiographical tradition of witnessing and testifying, and by their embodied experience. They bring all of themselves to their practice and to their teaching.

I have felt myself transformed by meditation—how the seemingly simple act of focusing on my in-breath and my out-breath offers me spaciousness even while living within a society that would have me contract, to the point of stopping my breathing. And yet I, along with millions of others, descendants of ancestors who were held captive on this land out of time, continue to breathe. We breathe for ourselves, we breathe for them, we breathe for those who are yet to arrive. We recognize and realize our interconnectedness. In doing so, we free ourselves from the delusions of separation, greed, and hatred that continue to hold so many of our minds and spirits captive and that are at the root of much of our suffering.

My aim in this book is to explore the message of liberation that contemporary women of African descent offer in their unique ways and through their bodily and spiritual lenses. I see their work as a legacy of our ancestors who for centuries used their voices, pens, and bodies to advocate for our individual and collective physical, mental, and spiritual freedom.

Although it may seem that the Buddhist women whose work I explore in this project speak and write through a spiritual tradition that is foreign to them, in fact they are continuing a long tradition of adopting and adapting spiritual teachings that resonate with our experience. We find it in African diasporic people's adaptation of religious systems that were imposed upon us under slavery and that we deployed in the service of freedom. This practice can be found in the US context, for example, in Nat Turner using the Bible to fuel his organized resistance to slavery and in Bishop Richard Allen's adaptation of Christianity to found the African Methodist Church. It is also evident in the Caribbean and Latin, Central, and South America in the syncretizing of the Catholic saints of the colonizers with the African ancestors and spirits who, having made the Middle Passage journey with their descendants and adherents, flowed into new spiritual traditions. Candomblé practiced in Brazil, Vodou in Haiti, and Santería in Cuba are evidence of these innovations. Mason speaks to this tradition of adoption, adaptation, and creation in her remarks about The Gathering II, the second national assembly of Black Buddhist teachers and practitioners, which took place at Spirit Rock Meditation Center in California in fall 2019. There she said,

> When Black people come together, we do it the way we do it. Our ancestors are always with us. When blackness and the buddhadharma come together, that intersection is a whole other buddhadharma. It's the tenets of the Buddha without a doubt, but our cultural mashup is something that is uniquely ours and involves celebration, music and ancestors. It involves all of who we are. We don't leave anything outside the door.[7]

Indeed, in Black people's ongoing pursuit of our bodily and spiritual liberation, we bring our full selves. In fact, the work of liberation demands that we bring our whole selves both to the cushion and beyond. As such, we light candles and pour libations for those ancestors known and unknown. We bring the Buddha alongside Harriet Tubman, Frederick Douglass, Nina Simone, Alice and John Coltrane, Audre Lorde, and James Baldwin to the circle—those who journeyed, who gifted themselves as conduits to our physical and spiritual liberation. This book relies on the writings and utterances of six Black women Buddhist practitioners and teachers to explore the many ways they carry on the legacy of their ancestral freedom seekers. In it I think through how they bring not only their blackness (with all of the history that comes with it) but also their womanness (with all of the weight and connection that that designation and identification carries) to their spiritual practice.

I begin with Jan Willis's autobiography, *Dreaming Me: Black, Baptist, and Buddhist—One Woman's Spiritual Journey*, which tells of her journey from a childhood of racialized trauma in the southern United States to become a leading scholar of Buddhism. Her writing has been invaluable to my putting my own experience as a woman of color, albeit from the north in the late twentieth century, into perspective.

I continue with bell hooks, well known for her writings on a number of subjects, including feminism, love, and cultural production. Although her Buddhism is not as well known as other aspects of her life, she wrote and spoke extensively about her Buddhist practice and offered an expansive way of being with and practicing the dharma. I conduct a close reading of her biomythography, *Bone Black: Memories of Girlhood*, and one of her last offerings, *Belonging: A Culture of Place*, in relation to several of her other writings as examples of her commitment to contributing to humanity's collective liberation.

Osho Zenju is my teacher, and her work has been immensely instructive for me. Through close readings of several of her texts, all of which contain autobiographical elements, I explore her expressed need for her racialized, gendered, sexualized, and aging body and "attendant social injustices" to be validated and addressed from within her dharma practice. As she states, attending to her full self has enabled her to move from the wounded tenderness resultant from living in the US to arrive at a place of loving, healing tenderness.

I begin my chapter on Zen priest Rev. angel Kyodo williams with her first book, *Being Black: Zen and the Art of Living with Fearlessness and Grace*, which reads for me like a love letter to African Americans. I then explore the work that she does with her coauthors of *Radical Dharma: Talking Race, Love, and Liberation* and with her organization,

Liberated Life Network. I see her work with Liberated Life and other organizations as a moving beyond writing and talking to enacting a commitment to ushering all who are interested into our individual and collective liberation.

I then read the meditation teacher and healer Spring Washam's *A Fierce Heart: Finding Strength, Courage, and Wisdom in Any Moment* as an example of her willingness to enter the fire of transformation in order to bring back the gift of spiritual liberation to all who choose that path. Part of what is interesting about Spring's way of communicating the wisdom of the dharma, infused as it is with her humor, is that it hits lightly at first. This style makes her work approachable, and with her guidance, the dharma in all of its depth becomes accessible to broad audiences.

Finally, I discuss the former Buddhist nun Faith Adiele's *Meeting Faith: The Forest Journals of a Black Buddhist Nun*. To me, this book speaks most directly to the sense of hypervisibility and invisibility that Black women experience in majority white sanghas. Her writing helped me see that such sanghas, as microcosms of larger American society, share in our society's founding on white supremacy and othering.

All six of these women provide us with candles for the darkest parts of our souls until we can light those flames ourselves. There is an implicit trust—evidenced by the fact that they write and keep writing, speak and keep speaking—that we will find the light that is already within us. They act as guides to those who are on the path, fully embodied, not just for themselves but for the liberation of all beings.

In doing close readings of these women's work, I hope to elucidate the ways that their truth-telling is an inheritance of the African American tradition of speaking truth to power in the service of Black people's liberation as a condition of universal collective liberation. *Lifting as They Climb* explores how these women's work draws from the ancient African philosophy of *ubuntu*, a philosophy based on the premise that

8

"I am" *only* because "we are."[8] As the literary scholar James Ogude explains, "Ubuntu is rooted in . . . a relational form of personhood, basically meaning that you are because of the others . . . as a human being, you—your humanity, your personhood—you are fostered in relation to other people."[9] Contrary to western individualism, the concept of ubuntu encourages forging and strengthening one's relationship with their community and upholding and honoring that relationship.[10] This spirit of ubuntu has sustained African Americans for centuries and continues to do so.

As I explore in detail in part two of this book, these women carry on the legacy of nineteenth-century African Americans who, having won their own freedom from slavery, went on to risk that freedom in order to pen their autobiographies. These brave souls understood, first, that their own freedom was hard won and always in jeopardy, and second, that it was circumscribed by the system of slavery that not only continued to operate in the American South but permeated the entire country's economy, culture, and politics. Finally, although they had managed to free themselves from their physical chains, thousands of their siblings remained fettered. The women whose work I explore in these pages, likewise, understand that the system of white supremacy on which this country was founded and that endures continues to circumscribe Black life. As such, they understand that their freedom is inextricably bound up with the vast majority of us who remain ensnared by the delusions that keep this system in place. An underlying premise of this project is that the women who are its focus, like their literary ancestors, have a foundational commitment to collective liberation as inextricable from their own.

Disruptions and Connections

Although it started off from a place of "business as usual," this project has transformed into one that is unlike any that I have undertaken.

In fall 2019, months after I had finished a draft of this manuscript, I accepted an invitation to contribute to an anthology on the work of the Haitian filmmaker Raoul Peck. Because he is one of my favorite artists and I have written about his work before, I was happy to do so. Just after the anthology was published, I received an email from Raoul, who had learned about it from a friend of his. Without going into the details of his gently rendered admonishment, I will say that my most important takeaway from the email was that it was not okay for me to continue with business as usual. It was not okay for me to write about the living without their consent or input. I am a Black woman who professes to be invested in Black liberation. Raoul pointed out my hypocrisy.

I immediately knew that there was no way I could continue with this project without giving the women about whom I was writing a say in it. So, with my heart in my throat, I emailed each woman and asked them if they would be interested in reading their individual chapters. Jan Willis was the first to respond with not only a yes but a decision on her part (unbeknownst to me) to introduce me and my work to an editor at Shambhala Publications. Osho Zenju also not only said yes but she too (unbeknownst to me) contacted the editor at Shambhala. She then invited me into conversation about the project and beyond. Spring Washam also said yes and scheduled a Zoom meeting with me to answer any questions that I might have. Faith Adiele, in her characteristic generously playful way, also said yes and offered questions in the manuscript to support my discussion of her work. Although I never heard back from Rev. angel, I attend Liberated Life's gatherings on a regular basis. For the past few years I have come to joyfully anticipate New Year's Eve because it means gathering together in community from about 10 p.m. EST, New Year's Eve, until 1 a.m. New Year's Day in Rev. angel's invitation to be fully present to life. I also never heard back from bell hooks. Although I hoped for a response, I didn't really expect one. It was only in December 2021 when I learned of her passing that I understood that she had been ill.

Part of my resistance to reaching out to these women comes from my training as an academic, where we're encouraged to work alone and to come out on the other side "the expert." There was also my ego, which it turns out is really big. And there was huge vulnerability in sharing what I wrote with the people I was writing about. What if they hated it?! What if they didn't want me to write about them? What if their chapters came back covered in red with demands for major revisions? What if I had to scrap the whole project after devoting at least a year of my life to it? In fact, none of my fears were realized. Rather than being constricting, inviting these women into the process of shaping this project has been expansive. I have been held in love and also held accountable in ways that I never have been before. That sense of love and accountability has brought into relief the freedom that comes out of working in community rather than in isolation or secrecy. I saw that if I was committed to telling our own stories, as I profess to and as Raoul encourages, then I needed to start from a position of transparency. I needed to work with an openness to truly living into the interrelatedness of the women whose stories I wanted to uplift as well as with those who would pick up this book. This commitment to transparency also led me, with my editor's gentle encouragement, to include much more about myself in this book than I initially had—again, not the standard approach in academic writing. Although sharing freely from my own life story feels vulnerable, I do so throughout the book to show how much resonance and guidance I have found in these women's lives and writings. It is my humble attempt to join them in their courageous commitment to opening paths for others.

All of this opening happened during COVID, when we were forced to slow down, to turn inward, to reflect, and to be bold in our reevaluation of our priorities. In that sense, it was a good time to consider what gives us life. Over the past few years, spending time in these women's company in person, over Zoom, and through their writings has invigorated my commitment to the goal of freedom. I think it's also no accident that the call for me to rethink the way that I went about this project came from Raoul. Raoul is from Haiti, the first Black republic in the world—a title earned from an enslaved people's revolution when every country surrounding it was in the throes of colonial brutality. Haiti is my soul home, a place that sings to me all the time. Here, once again, she had called me home to myself.

I am grateful to my global ancestors who have brought me to this place. I am grateful to these women who have so generously shared their stories. I am grateful to have found Black women who, in acknowledging and testifying to their particular embodied suffering as well as documenting their path to awakening, have given me and others like me permission to acknowledge our own suffering and to find our liberation through it. I am grateful that these women have written and spoken about their experiences with the Buddha's teachings from their unique perspectives. Their generosity has gifted us with lamps in the darkness of our own paths to liberation—lamps that will be passed on to future generations. May all beings benefit from this offering.

PART ONE

1

JAN WILLIS

Carrying On the Tradition

THE HEROINE'S JOURNEY often grows out of a deep dissatisfaction with the circumstances and conditions with which she is faced. The heroine looks to connect to something greater than herself to realize her life's purpose. She also understands that she must leave the dis/comfort[1] of her home in order to undertake the trials and learn the lessons that are necessary for her to return to her community—in whatever ways she envisions it—to make it better. She is intimately aware that the lessons she learns are not to be hoarded but must be shared with others who might benefit. It is the dis/comfort that sends her out into the world, and it is her commitment to collective liberation that brings her home, transformed and ready to teach others what she has learned.

This chapter is devoted to the work of Jan Willis, whose life exemplifies the heroine's journey. At a time when the vast majority of African Americans identified as Christians or members of the Nation of Islam, Willis decided to study Buddhism. She has been central to shaping the field of Buddhist studies and to highlighting the voices of

African American Buddhists in the United States.[2] The writer Emily Cohen has called her "an illuminating example of the richness that is brought to spiritual practices and religious traditions when women of color have a space and place to center their stories and voices."[3] More than that, for Black women like me, Willis stands as a beacon of possibility for forging one's own path.

Although she was raised in the South and I in the North twenty years apart and with significant differences in our journeys, I immediately recognized much of myself in Willis's life—especially her struggles and triumphs as a light-skinned, intellectually precocious Black woman whose childhood and adult life have involved facing up to America's racism and engaging in an intense search for true belonging. Neither of our stories are over. I am relatively new to Buddhist teachings and even newer to the possibility of embracing my multiple spiritual identities. Although Willis's autobiography—*Dreaming Me: Black, Baptist, and Buddhist—One Woman's Spiritual Journey*, which forms the focus of this chapter—ends at a point when she has made peace with her inherited Baptist faith and her adopted Buddhist practice, she continues to teach, publish, and evolve as a human being. In the African American tradition of lifting as we climb, she supported this project in ways that I can only hope to pay forward as my own journey continues.

Jan Willis: A Brief Biography

Janice Dean Willis was born in Ensley, Alabama, in 1948, the younger of two daughters of Oram Willis, a steelworker and deacon in the local Baptist church, and Dorothy "Dot" or "Dor-thay" Willis, a homemaker. As a child in the South, Willis faced one primary challenge: being born a light-skinned African American. Her skin was so light that her paternal origins were called into question, and throughout her childhood she carried the burden of being nicknamed "white gal" because of it. But she was not, of course, taken as a "white gal" by the local white community.

As an African American in what she has described as "the most segregated city in America at the time," she was repeatedly subjected to Jim Crow racism and its concomitant threats and enactments of violence.[4]

In 1950, Willis's parents bought a home in Docena, Alabama. A year later, her father's parents, Belton and Jennie, bought a house on the same street; the following year, her uncle Lamar bought a house next to theirs. As such, even though the threat of white violence was ever present, Willis grew up with a sense of relative safety.

Willis's education through high school was in the segregated schools in Docena, where her status as an academically talented child was both a gift and a curse. While it allowed her to skip a grade, it also created a rift in her family. Her father encouraged her intelligence, but her mother seemed to be jealous of it. It also meant that she was separated from her age-mates, which contributed to her sense of isolation and alienation from her community. Finally, it meant that she was singled out to "perform" for the white school superintendent when he visited the district. On one such visit, after Willis correctly answered a question from the superintendent about the ionosphere, he said to her principal, Ms. Jackson, "Well, . . . I see you have a smart one here!" "He might as well have said, 'a smart *pickaninny*,'" Willis writes. "I was more than angry."[5]

She attended Westfield High School, where she continued to excel academically, earning a full scholarship to Cornell University in Ithaca, New York. Two things happened as a result, which together speak to the ambivalent relationship that white America has with Black achievement. First, shortly before she was to leave for college, she was one of four Black students selected to represent the school in a nationally broadcast television program narrated by Walter Cronkite. Second, when news of her admission to Cornell spread in her local community, her family received a late-night visit from a group of Klansmen—made up of men, women, and *children*—who burned a cross in the alley across from their house.[6] While she and her fellow students' accomplishments were nationally celebrated as the result of the "grace" that America extended to Black people, locally they were seen as a threat to the white power structure. The experience of the Klan's visit was pivotal to Willis's burgeoning interest in the delusions of hatred and separation. With the Klan assembling outside her home, she remembered her father's shotgun in the closet but knew that she wouldn't be able to shoot it, nor did she want to. What she wanted was to talk to the people assembled outside her family's home: "To convince them that they were making a mistake; to show them that we were a family, *just like them*; that we were *human beings, just like them*. I wanted to *teach* them. I wanted them to know that I knew about the community of creation—what I'd experienced at my baptism—that we were all connected, all one family."[7] She concludes that fear kept her from expressing her heart. Readers like me who were born and raised in the US experience relief that she kept quiet, for we know too much about the fates of men, women, and *children* who have spoken their hearts in the face of angry, hate-filled mobs. Although that act of terror was a source of suffering for Willis, it was also a moment of clarity in which her desire to teach took root.

Another pivotal experience that she had while still a high school student came in 1963. Then, at the height of the civil rights movement, she and her sister, Sandy, and their parents marched with Rev. King in the Birmingham campaign. She faced fire hoses and police dogs but also experienced the joy of marching with leaders like King and Rev. Ralph David Abernathy as well as others of her generation. Despite the suffering she endured, she felt inspired to commit herself to working toward a more peaceful world.

Willis got to Cornell University by way of Telluride House, a living and learning center near campus, when during her junior year in high school a recruiter visited seeking gifted students for their summer program, and she was accepted. About the experience she says, "It was the first time I had left Alabama . . . and the first time I'd been in a mixed-race learning environment." She adds, "It was as if [the recruiter] reached down into the Jim Crow South and liberated me. . . . I know how different my life could be if it had not been for that."[8] Her participation in the Telluride House program led her to apply to Cornell, which accepted her with a scholarship, making her the first person in her family to attend college.

At Cornell in the early 1960s, she found herself facing isolation from the largely white student body. She sought refuge in the Telluride House and, later, in the Black student movement, which she joined shortly after arriving on campus. She had a love of philosophy and a burgeoning interest in Buddhism, both of which she was introduced to while a student at Cornell. Those influences soon paired with watching anti–Vietnam War campaigns, including the televised self-immolation of Buddhist monks and nuns to protest the war, leading Willis to join a study-abroad program to India through the University of Wisconsin–Madison in her junior year. Willis was the only African American in the program, and she threw herself into her first experience abroad, studying Hindi and Buddhist philosophy and undertaking a research project on contemporary Hindi poetry. She also learned to play the sitar. Her smoking habit allowed her to spend time with rickshaw drivers, which gave her a different view of the country than if she had remained within the confines of the university campus. Her eyes were also opened to international political struggles when, from 1967 to 1968, she witnessed Hindu-Muslim riots in the country and a growing anti-English sentiment on campus.

During and after the Chinese takeover of Tibet in the 1950s, tens of thousands of Tibetans fled their country, most of them going to India. Willis encountered Tibetans living in exile, some of whom invited her to visit their monasteries. There, seemingly for the first time in her life, she felt a sense of belonging: "I found a warmth and acceptance here that somehow, so far from rural Alabama, made me feel at home."[9]

After the formal educational experience of her study-abroad trip ended, the students were allowed to travel elsewhere in Asia. Willis chose to visit Nepal, and there she found an even deeper sense of belonging. During her first days in Nepal, she met a Tibetan monk, Lobsang Chonjor. During their first meeting, which took place in a small dress shop, he looked her directly in the eyes and, pointing at her, pronounced in English, "You should stay here and study with us." Willis writes of the encounter as feeling as if, in the words of Stevie Wonder, "the love bug bit me."[10] This was one of her first inklings that her destiny was tied to Nepal.

Willis returned to Cornell for her senior year in 1968 where she was again faced with the cancer that is US racism. In response to a KKK cross-burning on the lawn of a house occupied by Black women on campus, she and approximately 150 other Black students took over Willard Straight Hall, Cornell's student union. An armed stand-off between the group and the administration ensued. After it ended peacefully, she was appointed minister of women's safety, becoming the only woman with a leadership role in the Black Student Alliance, the organization that had called the students to action. In that capacity, she was able to meet members of the Black Panther Party (BPP), including Fred Hampton, whom she later learned was murdered by the FBI and the Philadelphia Police Department. Recalling those days—holed up in the Black Studies House, surrounded by guns—as another critical moment in her life, she writes, "I now recognized that I was scared to death of guns, preferring peace much more than a piece."[11]

Sensitive to the choice that Willis was faced with between the armed struggle that the BPP advocated and the peaceful route that Rev. King's movement represented, her thesis advisor offered her a way out. She could be admitted to Cornell's graduate studies program in philosophy and granted her first year there in absentia. This would allow her to return to Nepal on a University Traveling Fellowship. Willis accepted the offer and returned to Nepal, where she met her long-time teacher, Lama Thubten Yeshe.

After a year and a half in Nepal working closely with Lama Yeshe, in 1970 Willis decided that she wanted to teach and entered the doctoral program in Indic and Buddhist studies at Columbia University. In January 1974, at the age of twenty-four, she took a tenure track position in religion at the University of California, Santa Cruz (UCSC). While there, she finished her dissertation, a translation and analysis of a fourth-century Buddhist philosophical treatise, earning her PhD in 1976.

Although she loved her students, she realized that UCSC was not the best fit for her. Many of her students, though bright, "had been educated in California public schools that shunted them into vocational fields" rather than academic tracks. She says, "After three and a half years of teaching, counseling, and offering extra writing support to students, I was suffering from burnout."[12] The other issue was that UCSC was designed to be the state's experimental, interdisciplinary campus, leaving Willis longing for the intellectual stimulation offered by departmental structures. Following a year as a visiting professor at Wesleyan University in Middletown, Connecticut, she was offered a tenured position there at the same time that she was awarded tenure at UCSC. Willis chose Wesleyan and spent much of her teaching career there. Today, she is a visiting professor at Agnes Scott College in Decatur, Georgia, where she lives.

The author of many articles and texts on Buddhism, Willis has also received several honors and accolades throughout her career, including Wesleyan University's Binswanger Prize for Excellence in Teaching. She has been named one of Thirteen Distinguished Leaders of Faith-Based Health Initiatives by Aetna Incorporated, listed among *Time* magazine's "Six Spiritual Leaders of the Millennium" (2000), and featured in *Newsweek* (2005). *Ebony* magazine named her one of its "Power 150" most influential African Americans. She has also been a frequent contributor to the "On Faith" blog cosponsored by *Newsweek* and the *Washington Post*.[13]

The Memoir: A Heroine's Journey Within

Willis's memoir is divided into five parts: "Birth," "Odyssey," "Choices," "Becoming," and "Return." Four of the five parts begin with a recurring dream about lions that serves to anchor the narrative: "Dreaming Me, I–IV." The last part of the narrative, "Dreaming Me, V: The Lioness's Roar" stands alone and resolves the meaning behind the dream. The text follows the script of the heroine's journey of birth, exile from her community, trials and transformation, and, finally, rebirth and reintegration into her community. In Willis's version of this journey, she is reborn first as a student, then as a teacher, and finally as her parents' daughter. Her emotional and physical journey is echoed in the narrative's form, beginning with her physical birth in 1948 in Alabama, a place circumscribed by Jim Crow laws and informal race-based rules of behavior. It ends with her taking up her role as a global citizen and claiming her full self as Black, Baptist, and Buddhist.

Transgenerational Trauma in Willis's Birth Story

Willis's exile is multilayered and reflects the complicated experience of African Americans, especially of Black women. She surmises that the sense of loneliness and alienation that she has felt for much of her life began the moment that she was born. As noted above, Willis emerged from the womb as a very fair-skinned person to two brown-skinned parents in an African American community. Immediately upon her birth, people remarked on her "white features" and blond hair, using them to call her paternal origins into question and bringing up the charged possibility that her father was actually a white man. This experience started her on an emotional and psychological exile from her community that would haunt her for many years. In her initial chapter, "White Gal," she writes that she believes that even as a newborn, she could sense her "troubled welcome" into the world. With time it became clear that she was her father's child, but, she remarks, "there's a funny thing about doubt, anger, and denial once unleashed: in spite of later correction and understanding, they are not so easily relinquished."[14] She attributes her childhood moodiness and sensitivity to that early mixed reception.

Willis's paternal grandfather was among those who questioned whether she was the child of a local white man. As Willis relates, imitating Black vernacular speech, her mother's calm and relief after giving birth to a healthy child were shattered by the Black nurses' aides who declared, "Dat baby jes as sure white as dat white daddy dat fathered her."[15] They then instructed her to look out for her husband if she valued her life. In *Black Religion: Malcolm X, Julius Lester, and Jan Willis*, the religious studies professor William David Hart observes about the matter, "If infidelity was the injury, then the 'fact' that the father was a white man was the supreme insult in Jim Crow Alabama where the only thing a black man owned was his dignity and even the title to that property was precarious."[16] While Hart briefly considers the hurt that Willis's mother must have felt when such an accusation was hurled at her, he seems more preoccupied with the trauma suffered by Mr. Willis than that suffered by Mrs. Willis. Indeed, both Black men *and* women suffered under slavery and its aftermath.

Willis clearly empathizes with her mother when she muses, "My mother's hurt and sorrow in all this cannot be fathomed."[17] Willis introduces two important elements of what such an accusation would have meant to her mother. One is the lack of control that Black women had over their productive and reproductive labor during slavery and in the post-slavery era. This meant that, like the Black man whom Hart identifies as having only ownership of his dignity, the Black woman also suffered with the precariousness of that "property" under Jim Crow. As the Combahee River Collective, using the rape of Black women by white men as an example, argues, "We know that there is such a thing as racial-sexual oppression which is neither solely racial nor solely sexual."[18] If we consider the very real danger to Black womanhood posed by white men's use of rape as a weapon of political oppression, then we must account not only for the initial violation of the Black woman's body, mind, and spirit when she is raped but also for the secondary violation of giving birth to the result of the assault. Thus, while we can understand and empathize with the Black husband whose dignity is rightfully injured by the suspicion that his baby had been fathered by a white man, we must resist the urge to do so at the expense of the Black woman. She too has suffered many raced and gendered assaults against her dignity and subsequently faces judgment from both within her community and outside of it.

As readers, understanding this broader context of Willis's birth helps us widen our lens to see that her individual experience of childhood suffering is inextricable from that of the larger Black collective. Even though it hadn't actually occurred to her mother, the suspicion of racial-sexual violence in Willis's conception typifies the deeply subconscious and transgenerational trauma that African American people suffer as a result of the ambivalent (to put it mildly) relationship that Black people have with the United States. Our ancestors were brought here as chattel laborers. As such, we were never conceived of as "belonging" in the nation that we helped to build. And if we think of ourselves in terms of continuity of Spirit (for matter is neither created nor destroyed), then we also understand that our collective sense of exile began when we stepped onto these shores. We were not meant to live past our usefulness as fodder for white "progress." When we did survive, following the end of slavery, the US government, under the auspices of the Great Emancipator (Abraham Lincoln), quickly proposed (re)patriating us to Sierra Leone, Liberia, and Haiti. Some of us left. Those who stayed often experienced psychological and emotional exile even when we were granted citizenship. For those of us who are awake to our exiled state, we are acutely aware of the trials that we have endured and that compel us to return to our communities (however we define them), hoping to contribute to our liberation from our perpetual collective sense of exile from this nation.

What I'm describing is an example of transgenerational trauma, a topic many scholars have explored.[19] The insight meditation teacher Ruth King, for example, makes a direct connection between ancestral memory and our present-day experience of the self·

> We could say that our nervous system, the heart of relational well-being, is literally the skin that shapes and defines what we typically refer to as a self, hardwired with cellular memory. The very fibers of our being are being passed down from our ancestors. . . . Given the sensitive membrane that defines us, this gift from our ancestors, we can perhaps comprehend how intimately woven our nervous systems are to past and present conditioning, including racial conditioning. This may explain why we feel anxious or frightened when we come into contact with certain races but can't readily explain why.[20]

King's attention to ancestral memory and present-day conditioning is important to consider in relation to the way that Willis's first moments of life came to haunt her into adulthood. Even though she was new to the world, she felt the potential for rejection by her father on a visceral level. Her body began keeping the score at a time when her mind was not ready to.[21] In reflecting on the particularity of the experience of racism and sexism on Black women, Willis writes, "Historically, I was both the victim and the child of rape conceived in terror."[22] Attending to the collective experience of violation and the denial of personhood, she names its victims this way: "*Everyone* in the whole sordid history of slavery and racist oppression and all blacks are subject to its enduring legacy: black women unable to fend off white rapists; black men unable to protect their wives and partners."[23] In a gesture of forgiveness for the harm that was inflicted on her by the doubt surrounding her paternal origins, she concludes that the pervasive history of white sexual violence against Blacks in the US meant that "the questioning of origins, though painful, was unavoidable."[24]

Willis thus eventually came to understand that there was a larger societal source for her low self-esteem and alienation from her family and community—feelings that plagued her in childhood and beyond. Because there was no way for her to understand those things as a child, an internal sense of exile took hold. As difficult as that was, it was also partly responsible for her precociousness and the inquisitive nature that made her "strange and dangerous" to her community.[25] Before we move deeper into Willis's memoir, let's pause for a deeper look at Docena as a site of racial trauma in the American context.

Sites of Trauma

In the American popular imagination, the South has historically been the region most readily associated with racial trauma. This is, of course, not the whole of it. We know that the racism that was practiced in the South was often more blatant because it was *de jure*, promulgated and enforced by law. But in the North, *de facto* racism could be equally deadly and *was* equally effective at undermining African American self-esteem, self-determination, and opportunity. In Willis's memoir, then, Docena functions as a site of trauma that has regional, national, and, as she would learn during her time in India, international implications.

In several of the early chapters of her memoir, Willis gives examples of how racism wounded her southern Black community. It was found, for example, in her childhood experience of media blackouts of African American progress, including her own appearance in a nationally broadcast documentary, while white supremacist ideals were promoted. It was found in the racist epithets that issued from the mouths of white children as well as the terrorism enacted by the Ku Klux Klan, charged with keeping Blacks "in their place."

A stronghold of the KKK, Docena was a place where multiple individual and collective historical and cultural realities intersected. These intersections can be easily traced to the history of slavery in the area and in whites' desire to maintain power over African Americans by deploying various forms of violence after slavery as the institution ended. In this way, it can be considered a site of African American trauma.

By "site" I mean not only the physical place in which one dwells but also the human beings who benefit from and uphold that site or, in the case of white supremacy, are its gatekeepers. Thought of in this way, we may include the people who haunt the memories and imaginations of those who have been victimized as sites of trauma. As such, "site" extends beyond place to include people as well as sights, sounds, smells, and so forth.

In his writing on Willis, Hart maintains that the terrorist organization "embodies the inhumane desire to degrade the lives of black people. The psychic terror they inspired in Jan and other black people crippled some and left others with visible and invisible scars."[26] As an example of a site as "people" on which one can dwell, the KKK's infringement on Black life is something that Willis returns to repeatedly in her narrative because of the group's insistence on insinuating itself in Black life. Willis writes,

Every so often, Docena's Klan reminded us blacks of our "proper" place. Their tactics were simple: they reminded us of who was boss by instilling in us fear of the consequences of us ever forgetting it. None of the blacks who lived in Docena were spared the Klan's reminders. On a fairly regular basis, to prevent our forgetting, there were drive-throughs and cross-burnings, terrifyingly enacted by the Klan. The messages were crystal clear: Don't get out of line! Don't begin to feel safe![27]

In *Quiet As It's Kept: Shame, Trauma, and Race in the Novels of Toni Morrison*, the scholar J. Brooks Bouson argues that these types of "white racist practices" work to produce a "learned cultural shame" that is a deeply entrenched quality of contemporary Black identity and of the "collective African-American experience."[28] Willis asserts, "The unimaginable psychic terror would prove effective in helping to cripple my self-esteem and the self-esteem of many black people." Immediately after this statement, Willis concludes the chapter with the line: "I am witness to their scars."[29] This statement is her way of testifying, and it marks her role in helping to free Black people from our collective trauma in a way consistent with the historical role that African American autobiography played for those who were enslaved. "I am witness to their scars" is a refrain we find in countless slave narratives in which the authors tell their stories of escaping to freedom as inextricable from that of those who remained in bondage.

The Talk

As we have seen, white supremacy formed part of the context for Willis's childhood struggles with self-esteem. In "The Talk," another of the chapters in part 1 of her memoir, she describes more ways that Jim Crow circumscribed Black life. For her it was symbolized by the difference between the "whites only" water fountain and that for Blacks at the commissary where she went to pick up her family's mail. Her trips to the commissary were also when she learned how early white children began to receive training in racial hatred and how white hatred contaminates and distorts Black people's sense of ourselves.

As Willis made her way to the mailroom, a little white girl who lived near the commissary repeatedly called her a "dirty nigger." The child, who was only about four or five years old, would be in her backyard, "barefoot and clothed only in some skimpy top and panties . . . her legs . . . usually very dirty, spotted or smeared with dried mud."[30] Although the child's family was perhaps poorer than Willis's, and she was, at the very least, not well cared for, she had been taught that her whiteness made her better than any Black girl. Willis's father, in response to his daughter's tears, decided to give her and her sister, Sandy, "the talk" about white people not being any different from and no better than they were. But, as Willis notes, the talk was too little, too late and had the opposite of its intended effect. "Far from building my self-esteem," she writes, "the fact of its being given at all had only confirmed that there was a difference between blacks and whites, and that that difference had hateful, and possibly dangerous consequences."[31] She concludes that it would be better for Black parents to head off such talks by telling their children "*every day*, from the time they can understand the language, how special, bright, talented, and all-around how wonderful they are."[32] Such assurances would fortify them so that when hurtful words are hurled at them, they can reply with compassion for the person. This approach has the potential to dull the experience of violence, thus protecting the child from the low self-esteem and self-hatred that such attacks can trigger—and that Willis suffered for years and spends much of her memoir recounting.

Although Willis tells the story from a personal point of view, "the talk" will be familiar to most African American readers. It functions as a rite of passage for African Americans, an addressing of racism that takes place within the safety of the family unit before children must face it outside. Incidents such as Willis experienced with the little white girl, and her father's response, impinge in a fundamental way upon African American identity formation, with far-reaching implications for the way that Black people see ourselves and how we relate to one another, to white people, and to people of other races. Not only that, but it affects how we show up in the world on a daily basis. Our constant contact with the world of hostile whiteness can bring about a sense of alienation or lack of attunement to our bodies' internal logic—what the political scientist Melissa Harris-Perry describes as trying to stand up straight in a crooked room.[33] Black people, and

Black women in particular, are always off-balance because of the many stereotypes that affect how we move through our lives. We're always trying to figure out which way is up. As the Buddhist scholar Sharon A. Suh observes, "The compromise made by our bodies to accommodate whiteness by growing smaller, less threatening, less confrontational is also a survival tactic, one that has the further effect of also reinforcing the hegemony of whiteness which insists on an unequal distribution of power." Suh rightly concludes that "Our bodies have been traumatized by white supremacy."[34]

I have never felt like I belonged in this body—at least not while in this country. I was born twenty years after Willis, in 1968. That was the year Rev. Martin Luther King Jr. was assassinated. Only one year later, Fred Hampton—a handsome and charismatic leader of the Black Panther Party, whom Willis met while at Cornell—was murdered by the United States government. Two years later, Dr. Angela Y. Davis was fighting for her life.

America's anti-Black racism made it more than apparent to me that I wasn't meant to feel like I belong in the wider US. But, like Willis, neither did I feel I quite fit into my own community. Born in Queens, New York, I experienced a deep sense of alienation from those around me and, like her, this was in part due to being born with lighter skin. In my neighborhood, Black was the thing to be, and my early years were characterized by huge afros, Black-power signs, dashikis, and bean pies. Being lighter-skinned, I was often called "red bone" and teased about my fair skin. As far as I know, both of my parents were dark-skinned, as are my older brothers, Jeffrey and Clint. Fortunately for me, I have an older sister, Lisa, who is light-skinned like me, the youngest. My oldest brother, Jeffrey, took to calling me Whitey Ford, the name of a white New York Yankees baseball player who hailed from Astoria. And because I fell in love with language early in life, I was often accused of "talking white" by my peers. Although my mother, for the most part, encouraged my precociousness, my neighbors' and classmates' teasing left an indelible mark on me. Their taunts were hurtful and made me feel like I didn't belong there.

I must say, however, that despite the ribbing and taunts from my brothers and neighbors, I never felt like I was in *danger*. I chalk this up to being born in the North in the late twentieth century at the height of the Black power movement. Rather than the news blackouts that Willis experienced in her childhood, we had a radio station, WBLS, that celebrated Black achievement. It was almost always on at our house. The Nation of Islam, which preached Black self-determination, had several thriving restaurants nearby. The KKK would not have dared come into our neighborhood. Finally, I was the youngest sister of two brothers and a sister who were popular, so I was protected.

However, school integration had done something very interesting in the North at that time. Although our student population was Black and brown, the vast majority of our teachers were white. I was lucky that while most of my teachers right up through high school were white, there was a smattering of African Americans educators who left a deep impression on me. One was my fourth-grade teacher—an elegant, tall, caramel-colored woman with a clean-shaven head. The year that I was in her class, the King Tutankhamun exhibit came through New York, and we went to see it. What I remember most about the lessons around the exhibit was the story of the curse placed on King Tut's tomb. I loved knowing that European men, believing themselves invincible and driven by greed and a desire for fame, were "put in *their* place" by an African force that they could not control.

The second was my high school English teacher—a dark-skinned older gentleman, also bald. He wore a bowtie and suit jacket every day and kept a stash of ties in his classroom because he insisted that each boy wear a tie in his class. He absolutely loved the plays of William Shakespeare and would jump around and act them out for a classroom of students who couldn't care less about Brutus's betrayal of Caesar.

Such teachers were incredibly potent in their allowing me to see myself in them. They were definitely top-notch. And they were my version of a positive force I also find in reading Willis's memoir—the fortification of Black children through Black-led education.

Fortification through Education

Willis's memoir offers many instances of the devastation caused by white supremacy during her childhood in Docena, and it is true that trauma characterized much of Black life during the Jim Crow era. Yet it is also true that Black people have always found ways to fortify ourselves and the next generation using the very tool that was forbidden to our ancestors under slavery: education. We took the opportunity of the segregation that was imposed on us during the Jim Crow era to educate our children at home and beyond in ways that nurtured not only their minds but also their spirits.

One of the ways that Willis's sense of safety was fortified was through the protective circle that was drawn around her in her community. This sense of safety came in part from the fact that her paternal grandparents and uncle bought houses on the same block as her parents when the Willises moved to Docena: she was surrounded by family in quite a literal sense. She also found a strong sense of community in the care that was extended to her by her teachers, even though some of them were afraid of her because of her reputation as the school's Little Miss Know-It-All.[35] She maintains that Docena's segregated schools provided her with a great dual education—dual in the sense that the teachers, whom Willis calls "top-notch," were on a mission not only to teach their young charges what they needed to know for the world but also to strengthen their spirits.[36] In Willis's experience, what her segregated and unequal schools lacked in material resources they made up for in the care and attention that students received.

This kind of revolutionary education—in which Black students saw themselves reflected, their humanity acknowledged and cherished—armed students with the tools they needed to function in a world shaped by white supremacy. It also meant students received a supplementary education beyond the prescribed curriculum, one that exposed them to Black greatness, fed their imaginations, and nurtured their spirits. "When we studied world literature, we studied black literature alongside it; when we learned history, we heard about the blacks who participated in it," writes Willis. "Whenever we sang the national anthem, we followed it with the Negro national anthem. We were schooled in the memorizing and performance of black poetry."[37] This kind of education, in which men and women who looked like her were held up as role models, made a lasting impression on Willis and her peers. It not only enlivened their minds but also their hearts and bodies, as Willis makes clear in her visceral memory of such lessons: "Even now when I recite James Weldon Johnson's 'Creation,' I stretch out my arms and stamp my foot at key points in the poem. Many of my black peers today, educated at the same time, make exactly the same gestures."[38] Such an education, felt in the body, was a powerful antidote to the trauma that living under the boot of Jim Crow engendered. Another such antidote was the Baptist church—a place Willis felt loved and embraced, though it was not without difficulty for her.

Religion's Double Edge

In "The Holy Opens Its Arms to Me," another early chapter of her memoir, Willis eloquently describes her fraught relationship with the Baptist church of her childhood. She spends much of the chapter describing how her mother forced her to go to church and to be baptized, as well as her fear and trepidation around the ritual of baptism. "When my turn came, I balked," she remembers. "The steps were wet and cold to my bare feet. Two deacons took each arm to lead my trembling body down. I looked up in desperation, wanting to flee; but among all the wide-eyed faces my eyes settled on my mother's stern expression. It said silently but firmly, 'Go on, young lady. Get in there!'"[39]

Willis did in fact "get in there," and in doing so she experienced love that extended to her and was expansive in a way that "dissolved all fears" and that made her feel like she belonged to a family as big as "all creatures who breathed, and cried and struggled and sang." She confesses, however, that her sense of expansive connectedness ended the very next day when she was confronted with "the racism of the everyday world" she inhabited. Toward the end of the chapter, she notes that "it would take many years and a trip halfway around the world before I again experienced anything like the grace and serenity of that joyous immersion into community."[40]

Like Willis, growing up, I had a difficult relationship with the Black church. I loved the pageantry of Sunday morning with the women—my mother front and center—stepping down the aisle in the most elaborate hats that I have ever seen. I also loved watching the ushers in their crisp white uniforms, one hand always tucked behind them, leading congregants to their seats. I appreciated the delivery and cadence of the minister's message even if I didn't agree with his view of fire and brimstone. And I was seduced by the call and response that let us all know that we understood something that only those who had gone through our trials as Black people in this country could understand. Like Willis, I also experienced uneasiness as the congregation got swept up in what she calls "a mysterious spiritual frenzy that began gradually but soon rushed ahead uncontrollably to its cathartic end."[41] For me, my signal to make my way toward the exit was the cold sweat that would break out on my forehead and in my armpits as the preacher took off running down the aisle. Keeping one hand on his microphone, he used the other to reach out and slap some eagerly awaiting congregant on the head. Down they would go, arms outstretched as they caught the Spirit. I was terrified of falling within his line of vision and becoming one of those (un)lucky souls whose dress ended up around their waist, their carefully pressed and curled hair a mess, with no memory of who they had clocked during their communion with God. Thankfully that never happened to me because, like Willis's mother Dorothy, I was a subdued attendee. But I was not unmoved: listening to the choir and witnessing as the Spirit swept so powerfully through my family and neighbors, I often surrendered to silent tears.

Years later, while attending Vodou ceremonies in Haiti, I had similar experiences. As the drummers heated up and the spirits made their presence known, I would find myself swaying back and forth, crying quietly. After one such experience, my boyfriend at the time, a *sèvitè* and drummer who had been at a ceremony with me, announced to our friends that I had been possessed. He went on to inform me—and the others agreed—that spirit possession does not only show up as the battle that is so recognizable as a spirit mounts their horse.[42] Possession shows up in many ways, with crying being just another expression of their presence.

Today when I am in sanghas led by people of color (POC) such as Osho Zenju, Margarita Loinaz, or Devin Berry, I am often driven to tears. The tears well up with the recognition and sheer gratitude that I have found My People. As with my experiences in the Black church and in Haitian Vodou ceremonies, in POC-led sanghas I tap into the truth of who I am. I am seen. I am known. My suffering is acknowledged, and I get glimpses of the path to my liberation. How could I possibly choose between my African American spiritual tradition that I inherited and those that I have found and that have found me along my path to awakening? It is impossible. To do so would be to forsake a part of myself. It would be to willfully separate myself from my wholeness, which is inextricable from the fullness of my community in its many different and varied iterations.

This sense of finding home is something that Willis speaks of repeatedly in regard to her experience with the Tibetan Buddhists she met in India and in subsequent encounters with Buddhism. Describing her visit to the Buddhist monastery while living in India, and later when she received her new name as part of a ritual of committing to Buddhist practice, she writes, "I liked this warm and welcoming community. . . . In the midst of these Buddhists, I felt the hard shell of my rigid self beginning to soften."[43] The name that she was given, Joy of the Dharma, speaks to her potential to be an example to others of relief from suffering and the joy that one finds along the dharma path.

Although Willis's sense of Buddhism as a home came quite naturally, it took decades longer for her to be able to experience the Black church of her childhood that way again. In "Church with Daddy," a chapter near the end of the memoir, she describes how, after many years of being away, she accompanied her father to church. About her reasons for not having stepped foot inside a Baptist church in the previous twenty years, she writes, "As a child I had argued against the hypocrisy and money-grabbing of preachers. As an adolescent and wiseacre college student, I'd rejected the whole of Christianity as the white man's way of subjugating all blacks and of denigrating our African cultural and spiritual roots."[44] While there were certain parts of the scripture that she appreciated, growing up in the segregated South, where people spoke of loving their neighbors while deliberately causing them harm, led her to turn away from the religion.

I confess that I, too, am ambivalent about Christianity's meaning in the Black community. Historically, Europeans used it to justify Black enslavement. Today, the often-espoused belief that good and "obedient" Christians will get their just rewards in heaven makes me wonder if Christianity contributes to maintaining Black subjugation. That suspicion is not allayed by the preponderance of liquor stores and check-cashing places alongside churches in impoverished Black communities. But I am also in awe of our deployment of Christianity as a tool in our quest for freedom across the centuries. When white Christians treated us like second-class citizens in their churches, we founded the African Methodist Episcopal Church. Nat Turner looked to the Bible to justify his Southampton uprising in 1831, and Harriet Tubman looked to God to guide and protect her as she led approximately seventy men, women, and children to freedom. Contemporarily, many of us continue to seek refuge and strength in the church when "the racism of the everyday world" threatens to undo us.

Attending church as an adult who had for many years studied and practiced a "foreign" religion allowed Willis to see her homegrown religion in a new light: as a solace for her father, "a joyous place," "holy ground."[45] She claims the congregation as her own, and for the first time in the narrative, declares, "In this black Baptist sanctuary I, a Black Buddhist, had come home."[46]

From Internal Exile to External Departure

In the chapter titled "Having Crossed the Line," Willis writes,

> I sometimes wondered, as a child, why I had been born in this
> particular body, this family, this place. The whole thing of it
> never seemed quite right. I was born with black skin when
> having that attribute meant coming to know rejection for
> no good reason whatsoever. I was smart and quick-tongued,
> which seemed to place me at odds almost immediately with
> those around me.[47]

Her narrative is replete with examples of the myriad ways that she was made to feel like she did not belong in her body in that place at that time. As we have seen, from birth she experienced a sense of alienation from her family—first from her father as a consequence of her skin tone and then from her mother as a consequence of her intellectual prowess. In school she was feared on one hand and tokenized on the other. As someone who early on sensed the interconnectedness of all beings, living within a community marked by division, hatred, and othering, Willis was left feeling at odds with those around her. Her departure to college, travels overseas, becoming a Buddhist practitioner, and finding her place as a professor of Buddhist studies all constitute aspects of the external side of the exile she had felt internally throughout much of her childhood.

A Different Kind of Education

Willis was able to escape Docena—physically, if not yet psychologically— by leaving home to attend Cornell, a "*snooty*" northern Ivy League university. As she remarks about her unusual choice, "Of the 234 students who graduated in my senior class, only four of us went on to college, and only I ventured northward."[48] She had worked hard to earn her scholarship to one of the top universities in the nation, but the nature of white supremacy, especially during that time, meant that her accomplishment was shadowed by the sense that divine providence had a hand in it. "I know how different my life would be if not for that," she says.[49] Her assertion echoes Frederick Douglass's narrative, in which he ruminates on being plucked from the brutal plantation of Colonel Lloyd, where he had suffered in his early years, to travel to the home of Mr. and Mrs. Auld in Baltimore, where he was exposed to the power of the written word. He saw his move to Baltimore as laying the foundation and opening the way to all of his subsequent prosperity, believing it "kind providence" that intervened on his behalf. Moreover, he states that he always knew in his heart of hearts that he would not remain enslaved:

> From my earliest recollection, I date the entertainment of a deep conviction that slavery would not be able to hold me within its foul embrace; and in the darkest hours of my career in slavery, this living word of faith and spirit of hope departed not from me, but remained like ministering angels to cheer me through the gloom. This good spirit was from God, and to him I offer thanksgiving and praise.[50]

Willis expresses a similar sentiment when she says at the beginning of "Having Crossed the Line," "I could have been no more than four or five when I formed the strong determination that I would not be raised up to adult life in Alabama; I was not going to live in a place that asked me to squash my dreams and ambitions."[51] It seems clear that she believes that divine providence had a hand in making sure she was able to fulfill that promise to herself; that she was destined to be plucked from her small town in Alabama to have opportunities and experiences that would lead her to becoming a leading scholar of Tibetan Buddhism.

Although I would by no means compare myself to Douglass or Willis in terms of the reach of their many contributions to Black liberation, I have no doubt that my life has been deeply shaped by a force greater than myself. I have always known in my bones that I was destined for more than an unfulfilling life in Queens. I am confident that it was divine providence that brought me from a "failing" high school, named for the US president Andrew Jackson, to attend with a full scholarship a "snooty" college in upstate New York. Hamilton College gave me the opportunity to travel to Haiti, a country—a whole world, really—that has shaped much of my intellectual, professional, and imaginative life. With the gifts and opportunities that I have been afforded since graduating, I have been able to help shape my own students. Through my research, I have been able to elevate the gift of claiming freedom that Haiti has given the world and especially those in the African diaspora.

As I write this, I am also keenly aware that Douglass's, Willis's, and my experience as members "of the chosen few" are also evidence of the way that white supremacy maintains itself. The plucking of a few "exceptional" ones from the masses to stand as examples of achievement in a country built on exclusion upholds a system that throws away the majority of our brothers and sisters to poverty, drug addiction, and prison.

At the same time, I am reminded that those who are committed to upholding white supremacy find such examples intolerable. For Douglass, this initially occurred when Mr. Auld found out that his wife was teaching young Frederick to read and write. His warning that "if you give a nigger an inch, he will take an ell," and instructing her in the importance of keeping enslaved people ignorant, not only put an end to the lessons but turned Mrs. Auld's heart into stone. Her "lamb-like disposition gave way to one of tiger-like fierceness," in Douglass's words. She became more vigilant than even her husband in maintaining Douglass's ignorance, watching him like a hawk to make sure he did not have access to reading.[52] As we've seen, white members of Willis's community were so angered by her achievement that the Klan burned a cross in the alley across from her family's home. For my part, one of my most painful experiences with Hamilton's majority white student population came when, postgraduation, I was invited back to my alma mater to celebrate the legacy of Joseph Spurlarke (class of 1889), the first African American to attend the college. There was a ceremony at the library in which I was invited to speak, and a photo and plaque of him was hung in the lobby. Several days after I left campus, I learned from my mentor, Dr. Andrée Nicola McLaughlin, who was still there, that in the middle of the night, someone had entered the library and placed a used sanitary napkin with the words "Eat Me" over the photo. The memory of that violence stings to this day.

Willis's experiences as an undergraduate in the Black Student Alliance and with the Black Panthers broadened her horizons and helped her gain confidence. However, she remained haunted by the traumas of her childhood and plagued by low self-esteem. The disruption of identity formation and continuous assault against Black personhood that racism engendered were not something Willis, or anyone, could simply undo. Writing about the enduring impact of racism on identity formation in her own life, the scholar Meta Y. Harris points out that as a Black woman who came of age in the Deep South during the civil rights movement, she had a deep concern for how Black people were perceived and judged, especially by people who knew nothing about them.[53] In many ways we see this same concern haunting Willis in both the South *and* the North. We see it, for instance, in her experience of having to perform for white school superintendents as a child in the South, and we see it later when, as a tenured professor in Connecticut, she is shunned by a white clerk who assumes she cannot afford a high-end gift that she wants to buy.

This concern even follows her halfway around the world when in India during her junior year abroad, the owner of a dry-food stall asks to which caste she belongs. Eager to distance herself from India's strict and repressive caste system, Willis tells the inquirer that she is American. "We don't have castes in America," she explains. "I am a black American."[54] Rather than receiving the apology she expects to hear in this "one-street town of Lanka," she instead hears, "Oh . . . American Negro. So sorry, madam. I am so sorry."[55] The sympathy that was offered to her at that moment made her aware of the way that African Americans were perceived abroad. Willis calls the encounter a "sobering awakening" in which she was forced to confront the whole notion of caste—both the system in India and her own denials about its existence in America.[56] Though in a faraway country where Willis thought a simple shopkeeper would know nothing about the deplorable treatment of African American people, she is forced to confront the long-denied trauma of having come of age in a racial caste system in which *she* was an untouchable.

When Willis is able to see that the system that she disparaged abroad was also alive and well in her country—and, as such, lives inside her—her perception shifts in a way that would remain with her. We see it decades later, for instance, in an article titled "We Cry Out for Justice" that she wrote in response to US police violence against Black men. In that article Willis makes an important distinction between two Buddhist exercises found in the Buddhist scholar Shantideva's exploration of true compassion in *Bodhicharyavatara* (*A Guide to the Bodhisattva's Way of Life*): one of "exchanging self with others," or walking in another's shoes; and "equalizing self and others."[57] She criticizes the first exercise as being akin to pity, offered from a position of superiority. This would seem to be the emotion that prompted her response to the inquiry about her origins in India. What she learned from that exchange was the value of the second exercise, actualizing "our equality with others: neither our superiority nor our inferiority but our equality with them."[58] She declares that "only this flash of insight is capable of truly liberating us."[59] It was the encounter far from home where Willis relearned the important lesson of interconnectedness that she had glimpsed in her run-in with the Klan as a teenager.

By the time she wrote that article, Buddhist teachings had given Willis the tools to access a sense of equanimity that relieved her of the destructive worldview that keeps people separated and prone to othering. This sense of interconnectedness began during her childhood with her baptism and resurfaced during critical moments in her life, such as during the Birmingham campaign. It was when she visited the Nepalese Buddhists living in exile in India, however, that she began to see the contours of the Buddhist spiritual path she has walked ever since.

Meeting Lama Yeshe, Meeting Herself

Willis's teacher was Lama Thubten Yeshe, a Tibetan Buddhist monk born in Tibet in 1935 in the town of Tölung Dechen. His birthplace was not far from the Chi-me Lung Gompa, home to about one hundred nuns of the Gelug tradition whose learned abbess and guru had passed away a few years before. A lama known for his psychic powers visited the nuns at the time of Lama Yeshe's birth and named him as their reincarnated guru. Following the lama's advice, the nuns traveled to visit the young Lama Yeshe and bring him offerings, eventually inviting him to the convent to attend ceremonies and religious functions.

From a very early age, Lama Yeshe expressed the desire to lead a religious life. Whenever a monk would visit his family's home, he would beg to leave with him and join a monastery. Finally, when he was six years old, his parents permitted him to join Sera Monastery, one of three great Gelug monastic centers, where he remained until he was twenty-five years old.

In addition to the spiritual instruction he received based on the educational traditions brought from India to Tibet over a thousand years ago, he was also initiated into the tantric tradition, reputed to provide a powerful and speedy path to the attainment of a fully awakened and purified mind.

This phase of his education ended in 1959 when, in the words of Lama Yeshe, "the Chinese kindly told us that it was time to leave Tibet and meet the outside world." Escaping through Bhutan, he eventually reached northeast India where he met up with many other Tibetan refugees and continued with his studies until, at the age of twenty-eight, he received full monk's ordination and then moved to Nepal.

In 1965 Lama Yeshe began teaching Western students at a time when such a thing was frowned upon. Nonetheless, he developed a following that continued to grow, eventually resulting in the founding of several institutions. Willis met Lama Yeshe in 1969 when she traveled to Nepal to live for several months. She describes him as "a wise and gentle man who would change my life forever."[60] He remained her primary teacher for many years.[61]

Willis's relationship with Lama Yeshe can be considered another aspect of divine providence working in her life. Their meeting had been predicted by two strangers who came to visit her while she was visiting a friend when still in India. She relates the experience of hearing about Lama Yeshe for the first time from one of the men:

As he continued to talk, I began to experience a strange, though pleasant, sensation. It was unlike any sensation I had ever experienced before: a sort of warm tingling feeling that began at the nape of my neck and then radiated downward and outward to encircle my whole body. Then, as though I had suddenly stepped into an invisible field of electricity, I noticed that the hairs on my skin stood up erect.[62]

Willis had a strong sense of a preordained relationship with Lama Yeshe, yet when they met, she found it difficult to share the truths of her life with him. In the chapter "Meeting Lama Yeshe," she includes a list of regrets about not being truthful about why she had come to see him. Their meeting marks the first time in the memoir that Willis confronts the ways in which being a Black American carries with it generational trauma. Her list of pain points is easily recognizable to her African American readers, even this far into the twenty-first century. She writes, "I should have told him the truth when he'd first asked; should have blurted out that I suffered; that I was often frustrated and angry; that slavery and its legacy of racism had taken their tolls on me; that I had come seeking help in coping with feelings of inadequacy, unworthiness, and shame."[63]

In the ensuing chapters, Willis lets us in on just a few of what we can be sure are Lama Yeshe's many gems of wisdom. At the end of a chapter titled "This, Too, Is Buddha," she states how critical her relationship with Lama Yeshe has been to her healing:

I had come to Lama Yeshe loaded down with guilt, shame, anger, and a feeling of utter helplessness. I couldn't think or see past the rage I felt from the untold indignities I'd experienced in life prior to meeting him. Such anger had crippled me in countless ways and had almost sent me down the path of violence. Yet, wounds like mine had a flip side too, a false and prideful view of entitlement: Look at all that I've endured. I'm great. In time, Lama Yeshe would find a way to pull the rug out from under that pride.[64]

The chapter that follows that important lesson, "The Test," is full of the personal lessons offered to Willis by her teacher. Ever aware that her story is not just her own, she repeatedly connects the lightening of her personal burden of the trance of unworthiness and low self-esteem to the possibility of liberation that Buddhism offers to the Black collective:

> It is the trauma of slavery that haunts African Americans in the deepest recesses of our souls. This is the chief issue for us, the issue that must be dealt with head-on—not denied, not forgotten, not suppressed. Indeed, its suppression and denial only hurt us more deeply, causing us to accept a limiting, disparaging, and at times, even repugnant view of ourselves. We as a people cannot move forward until we have grappled in a serious way with all the negative effects of this trauma.[65]

Living on the other side of the world in Nepal, she gets to the heart of not only her own suffering but that of thousands of us who live with the question that the historical trauma of slavery elicits: "How to stand dignified, yet humbly, in the world."[66]

Indeed, looking around me, I reflect on how the everyday violence that Black people face in enduring so-called microaggressions is inextricable from the larger violence of police brutality. I reflect on the unequal distribution of wealth and access in this country, and on the ways that the COVID pandemic exposed the equally deadly pandemic of racism. These and so many similar reflections make it clear to me that our ability to access our innate dignity, coupled with the graciousness found in humility, is not outside of ourselves. In fact, we cannot *afford* to look outside of ourselves. These qualities are only found when we turn inward and seek guidance from our internal wisdom. So that no matter what we face in the world, we are able to resource ourselves and stand strong like a Bodhi tree, or like an African baobab tree, solid against the worldly winds.

From 1980 to 1981, Willis returned to Nepal on a National Endowment for the Humanities Fellowship to collect the oral histories of certain living Tibetans. While she was there, Lama Yeshe asked her to translate the lives of several Buddhist saints who had gained full enlightenment in a system known as the Ganden Oral Tradition, or the Gelugpa Mahamudra. Through her work on the saints, Willis learned about the Great Seal Retreat, an arduous undertaking that is believed to result in the practitioner's enlightenment. Although she initially turned down Lama Yeshe's invitation to undertake the retreat, she eventually changed her mind. At the moment that she agreed, Lama Yeshe performed a gesture that resulted in Willis feeling "something quite simple and quite extraordinary at the same time, something akin to grace. A vast blissful calmness. A stillness that was, in its immensity, all of a piece and all peace-filled."[67] She likens the experience of peace to what she felt when she emerged from the baptismal waters of Docena as a child; it was a fitting way to begin the closing of a critical time in her life, by returning to the beginning. Unlike in Docena, though, the "racism of the everyday world" did not descend to steal her bliss.

Although she had to end the retreat early for health reasons, she came to a profound awareness about the nature of awakening. It marks another critical moment in her transformation, and one she felt compelled to carry forward. Testifying to the power that she has gained from her Buddhist practice, she says, "When I look back at myself, at the timid and insecure self that first arrived before Lama Yeshe, I can clearly see how I have changed, how I have become less fearful and more confident and capable. These changes occurred in small increments and over some time." Then, without missing a beat, she speaks directly to the reader, saying, "The point is to allow them to happen, without grasping and attachment; to have faith that positive change will come and, in the meantime, to try and be gentle with yourself. It is like this for all the Buddhas throughout the ages." Finally, bringing herself into the collective circle of potential enlightened beings, she says,

"They were each, at the beginning of their journeys, beings just like us: tossed and pummeled by ordinary fears, worries, and insecurities. And yet with steady and patient practice, they each became Awakened Ones." As Willis has done throughout the telling of her story, she reminds us that "they have given us a model of moderation to follow." And like a teacher encouraging her students, she finishes by asserting (we can imagine, with a wink), "If we practice as they did, who knows? We might just become the next Buddhas."[68]

The Heroine's Return

Willis's exile and return were not single events. Modern-day rites-of-passage journeys very rarely are. Rather, they often look more like two steps forward, one step back as the emerging adult finds their footing out in the world. Sometimes these returns are cultural in nature—for instance, in becoming comfortable with the language that we need to use to communicate with loved ones even as we occupy different spaces in other areas of our lives. An example of this is in a story that Willis includes toward the end of the memoir about the code-switching that she does with her family. Willis talks about how, even as a grown woman, whenever she phones home, her language changes immediately. She says, "I speak with my family in our familiar dialect—not the slow drawl of white southern speech, but the laughter-filled dialect of black speech. My colleagues and students might not be able to understand me. And after lengthy trips home, I've joked with my closest friends about worries that I might not be able to shed this dialect when classes resume."[69] The intimation of celebration makes Black southern speech special: it is laughter-filled, rooted not only in struggle but also in the joy that comes from community and communion. The warmth that comes through in her description also signals her psychic and emotional return to her home.

There are also times when the lessons that one needs to learn can only be found at one's starting place with all of its fraught relationships.

At such times, the return may not only be psychic and cultural but also physical. An example of the joy of return found in Willis's physical return to her southern roots is in her recounting of her decision in the late 1980s, at around the age of forty, to undertake research on her family history and genealogy—a project that would take four years. She opens the chapter "My Search for Kin" with her mother's elation when she announced her plans to do the work. She says, "I can still see the joy that came over my mother's face when I first proposed the project. 'Oh yeah! *Do* it, Dean! Write a book about *us*!'" Highlighting Willis's status as a kind of prodigal daughter finally returned home, her mother grinned from ear to ear. She went on to add, "'Yeah, a book about us. No need to wade through Sanskrit or those other languages.' She was relieved."[70] Her mother's comment on language also speaks to her perception of her daughter returning home to the fold, an issue that had haunted Willis since she had left for college many years before.

But while her mother's enthusiasm made Willis feel affirmed, she was soon to learn that her decision to return to the South also raised the ire of her white neighbors, who believed that during her absence, Willis had "forgotten her place."

The Dark Side of Sankofa

By the time Willis embarked on the genealogy project she was well established in her career: a successful professor and respected scholar of Tibetan Buddhism. She felt ready to look at her family's past and confront the roots of the transgenerational trauma she had carried all her life. That trauma would indeed resurface when she learned that her "maternal great-grandfather was *white*."[71] Although there is no way to know what kind of relationship Willis's maternal great-grandmother had with her great-grandfather, given the exploitative power relations between white men and Black women that prevailed at that time, we can surmise that her great-grandmother was a victim of rape. But it was not just the circumstances of her grandmother's conception that disturbed Willis. It was the way that the information was delivered to her: through a white woman named Becky James, a local historian, whom Willis repeatedly encountered in the course of her research and who reveled in being able to inform her of her heritage.

On what Willis calls "the fateful day," she suspected that James might know who her mother's grandfather was. When she finally mustered up the courage to ask James directly, James smugly revealed not only his name but also the fact that she had known it throughout the whole four years that she had watched Willis research her family history! Reflecting on the suffering that ensued when Willis received the information, she characterizes James's look as "like a devil licking her chops,"[72] one that produced strong feelings of hatred in her.

Along with "licking her chops," James—in a move that has been repeated for centuries when whites learn of the mixed-race heritage of an intelligent or successful Black person—identified Willis's white heritage as the source of her intellectual acumen.[73] With this encounter, which Willis relates almost three hundred pages after she initially shares her perception of her white heritage as a cancer, the reader finally understands the traumatic experience that shaped that perception.

Suffering a profound rage at the information delivered hatefully by James, she sought out the counsel of her friend, Lama Pema, who advised her that the hate she felt was part of her own mind. It was empty and needed to be let go. It was the advice that Willis wished that she had gotten when she was a child before she was harmed by being called a "nigger." Rather than producing in her a desire to prove that she was as good as a white person, Lama Pema's advice allowed her to practice non-attachment. He signaled that James's hatred was not Willis's to carry; she could let it drop so that she could do the important work that she was destined to do. Although Willis does not say what she did with the advice, we can be sure that by the time she received it, she was at a place in her life where, at the very least, she could detach herself from the woman's hateful intentions rather than internalize them.

The sentiment of this instruction issued from a Buddhist lama can also be found in the African American tradition—for instance, in the Reverend Martin Luther King Jr.'s message about the destructiveness of hatred in his sermon "Loving Your Enemies." There he explains how hatred is not only harmful to the object of hate but also to the one who hates, acting like an unchecked cancer, corroding the personality and eating away its vital energy.[74] As Lama Pema told Willis, she had important work to do—work that would be impossible with hatred eating away at her heart and spirit.[75]

Willis doesn't directly address how she resolved her feelings of hatred toward James. In fact, the need to offer such a resolution is beside the point. If we think about her memoir as part of the legacy of the African American slave narrative—and I suggest we do—then the story that she imparts is meant as a lesson to the reader. She tells it so late in the narrative because she has provided us with over two hundred pages of examples of such hate-filled aggression alongside all the ways that she has learned to deflect them: through deep internal reflection and building her self-esteem. She arrives at that place of equanimity through her relationship with Lama Yeshe. In one of the final chapters of *Dreaming Me*, and in the essay "Buddhism and Race," she writes that when she looks back on her fifteen-year relationship with Lama Yeshe, she sees his main teaching as *confidence*— something that she lacked throughout her childhood and much of her adulthood.[76] Recall the story that she relates early in the text regarding "the talk," in which she asserts that the counsel her father offered was too little, too late; the damage had been done. In "Buddhism and Race," Willis mentions that Lama Yeshe called her "daughter." This reflection on her distant past with her father in the South alongside her recent past with Lama Yeshe clues us into the role that her teacher was able to play for her: he was able to reparent her in a way that fortified her against the vitriol that she faced as a Black American woman.

So, while the incident with James resurfaced much of the pain that she suffered as a child, ultimately she became confident enough in her worthiness to say to her inner child, "Well, too bad for those hate-filled people. The problem is theirs, not yours!"—precisely the words she wished her father had said to her.[77] The evidence of her moving on from James's assault is in her telling the story.

Letting Go

Much of the last part of Willis's memoir is about surrender: letting go of loved ones, labels, and "should" to embrace what *is*. In one of the final chapters, titled "Mama," Willis describes the process of saying goodbye to her mother. Dorothy Willis had by then suffered from Alzheimer's for many years, and she was in the hospital after developing a brain bleed from a fall off her back porch. When Willis got the call from her sister, Sandy, about their mother's hospitalization, she vacillated between praying to Jesus, saying mantras, and bringing to mind Lama Yeshe and the Buddha—none of which felt right. Finally she gave up fretting "over which tradition or ritual to employ" and decided to instead focus on her "object of meditation," her mother, and began saying a mantra that felt right to her.[78]

She was able to get a flight to Birmingham to visit her mother in the hospital during her final hours. Willis writes that, upon seeing her, "to my surprise, her eyes were open and they grew wider when I entered. She knew I had come and that I was there."[79] Although she and her mother had had a difficult relationship when she was growing up, in the throes of Alzheimer's, with death imminent, her mother recognized and welcomed her child home.

I found that same grace in November 2009, when after suffering several small strokes, my mother was hospitalized. I had just moved to Pennsylvania from the Midwest so I could see her more often. One weekend, my son, Reuben, and I made the three-hour bus trip to visit her in New York. She was sleeping as we entered her hospital room, her tiny frail body where once there had been a robust woman, full of life and always fighting. As my son and I settled down by her bedside, her eyes fluttered open and immediately widened as she recognized us. She wasn't able to speak, so we simply sat with her for a while, stroking her hand and her hair, telling her over and over again that we loved her until she fell back to sleep. She passed away a few weeks later. I remain immensely grateful that I—and more importantly, my son—had been able to be with her in her final days; that she knew that we were there and that we loved her. One of the lessons for me was that in the end, no matter how far afield we go, we recognize home in our loved ones. Honoring that connection allows us to do the work that we are meant to do out in the world.

Teaching as Practice

In the closing pages of her memoir, Willis also writes about her parents' visits to the various college campuses where she has taught. She recalls overhearing her mother one day tell a neighbor that her daughter got paid a lot of money for teaching just four hours a week. Willis chuckled at the contrast between her mother's perception and the reality of the life of a professor, which doesn't switch off at 5 p.m. like other professions. The story reminds me of my mother, who came to visit when I was a graduate student in Wisconsin. Like Willis's parents, she had a high school education, so the world of academia was a mystery to her, and she never quite grasped what it was that I was doing so far away. She was, nonetheless, very proud of me. This is true of many African American families. Those of us who are first-generation college graduates are charged with negotiating two different worlds, as translators.

Willis extends her discussion of this humorous challenge that she faced to some of the challenges she faces as "one of the first American scholar-practitioners of Tibetan Buddhism."[80] She is seen as an anomaly in her field because she is a Black woman, and the choices she made about what to study and teach were not expected of her. And let's be clear: the fact that she excels at what she does is a slap in the face not only to those of the "long-gone" Jim Crow South but also to those today across the nation who uphold white supremacy.

She addresses the ways that academia is wary of the possibility that people will use "their classroom as their pulpit to advance their own private sectarian views,"[81] and she is mindful of how easy it is to do such a thing. Nonetheless, she is authentic in her teaching through the lens of Buddhism. While careful to make sure that students distinguish between her and the subject she teaches, she admits that she considers teaching part of her Buddhist practice. As such, she hopes to convey to the students their commonalities and interconnectedness. She also hopes to have them "appreciate others and lessen their clinging solely to thoughts of themselves, to the extent that they can become better human beings and realize their true humanity."[82] As a visiting professor of religion at Agnes Scott College and a scholar who continues to give talks and publish articles and books (her most recent publication is *Dharma Matters: Women, Race, and Tantra*), Willis remains steady in her commitment to helping everyone who encounters her work to become better human beings and realize our true potential.

Lessons of Lions and the Power of Writing One's Own Story

Willis begins four of the five sections of *Dreaming Me* with some variation on her dream about lions, and in the last section she comes to terms with the significance of lions to her life path. "Sometimes frightening, but always awe-inspiring, the lions invaded my dreams and my psyche," she writes. "They clearly wanted in, though I tried hard for a time to suppress them. I believe the lions are me, myself. Perhaps they are my deepest African self. They are the 'me' that I have battled over since leaving Docena and venturing forth into a mostly white world."[83] In addition to the significance of lions to her African ancestry, she highlights their meaning in her Buddhist lineage: "In Buddhism, the lion's roar is the mark of the eloquence and power of the Buddha's speech. His eminent disciples, too, are often referred to as his lions. They carry on and embody the Teachings."[84] How beautiful to see Willis embracing the fact that she is a mighty lioness of Buddha, bravely venturing out into the world to spread the message of liberation.

In naming her memoir *Dreaming Me: Black, Baptist, and Buddhist: One Woman's Spiritual Journey*, Willis announces the uniqueness and particularity of her experience. Yet to read the book is to experience the Black tradition of the individual narrative standing in for the collective experience, such as we find, for example, in Douglass's autobiography, *Narrative of the Life of Frederick Douglass: An American Slave* or Harriet Jacobs's *Incidents in the Life of Slave Girl*.[85] In addition, rather than a dissolution of the self that some have interpreted as the Buddhist teaching of "no self," Willis, like the other women whose work I explore in this text, finds meaning in the words of the Buddhist teacher Dogen Zenji, who states that "to study the way of enlightenment is to study the self. To study the self is to forget the self."[86] As Osho Zenju Earthlyn Manuel reconstructs this teaching, "In order to forget the self, we must study it."[87] By studying her self within a US context and outside of it, Willis has been able to free herself from the hold that white supremacy and its resultant suffering had on her.

While the text moves relatively quickly from Willis's Black Baptist southern childhood during the Jim Crow era to her process of discovering and choosing Buddhism, she returns again and again to slavery and its personal and collective legacies. By dwelling on the scourge of American racism, which haunted her even as she traveled halfway around the world, she illustrates slavery's enduring legacy on both the individual and collective mind and heart of those who lived during the Jim Crow era.

Her writings since the publication of *Dreaming Me* have continued to speak to slavery's legacy, identifiable in the racial terror that continues to plague Black life in the twenty-first century. Her story, though a personal one, does what many autobiographies do: it "lives in the two worlds of history and literature, objective fact and subjective awareness."[88] Willis's personal life narrative traces her physical, mental, and spiritual journey. In the process, she draws on elements of the life narratives of her Tibetan teachers and friends, and she traces the United States' life narrative.

The impact of Willis's memoir on others is already amply evident. In the afterword to *Dreaming Me*, the activist and author Bettina Aptheker testifies to the importance to her of the section of the autobiography that focuses on Becky James, the white woman who withheld her knowledge of the identity of Willis's great-grandfather and then deployed it spitefully. Willis's sharing the wisdom bestowed upon her by Lama Pema—that the rage she was feeling should be seen not as external but as her own mind—allowed Aptheker to see that her rage, too, was the hatred in her own mind and that this "hook" trapped her mind in its negative cycle. From her own studies with Tibetan teachers, Aptheker was able to find her way toward more compassion and forgiveness.[89] In my life, Willis's text has let me know that I am not alone. She is my kin. And if she has been able to free herself from the chains of white supremacy, then so can I. So can we all.

Willis's text does the work of traditional African American autobiographies by helping to free others from the emotional and spiritual chains that bind us. As someone who has studied Mahayana Buddhism, a form of Buddhism dedicated to service, Willis offers her autobiography as an extension of her service to humanity, which we also see in her teaching and lecturing within and beyond the university classroom. As she says in the chapter titled "Teaching as My Practice," "I want my students to appreciate that we human beings share a great deal: we all wish to have happiness and avoid suffering. I want them to develop the ability to identify, and therefore to empathize, with other human beings, to be able to practice standing in another's shoes."[90]

2

BELL HOOKS

Being Love, Finding Home

ON JANUARY 22, 2022, I attended a daylong remote retreat dedicated to the teachings of the Black feminist writer and public intellectual bell hooks. The retreat, titled "Celebrating bell hooks and All about Love," was offered through East Bay Meditation Center (EBMC) and led by Rev. Liên Shutt, a Vietnamese American Zen Buddhist. Just a little over a month before, on December 15, 2021, hooks made her transition surrounded by family in her home in the mountains of Kentucky. She was sixty-nine years old. The morning of the retreat, I awoke to the news that the beloved Vietnamese Zen master Thich Nhat Hanh—Thay, as his students called him—had passed away at the age of ninety-five. Nhat Hanh, whom hooks named as one of her teachers, had lived thirty years in government-imposed exile but had returned to Vietnam in 2018 and settled in the city of Hue, at the same monastery where he had studied Buddhism in his youth. hooks had lived thirty years in a self-imposed exile in other parts of the US but had returned to her home state in 2004.

In "My Fate Is Kentucky," one of the opening chapters of *Belonging: A Culture of Place,* hooks positions her decision to return to her childhood home in later life in relation to her mindful living practice. She connects it to her vision for the way that she would die:

> If one has chosen to live mindfully, then choosing a place to die is as vital as choosing where and how to live. Choosing to return to the land and landscape of my childhood, the world of my Kentucky upbringing, I am comforted by the knowledge that I could die here. This is the way I imagine "the end": I close my eyes and see hands holding the Chinese lacquer bowl, walking to the top of the Kentucky hill I call my own, scattering my remains as though they are seeds and not ash, a burnt offering on solid ground vulnerable to the wind and rain—all that is left of my body gone, my being shifted, passed away, moving forward on and into eternity.[1]

While I have no way of knowing if "the end" that bell hooks imagined materialized, I believe that she made her transition from a place that she thought of as home; a space of belonging. It strikes me as a wonderful way to make one's way from this realm of existence. Her desire to have her body scattered among the hills that she loved, to return to the earth that gave birth to her, reflects her deep connection to the natural world, which she wrote about often. The way she envisions her being "moving forward on and into eternity" is deeply reminiscent of Nhat Hanh's teachings on the fundamental interdependence, or "interbeing," of all things, which casts death in a totally different light. Her use of the term *vulnerable* to describe her body's relationship to the land denotes a surrender to its wisdom; that the elements will take her where she is needed so that she can continue to serve her highest purpose: planting seeds of liberation.

By the time the day of the retreat arrived, I had spent weeks simultaneously grieving her passing and celebrating her life. I looked forward to being in community where I would be able to follow some threads that connected hooks's life and work to those of Nhat Hanh.

The connection between the two was fresh in my mind because I had recently reread the transcript of a conversation that hooks had with Nhat Hanh, featured in the March 24, 2017 issue of *Lion's Roar* magazine. In returning to the conversation two years after I had first encountered it, I was struck by how open and, dare I say, loving their communication was. At its base was a sense of care and affection for each other; a recognition of each other's humanity and preciousness. I felt their commitment not only to each other's awakening but also to those known and unknown who might read their words. It was clear that even though they were meeting for the first time, they trusted each other with their feelings and words, their strengths and vulnerabilities. These qualities that I sensed in reading the interview are what constitute the basis of love according to hooks.[2] hooks's conviction that "love is as love does" served as a guiding light for much of her work and more importantly, her life. This was also true of Thich Nhat Hanh. In many ways, I believe, they were kindred spirits. Although both are gone in body, they live on as major intellectual, creative, and spiritual forces.

When the Student Is Ready . . .

I first learned about bell hooks in the late 1980s when, during my sophomore year of college, two mushroom-eating visiting professors assigned *Ain't I a Woman: Black Women and Feminism* in their introductory women's studies course. That first encounter with hooks fell flat with me for a couple of reasons: First, I did not trust that the message of my liberation could come through white women. Second, although I was *in* college, at the time I didn't feel *of* it. I didn't quite know how I'd gotten there nor what I was doing there. As a barely eighteen-year-old Black first-generation college student from Queens, New York, at a predominantly white upper-class institution, I certainly didn't feel like I belonged. There was also the fact that I was not at a place in my life where I could appreciate the audacity of Black women. Although I was raised by an incredible Black woman, Lucille Pressley, and mothered by my older sister, Lisa, and my aunt Mary Jackson, I was oblivious to what it took for them to support their loved ones—the sacrifices they made on my behalf.

It was not until many years later when I revisited hooks—not in *Ain't I a Woman* but rather in *Salvation: Black People and Love*—that I began to appreciate the revolutionary work she was doing. (*Salvation* was the second publication in her series of three books on love. The first was *All about Love: New Visions* and the third was *Communion: The Female Search for Love*.) *Salvation* helped me recognize and appreciate the work of Black women in my life and in the world. By the time I read the book in 2001, shortly after 9/11, I was a single parent newly arrived at a competitive PhD program at the University of Wisconsin–Madison. I felt I needed saving. Reading the text, I was struck by how hooks's focus on the transformative power of Black love gently lifted me out of my head (where graduate students are told the true transformative work takes place) and dropped me into my heart. When I learned several years later that, quiet as it's kept, hooks was a practicing Buddhist, I knew that even though her memoir *Bone Black: Memories of Girlhood* and her three-book series on love were not explicitly about her relationship to Buddhism, they needed to be included in this work.

Read in relation to her other writings, *Bone Black* does implicitly what hooks's love series does explicitly: it moves us out of *just* our heads and into our bodies, where the heart resides. It is a profoundly nonlinear book, full of shifts in perspective and sudden leaps between different times. The disjuncture and disorientation that results from such a nonlinear narrative means that we must *feel into* what hooks is communicating. Reading her words thus becomes an embodied experience. This is one of the many gifts of the work she did in the world.

Her writings about her personal synthesis of Buddhism, Christian prayer, and Sufi mysticism (in several essays and in her collection of essays, *Remembered Rapture: The Writer at Work*) began as long ago as 1994. For me, an exploration of hooks's spiritual worldview is important to understanding her other work. As she wrote in her essay "Divine Inspiration: Writing and Spirituality," spirituality has always been the foundation of her experience as a writer.[3] Furthermore, her spirituality was integral to her activist work. For example, she spoke publicly about spirituality, including her own spiritual practice, as a way of giving young people hope.[4] Her dedication to sharing her personal story drew upon the African American tradition of bearing witness not only to our pain but also to how we get free. As she writes in a letter to her friend and fellow public intellectual Cornel West, "We bear witness not just with our intellectual work, but with ourselves, our lives. Surely, the crisis of our times demands that we give our all."[5] For hooks, bringing all of herself to her scholarly and activist work was both "political practice and religious sacrament—a life of resistance."[6] Her orientation was distinctly African American in the way that she drew upon Black people's long history of integrating our political work and our spiritual traditions. In other words, as a Black feminist, she lived the adage that the personal is political, and she extended its application to the spiritual realm. Such an approach rejects the compartmentalization that hooks recognized as a tool of "the imperialist white supremacist capitalist patriarchy," a phrase she used to describe the power structure that underlies the social order.[7]

hooks's commitment to giving the next generation hope is borne out in countless scholarly and cultural references to her work by both established and emerging thinkers and creators. Take, for instance, Carol J. Moeller's essay "bell hooks Made Me a Buddhist," wherein the author—a white woman—testifies that hooks played a considerable part in her discovery of other life-changing Buddhist teachers. hooks achieved this not only by exposing Moeller to Buddhism in the

classroom but also by "exemplifying a combined critical consciousness and mindful spiritual outlook that was and continues to be life-
sustaining."[8] In other words, hooks went beyond talking the talk to
the equally important work of walking the walk of Buddhist philosophy. In the public and supportive way she did this—lifting others as
she climbed—she carried on the work of the Black women activists in
whose footsteps she followed. Some of those women—including Sara
Oldman (her mother's mother), Rosa Bell (her mother), Alina Strand
(her quilting neighbor)—performed an activism that was known only
by their family and friends. It was nonetheless impactful as it helped
shape those, like hooks, who came after.

Although her spiritual practice included traditions that seem foreign to the African American experience, hooks nonetheless honored
those women's legacies. Moreover, as with the other women I write
about here, her focus on love opened up the primary community she
wrote about—Black people, and Black women in particular—to a liberating energy that was ultimately inclusive of everyone. She was a beacon of the revolutionary potential of Black women who stand in our
full power. I echo *Lion's Roar* associate editor Pamela Ayo Yetunde in
remembering hooks's influence on her own life: "Reading hooks gave
me permission to rebel, question, be authentic, speak my truth, love
myself and others, and be unapologetically critical as a Black woman."[9]
Many of us have tried to force ourselves into molds that never had us in
mind. hooks gave us permission to carve out our own spaces, ones that
honor where we came from and empower us to forge a new liberatory
path for ourselves. In doing so, we help light the lantern for others.

In these pages, I explore the ways in which hooks's writings and
teachings were integral to her steadfast commitment to contributing
to humanity's collective liberation. I offer an excavation of the ways
that her spiritual practice and the love ethic that drove her intellectual
and activist work intersected. In integrating my own story of my still-
unfolding awakening, I explore how when I, as the student, was ready,

she came. I can attest to her knowing that the end of her earthly body did not mean the end of her life, for as my relationship to her work evolves, she in turn shows up more and more in my life in new and meaningful ways.

The Making of a Love Ethic

In *Belonging*, hooks refers to the Kentucky hills as the place where her life began.[10] Born Gloria Jean Watkins to a working-class African American family in the small segregated town of Hopkinsville on September 25, 1952, she was the oldest of seven children: six girls and one boy. Her mother, Rosa Bell Watkins, worked as a maid in white homes; her father, Veodis Watkins, worked as a janitor.

hooks attended racially segregated public schools in the Jim Crow South. As we saw with Willis, hooks's education by Black teachers in an all-Black setting, rather than being limiting, was an empowering experience. There, her intellectual curiosity was nurtured. As she writes in *Teaching to Transgress: Education as the Practice of Freedom*, "We learned early that our devotion to learning, to a life of the mind, was a counter-hegemonic act, a fundamental way to resist every strategy of white racist colonization."[11] The love and support hooks experienced in her early childhood education fortified her to face the racism she experienced from the predominantly white staff and students she encountered when schools were desegregated in the 1960s. The two experiences, which she characterizes as the before and after, helped inspire her life's work fighting sexism and racism.[12]

After graduating from Hopkinsville High School, hooks attended Stanford University where she earned her bachelor's degree in English in 1973. In her women's studies classes at Stanford, hooks noticed a significant absence of Black women from the feminist literature the students were reading. That absence prompted her to begin writing *Ain't I a Woman* as a nineteen-year-old graduate student. The book, published in

1981, was groundbreaking in the way that it combined race, gender, and politics to point scholars and activists in the direction of a more inclusive way of viewing social activism. At the time, it was revolutionary, and it remains a popular work studied in many university courses.

hooks earned her master's degree in English from my alma mater, University of Wisconsin–Madison, in 1976. That same year, while attending the University of California, Santa Cruz, she took a position as an English professor and lecturer in ethnic studies at the University of Southern California. She earned her doctorate in literature in 1983. *And There We Wept*, a book of poems that she published in 1978, marks the first time that she used the pen name "bell hooks." The name is an homage to her great-grandmother, Bell Blair Hooks, who was known for speaking her mind. hooks chose not to capitalize any letters in her first and last names so as to focus on the importance of the *substance* of her writing rather than who she was.[13] Also, as the feminist scholar Beverly Guy-Sheftall notes, hooks's "choice to not capitalize her name captured her transgressive, oppositional self."[14]

hooks had read about Buddhist thought in high school, and at Stanford she encountered and came to love Beat poetry, which brought her into contact with the writings of the poets and Buddhist practitioners Jack Kerouac and Gary Snyder. She went on to visit Snyder's Zen center, the Ring of Bone Zendo in Nevada City, California, attending a May Day celebration. That was the point when she began engaging in what she called a "Buddhist Christian practice."

hooks had established her professional success as a writer and professor when she began feeling the call to return home to Kentucky. She made the move in 2004, taking a position as Distinguished Professor in Residence in Appalachian Studies at Berea College and founding the bell hooks Institute there. She wrote and spoke extensively about her fraught relationship to Appalachia. While she credited her commitment to self-determination and dissident speech to "the cultural ethos of the Kentucky backwoods, of the hillbilly country folk who were [her] ancestors and kin," she was also acutely aware of how her presence in her community brought into relief her otherness.[15] Nonetheless, she was committed to her chosen community, asserting during the keynote for Berea's Appalachian Writers Symposium in 2015, "I always take the motto, like the queer motto, 'We're here.' I feel that about myself as a Black person in the hills of Kentucky. I am here, and there's nothing but love within me for the world around me."[16] Her memoir, *Bone Black*, was one of the first places that she explored her complicated relationship to her Kentucky home.

Bone Black as Biomythography

Although most of hooks's writings contain autobiographical elements, only *Bone Black* can be considered an autobiography—or, more accurately, a biomythography. hooks, who was in her midforties when the book was published, described the writing similar to the way that the Black radical feminist and lesbian writer Audre Lorde characterized her text *Zami: A New Spelling of My Name*. hooks made the connection between what she did in *Bone Black* and Lorde's work in her essay "Writing Autobiography," noting that she was not as concerned with the accuracy of detail as with evoking in writing the state of mind, the spirit of a particular moment.[17]

The purpose of biomythography is not to retell one's life based solely on verifiable facts or events but to highlight the meanings behind or *embedded in* the facts or events. As hooks writes in the foreword to *Bone Black*, "This is autobiography as truth and myth—as poetic witness." She further explains that the text gathers together "the dreams, fantasies, experiences that preoccupied me as a girl, that stay with me and appear and reappear in different shapes and forms in all my work."[18] About the process of writing it, she says the memories from her childhood "came in a surreal, dreamlike style which made [her] cease to think of them as strictly autobiographical . . . it seemed that myth, dream, and reality had merged."[19] hooks relates that it was the query of her maternal grandmother, Sara Oldman (Baba), about how she could bear to live so far away from her people, that prompted hooks to begin listing the stories she told people when meeting them. In the process it became clear to her that she repeatedly shared the same tales she thought were significant and saw the process of putting those memories to paper as a way of bringing order to her life. It was her attempt "to stand back and see [herself] in a new way, no longer fragmented—whole—complete."[20] Emerging from those stories, *Bone Black* marked a shift in her relationship with herself and with her past, allowing her to become fully present to her life.

> Writing my girlhood life helped. It gave me new ground to stand on. . . . Poetic in style and tone, abstract even, I read and hear these accounts of my girlhood as though the speaker is in a trance, in a state that is at once removed and yet present. Much of my life away from Kentucky was lived in a trance state, as though I was always there and not there at the same time. Working to heal, to be whole, has been a process of awakening, of moving from trance into reality, of learning how to be fully present.[21]

The trance that hooks writes about is one with which many will be familiar; it is where the majority of us dwell. We go through the motions existing from one moment to the next with our minds either in the past or the future, but rarely in the present. I can attest to spending much of my life in a trance state, completely unaware of my inner life, let alone being present to my surroundings. But I have begun to wake up. Reading and writing about liberated souls like hooks has made the process easier. How grateful I am that their guiding lights exist. They help me know that I am not alone on this path.

As mentioned above, *Bone Black* is not a standard biography and makes for a disorienting reading experience. Here's an excerpt that typifies hooks's writing style in the book: In describing her and her siblings hiding in the family car from her father's mother, Sister Ray, who came to care for them while their mother was in the hospital, hooks refers to herself in the third person. She writes,

> Defiant, determined, they refused to budge even though they
> were beginning to feel afraid. Their resolve was weakening. . . .
> They wanted to relent but the particular little one, the one
> who was not her favorite, couldn't resist a last rebellious dis-
> play. She spit—right in the direction of that stern face. Only the
> rolled-up window kept it from reaching the target. Shocked,
> they opened the doors and ran, leaving her sitting alone con-
> templating the coming punishment.[22]

Even providing an excerpt from the text is difficult because each chapter, though short, reads as a self-contained narrative.

As someone who is normally averse to nonlinear narrative, preferring to have a story line to follow, I was surprised at how much I loved reading *Bone Black*. The dreamlike quality, the switching of pronouns, the seeming misremembering of the past—all resonated deeply. I understood the necessity of distancing one's self from a deeply painful childhood and was inspired to be gentle with myself for not being able to recall a lot of my own. In fact, it has long disturbed me that much of my childhood seems to be condensed into a few key moments revolving around the age of eleven. My eleventh year was one of profound internal and external transition; that year I entered a space of liminality in which I remained suspended even as the calendar years ticked by. I was no longer a relatively innocent girl (more on that later), yet I was many years from stepping into my womanhood.

In recent years I have tried to recover some memories, and through that process I've come to understand that the trancelike state in which I spent most of my preteen and teenage years was my mind's way of protecting itself from the trauma I experienced during that time. My meditation practice has helped in my re-membering the myself of today to that past. But even now, so far removed not only from the hurtful words and actions of others but also of myself toward myself when I didn't know any better, I experience the visceral need for distance. It is at those times that, like hooks, I will substitute "she" for "I" in my flawed remembering.

Like hooks, I also have siblings who have different recollections of the past and can fill in certain gaps in my memory. A recent example happened when I wrote a blog post celebrating the brilliance of the singer, classical pianist, and civil rights activist Nina Simone. In the post, I lamented not growing up in a household where the music of Simone was played. My elder sister, who follows my blog, called me up to tell me that I was wrong. Our mother did, in fact, play Simone's music. I listened, dumbfounded. How could I not remember that? What else have I misremembered and wrongly accused our mother of? While this gap in my memory may seem trivial, it is significant because it reframes my view of my mother, whom I always thought of as apolitical. The year that I was born, 1968, was a time of monumental social and political upheaval. I have often internally admonished my mother for not being in the streets marching with either Rev. King or Malcolm X. Now knowing that she sang along to "Young, Gifted and Black" and "Mississippi Goddam" helps me rethink her relationship to the revolutionary ethos that swept through our majority Black community in the late 1960s and '70s. It also makes me wonder what lessons seeped into my consciousness when I, as a young child, positioned myself under an end table at one of her raucous parties. While most of my life I viewed myself as an anomaly in my immediate family and community, the knowledge that the music of a revolution made its way into my developing consciousness brings into focus a few of the many early environmental influences on the paths I have followed.

For all of the childhood trauma that shapes the disjointedness of *Bone Black* and that hooks explores more lucidly in her other writings, she also testifies to the beauty that characterized much of her childhood. This beauty was found in her natural environment in the backwoods of Kentucky as well as in the quilting tradition that her grandmother passed down to her. Likewise, although childhood trauma propelled me into a kind of amnesia that persists, it exists alongside strong memories of my mother's warm hand enveloping my own as we trudged together down a snowy New York sidewalk, of her singing silly songs to me to make me know that I was loved, and, in the limited capacity that her Black southern heritage allowed, permitting me to speak my truth. In the small ways that she could, she encouraged my love of visual art and literature, letting me camp out in a corner in the kitchen reading a novel or drawing while she fried chicken, opening herself up to criticism from family members for "not making that girl do some work." She allowed me to dream even when she didn't understand what I was dreaming about. And although they did their requisite share of teasing of their baby sister, I must admit my sister and brothers also encouraged my dreams.

I am not sure that I would have been able to rise above the rebuke and teasing that hooks describes in *Bone Black*. For example, relating her family's reaction to her preference for reading instead of doing childhood household chores, she says, "It is my turn to iron. I can do nothing right. Before I begin I am being yelled at. I hear again and again that I am crazy, that I will end up in a mental institution. This is my punishment for wanting to finish reading before doing my work, for taking too long to walk down the stairs." Her family laughed at and mocked her, and though her mother's rejection would later drive hooks to pursue her deep study of love, its lacerating quality comes through in her description: "It is times like these that I am sorry to be alive, that I want to die. In the kitchen with my sisters, she talks on about how she cannot stand me, about how I will go crazy."[23] In that moment the pain of rejection from her family is so intense that she resorts to burning herself with the iron. Rather than her action evoking sympathy, her family pounces, seeing it as further evidence that she is headed for a mental institution. She says, "Already someone is laughing and yelling about what the crazy fool has done to herself. Already I have begun to feel the pain of the burning flesh. They do not stop talking. They say no one will visit me in the mental hospital."[24]

While her siblings taunted her, her mother doubled down on her harsh judgment of her daughter, telling her that her pain did not matter; she still must finish her ironing. How painful her family's taunting must have been; it seems to me that her self-inflicted wounding was all she could do to quiet the psychological and spiritual wounding that she suffered from those who should have protected her. How generous of her, then, to share the story. In relating it, she allows us to look into our own lives to confront past traumas. If we go on to read another of hooks's books, *Feminism Is for Everybody: Passionate Politics*, we can see where the ferociousness with which she defended children's rights came from. In the chapter "Feminist Parenting" she writes, "In a culture of domination where children have no civil rights, those who are powerful, adult males and females, can assert autocratic rule over children."[25] She concludes the chapter by advising, "Ending patriarchal domination of children by men and women is the only way to make the family a place where children can be safe, where they can be free, where they can know love."[26] In reading the two texts, I was able to reflect on the many times in my childhood when I was told to stop crying before I "was given something to cry for." And how I perpetuated that cycle of violence in my relationship with my own precious child. And to apologize. And then do better. This is part of hooks's revolutionary work, her transgressive pedagogy: she includes *everyone* in her revolutionary love vision, especially the most vulnerable, as it should be. In doing so, she models the courage and honesty that is imperative to the path of liberation.

hooks also described the process of writing *Bone Black* as trance-like. It seems that deliberately entering into that trance state helped surface memories that opened the way for her to wake up from the trance that she had unwittingly succumbed to. Her process can serve as a road map for others who seek to wake up from the trance of our complicity in the dominant culture that is built on and upheld through violence.

The result of that process is what the journalist Monique Judge calls "a transgressive form of writing, taking the idea of crossing boundaries as the basis of its form."[27] This transgressiveness comes through hooks's choice to vary the standpoint of her narrative delivery—sometimes in the singular first person, sometimes in the singular third person, and sometimes in the plural first person. According to hooks, the memories came to her in short vignettes, and each particular incident or encounter had its own story. The way that the biomythography unfolds feels to me like the working of Spirit. hooks describes it as "part of a cycle of reunion" that gave her the narrative in "bits and pieces of [her] heart"[28] and came together to form a whole, like a quilt. The process of remembering and writing was not unidirectional but rather reciprocal, or perhaps more appropriately, circular. hooks understood the stories that make up the narrative as also working on her, healing her, and making her heart "whole again."[29] Reading her work has served a similar purpose for me as I allow painful childhood memories to surface within the container of the Buddha's teachings of the Four Noble Truths, the first of which is "There is suffering." Without the support of Spirit, I'm not sure I would be able to hold them.

hooks said of her initial inspiration for writing her biomythography that she wanted to kill who she was without really having to die.[30]

Through her writing process, she could lay to rest the Gloria Jean of her tormented and anguished childhood. This desire to die to her past was, in part, indicative of her readiness to enter into another stage of her embodied experience. It was a rite of passage that marked her movement from metaphorical childhood to adulthood. As she says, "Once that self was gone—out of my life forever—I could more easily become the me of me."[31] Writing the biomythography was a catharsis, an emptying out of her past to make way for her rebirth as a more whole, healed, fully realized human being who could go on to do the writing around love that defines much of her oeuvre.

In the end, hooks did not need to kill her past. Writing the manuscript enabled her to look at her past from a different perspective and use the knowledge that she gained to grow and change in practical ways. In putting her story to paper, hooks was able to move away from seeing her childhood self as "the little girl who had to be annihilated for the woman to come into being" and instead to rescue that tormented and anguished child.[32] Put another way, writing enabled her to reclaim the parts of herself that had long gone uncared for and rejected, just as she had often felt alone and neglected as a child.

hooks's Childhood in Bone Black and Belonging

hooks was a Black girl who came of age in the Jim Crow South. As such, her life was circumscribed by southern white supremacy. In *Bone Black*, she nonetheless depicts a childhood seemingly shaped exclusively by her African American community. In the tradition of Nobel Prize–winning writer Toni Morrison's notion of bypassing the white gaze,[33] hooks writes of her childhood community, "White folks mean little to them. They pay them no mind. It is black people of all colors who are the center of their world."[34]

Likewise, in *Belonging* hooks writes, "Growing up in racial segregation I felt 'safe' in our all black neighborhoods."[35] We learn in that book, though, that there were instances in which white people and their cultural baggage penetrated the Black world that hooks's family and community created for themselves. Drawing attention to the particular danger that white men posed to Black girls, hooks goes on to discuss the few Black people, like her Baba, who lived in white neighborhoods. This meant that in order to visit their grandmother, hooks and her siblings had to make their way past white racists who taunted and jeered at them. The experience, which she calls "frightening and stressful," left an indelible mark on hooks.[36] While the children were taught to not see all white people as "bad," they were nonetheless socialized to be constantly vigilant of them. This socialization, a survival tactic, coupled with encountering racists who clearly meant them harm, was no doubt traumatizing. Yet hooks bypasses that trauma in *Bone Black*. There, the only hint that we have of such trauma is in a story that she includes of driving home with a white male friend when some other white men tried to drive them off the road. hooks leaves the interiority of the experience out of her telling of this story. Rather, she simply relates it as one part of the more important story of her relationship with the white boy. Although she does not dwell on the experience, the fact that she ends the chapter with the incident leaves a lasting impression.[37] I can't help but be reminded of the abolitionist and statesman Frederick Douglass who, in his autobiography, writes of not having much feeling when he learned after his mother's funeral that she had died. The passage has always haunted me, at least in part because, although he denies his grief at the news, his including it in the narrative's opening belies his professed disengagement. Similarly, hooks's way of relating her story in *Bone Black* haunts me for what is not expressed.

I write about the two books as if *Bone Black* preceded *Belonging*. In fact, *Bone Black* was published six years after *Belonging*. I suspect that the approach that hooks takes to similar material—one, a lucid recounting of her childhood, and another that is disjointed and disorienting—reflects the moving out of the head and dropping into the heart that takes time once someone has been trained in academia and that I discussed in the opening of this chapter.

In *Belonging*, hooks is able to take a step back to explore the interiority of her feelings about her interactions with her white neighbors and make larger observations about the lasting impact of such interactions. She writes, for instance, "Still many black people suffer post-traumatic stress disorder as a consequence of sustained racist exploitation and oppression. More than not that pain is ignored in our culture."[38] Read alongside *Bone Black*, *Belonging* connects her personal story of trauma engendered by living in a white supremacist society and the trickle-down effect of it to that of the collective, providing a more straightforward reflection on childhood experiences that were distorted by painful memories.

In addition to the personal catharsis they provided for hooks, *Belonging* and, later, *Bone Black* show us how events and feelings that seem unique to the individual may be shared by the collective. They point to larger structural issues that facilitate and cement the conditions that provide the framework for individual experience. In linking the individual with collective experience and bearing witness to her own and others' suffering, hooks pays homage to the African American autobiographical tradition. I have come to appreciate the different approaches that hooks takes to her individual work of waking up in the two texts. In doing so, she allows different entry points to the reader who is also seeking liberation.

Bone Black leaves off at the cusp of young adulthood, before hooks departed the South and traveled to Stanford University to pursue her undergraduate degree. She said about her decision to attend school in California that she was fleeing her southern upbringing. Her proclamation will resonate with many; it definitely resonates with me. Born to a single mother and raised in the North from the late 1960s until the late 1980s, my childhood was marked by disruption, displacement, and a profound sense of confinement. When college recruiters visited my "failing" high school and offered me a way out with a full scholarship in a place with trees and opportunity, I took it. The many places that I have traveled since that first sojourn have helped me to put my own before-and-after time in perspective. After decades of being alienated from myself, taking up a meditation practice allowed me to rejoin some of my fragmented memories to not only my current self but also to the communities I left behind. They have become integral to my thinking about what it means to be free. Again, reading hooks's memoir has supported my reexamination of my own difficult childhood. Being able to see myself in her story has illuminated a path to re-membering myself to my past; to experience release from a many-layered trance to step into a more awake present. If I were to write my own autobiography, it, like hooks's text, might very well be characterized by vignettes, changing narrative voice, and dream states. I would see the form as honoring and reflecting a ruptured consciousness that acted as a protective shield so that I could function in the world until I was ready and for which I am grateful.

The Site of Memory

I want to dwell here on the question of memory, positing that *Bone Black* deliberately plays with memory to illustrate the way that the "self" is constructed. Like Toni Morrison, who in her exploration of the role of memory in her work as a fiction writer, said ". . . memory weighs heavily in what I write, in how I begin and what I find significant . . . memories within are the subsoil of my work,"[39] hooks inquired into the central role of memory in getting *at* truth. She is transparent about the role memory played in her ability to accept and reconcile her past.

Morrison frames her writings as acts of literary archaeology.[40] She describes this approach to writing as "a way of journey[ing] to a site to see what remains and reconstruct[ing] the world that the remains imply."[41] This is exactly what hooks does in her biomythographical merging of "myth, dream and reality."[42] She conceives of her narrative as "evoking in writing the state of mind, the spirit of a particular moment."[43]

Another way that we see a convergence between Morrison's process and hooks's is in the deployment of their senses. Morrison describes her fiction-writing process as tracking an image from picture to meaning to text. hooks's way of releasing the memories locked inside her also depends on her senses, although in her case, she did not always begin with the visual sense. As she writes, part of *Bone Black* unfurled for her on the page after she encountered the scents of a Black man with whom she was having an affair—cigarettes, occasionally alcohol, and the smell of his body. In what she calls the "scent of memory," the combination of his Black maleness and the scents that surrounded him "in some mysterious way" provided her with a link to a past that she "had been struggling to grapple with, to name in writing."[44] The man's presence in her life cracked open the protective shells that contained the memories of particular events, releasing them to be explored for the deeper meanings that they held.

One of those memories surfaces in *Belonging* in which she spends a chapter lovingly discussing her family's close relationship to tobacco— not atypical for a southern family at that time. She writes,

> I cannot recall a time in my childhood when tobacco did not have meaning and presence. Whether it came from watching Big Mama smoke her pipe, or emptying the coffee cans that were used to spit our chewing tobacco, or watching Mama's mother Baba braid tobacco leaves for use to ward off bugs, or watching Aunt Margaret hand-roll tobacco or cigarettes and cigars, the odor of tobacco permeated our lives and touches me with the scent of memory.[45]

It would seem that the scent of her lover opened up memories that she had held at bay because of her painful childhood. The intimacy that she shared with her partner—being close enough to smell him—allowed her senses to lead her to the images, which then led her to the text. Her openness to that process allowed it to unfold in its own time. By writing about the crop in the way that she does—giving a history of it steeped in community—hooks helps us to understand the way that it has been bastardized and abused. Where now it is a source of sickness and death, it was once sacred medicine.

Interestingly, although in *Bone Black* we see an intense interest in sensorial connection to the past, hooks does not show much allegiance to her memories. In fact, she exposes the inaccuracy of one of her earliest memories of her relationship with her only brother almost as soon as she relates it. She writes of the two of them playing with a red wagon, noting that it was kept at their great-grandfather's house because he lived in an area that had sidewalks. Later, as an adult, she is told that what they had was not a wagon but a wheelbarrow: "She grew up and found that the red wagon of her memory had never existed," writes hooks. In fact, "Going through boxes of black-and-white photos, she found many of herself plump and unsmiling seated in a wheelbarrow with the boy-brother holding the ends as if at any moment he would dump her out."[46] It is not the accuracy but rather the *significance* of the memory that matters. That unstable object of memory serves as a symbol of what ended up separating them, forcing them into different worlds as a result of prescribed gender roles that, in hooks's child mind, made her brother hate her.[47] She remembers "waiting to hear the boy tell her when they were alone that he hate, hate, hated her because she was a girl."[48] Although she did not have the language for it at the time, the expression of hatred that she waited to hear from her brother was the result of the sexism that she experienced from her father.

In "A Place Where the Soul Can Rest," a chapter from *Belonging*, hooks describes the structure of the house where she grew up in gendered terms, with the porch being a feminine space. Disliking the presence of such a space where his six daughters would congregate, her father eventually "sheet-rocked, blocked up the door so that it became our brother's room, an enclosed space with no window to the outside."[49] hooks never mentions having a room of her own, despite being the oldest. It was a privilege that only her brother got to enjoy. The why of that privilege as well as the source of hooks's assumption of her brother's sexist thinking becomes clearer just two paragraphs later.

> To our patriarchal dad, Mr. V, the porch was a danger zone—as in his sexist mindset all feminine space was designated dangerous, a threat. A strange man walking on Mr. V's porch was setting himself up to be a possible target: walking on the porch, into an inner feminine sanctum, was in the eyes of any patriarch just the same as raping another man's woman. And we were all of us—mother, daughters—owned by my father. Like any patriarch would, he reminded us whose house we lived in—a house where women had no rights but could indeed, claim the porch. . . . Indeed, our daddy always acted as though he hated the porch.[50]

Is it any wonder, then, that hooks expected to be the object of her younger brother's hatred? That she saw an unspoken hatred for her in his eyes simply because she was a girl? That she expected to hear him speak words of hatred even though she never relates actually ever hearing them? I would say no. Rather, what is surprising is that she and her sisters did not internalize the hatred of their femaleness that they sensed from their father and that her brother surely picked up on.

hooks's telling of the story is an example of a function of memory that, as the literature scholar Jeanne Braham explains, "With all its biases and special needs, . . . yokes with the imagination—often through the medium of metaphor—to discover or create the 'felt truth' of a particular life experience."[51] The wagon/wheelbarrow rides that for hooks marked the rift in her relationship with her brother may be seen as a metaphor for gender inequality and trauma engendered by the patriarchy that showed up so intimately in her father's attitude toward the female members of his family. As hooks says, the biomythography was not so much an overview of her childhood as it was a creative revisiting of experiences that were deeply imprinted on her consciousness.[52] The memory of the wagon/wheelbarrow, however false in its detail, laid the groundwork for her later feminist work on gender.

By including the story in her biomythology and being transparent about the untrustworthiness of memory, hooks helped me question my own memories, like the presence and equally important *perceived* absence of certain music from my childhood experience. It speaks to the importance of centering one's personal experience as part of a commitment to collective liberation. Her honesty allows those of us who read her to be honest with ourselves in a society that is predicated on delusion. Such honesty can set us on the path to uncovering certain memories, which, left unexamined, weigh on our subconscious and, without our knowledge or consent, continue to guide our decisions and actions. To face such memories honestly is in and of itself a liberatory act.

What's Love Got to Do with It?

One of the questions that hooks returns to again and again in her writing is "What does real love look like?" This may seem like a simple question with an obvious answer. However, as hooks discusses in her love trilogy—*All about Love, Salvation,* and *Communion*—the vast majority of people have superficial and deeply flawed ideas of love, based in fantasy.[53] Moreover, as she notes in *All about Love,* most of the theorizing about love has been done by men, even as patriarchy and male domination of women and children stand in the way of love.[54] With these observations as background, she asserts that "profound changes in the way we think and act must take place if we are to create a loving culture."[55]

All about Love opens with hooks stating that it was the absence of love that made her understand how much love matters:

> At the moment of my birth I was looked upon with loving-kindness, cherished and made to feel wanted on this earth and in my home. To this day, I cannot remember when that feeling of being loved left me. I just know that one day I was no longer precious. Those who had initially loved me well turned away. The absence of their recognition and regard pierced my heart and left me with a feeling of brokenheartedness so profound I was spellbound.[56]

Invoking the image of Adam and Eve's banishment from the Garden of Eden, she continues, "No other connection healed the hurt of that first abandonment, that first banishment from love's paradise." That time in her life, when she went from feeling loved to unloved, was at the root of her subsequent suffering: "Like every wounded child I just wanted to turn back time and be in that paradise again, in that moment of remembered rapture where I felt loved, where I felt that sense of belonging."[57] The desire to recapture that sense of belonging haunted much of her life. As she says in the last chapter of *Belonging*, "All my life I have searched for belonging, a place that would become home."[58] She seems to have finally found home—a kind of return to the Garden of Eden—when, after thirty years in her self-imposed exile, she returned to Kentucky to live.

In an interview hooks did with Sharon Salzberg, one of the founders of the mindfulness meditation movement and a leading voice in lovingkindness, or *metta*, practice, she talks about being obsessed with the subject of love, adding that many of us, and especially those of us from dysfunctional backgrounds, have to learn what it is to love.[59] hooks's suffering around the absence of love that she experienced as a child and her subsequent search for it inspired her to turn to Buddhism, which in turn inspired her writing.[60] She notes in her interview with Salzberg that one of the things that she loved about Buddhism was the emphasis on practice, something that she believed is also necessary for love. This, she argues, was especially true in historical moments such as the one that we faced following the presidential election of Donald Trump. As a woman of color, she had the sense of people beaming hate at her and experienced fear in the presence of strangers.[61] Under such conditions, she was prompted to ask rhetorically, how does one practice love under such circumstances?

As hooks asserts in *All about Love*, "The intensity of our woundedness often leads to a closing of the heart, making it impossible for us to give or receive the love that is given to us."[62] While she may have been referring to interpersonal love—the love of a parent for a child or of one lover for another—this ability to give and receive love is also useful in the way that we think about our relationship to other humans, animals, and all sentient beings, as well as the earth, the spirit world, and the universe. Doubling back, however, to her acknowledgment that she often felt unloved by her parents and siblings, we can see that her love ethic reached beyond the interpersonal while being very much rooted in it. In that I see the lesson that the interpersonal cannot be bypassed. Rather, it may serve as a starting point for an expanded sense of love that is unconditional and available to every being.

"Waking Up to Racism"

Feeling the need to emerge from the shadows, in 1994 hooks "outed" herself as a Buddhist in *Tricycle: The Buddhist Review*. The article in which she did so, "Waking Up to Racism," was, on the one hand, a wake-up call to her white fellow Buddhist practitioners to recognize their role in perpetuating racism in their sanghas. On the other, it was a call to African American Buddhists to step out of "their place" and to "speak their experiences."[63] The essay contrasts white arrogance with Black humility with regard to Buddhist practice—without judgment.

She names the fact that, unlike her white comrades who have no qualms about journeying "in search of spiritual nourishment to the 'third world,'" "black people, and other people of color who have grown up in the midst of racial apartheid and racist domination often feel the need to stay home, to stay in their place."[64] This imperative for people of African descent to "stay in their place" is one with which hooks (like Willis) was familiar growing up when and where she did.

The article explores both white and Black Buddhists' role in fostering Black hypervisibility and invisibility. From the white American side of the equation, hooks looks to the role that imperialism plays in whites' ability to travel "anywhere in the world and claim ownership to walk on many paths."[65] She contends that because of "violent colonialism, continuing neocolonialism, and journeying rooted in compassion and good will," much of what has been found in the places that they travel to both gives life and takes it away.[66] She counsels recognizing and interrogating the simultaneity of violence and compassion that these seekers embody.

hooks took the opportunity of the article to begin an important and ongoing conversation about the many ways that white supremacy is perpetuated in Buddhist communities. Among them, in her own case, was being singled out by white Buddhists who questioned her interest in Buddhism. hooks deduces that such questions presuppose that while the questioner's attraction to Buddhism is natural, hers is not. She is the Other with no ancestral connection between herself and "other people of color and the cultures in which they search to find Buddhist truth."[67] hooks posits that this white suspicion is one of the reasons that African Americans have difficulty associating themselves with Buddhism. Such resistance, coupled with "the legacy of slavery and the spiritual uplift offered by the transformative message of antebellum evangelical Christianity,"[68] has led them to believe that "they cannot maintain a connection with their race and culture of origin and walk a Buddhist path."[69] Getting to the core of the issue, hooks explains, "To some of them, choosing such a path in this country has been synonymous with choosing whiteness, with remaining silent about racism for fear of being dismissed."[70] Such thinking is reinforced by Buddhist teachers whose teachings on "no self" or "nonself" potentially signal to African American students that their attention to race is "really not important."[71] As Osho Zenju observes, this conveys to such students that they are not as spiritually evolved as their white counterparts.

Jan Willis approaches this topic of belonging from a different, equally cogent perspective. When asked by "certain people" whether she feels a gap between who she is and what she does, she sees beneath the question to what is really at issue: "What does Buddhism offer to *any* African American?"[72] The question comes partly from the assumption that Buddhism is not *for* African Americans. As Willis remarks, "Some scholars have even suggested that the quiet meditative styles of Buddhist services are too sedate for people coming from such exuberant backgrounds as the black church."[73] But she and hooks, both raised Baptist, are among a growing number who are proof against the intimation of a monolithic blackness inherent in the statement. The fact is, there is no one way of being Black. Bringing our full selves to our Buddhist practice involves both silence and music. There is celebration in each of these approaches.

The question "Why Buddhism?" also comes from a belief that the tradition is too far removed from the concerns of African Americans, many of whom have for centuries sought relief in the Black church from their daily struggle of living in a white supremacist society. Willis's answer to the question is that Buddhism offers African Americans "a methodology for enhancing our confidence."[74] The issue of self-confidence or self-esteem is something with which hooks struggled on a daily basis. It is something millions of African Americans continue to struggle with as a result of growing up and living in a white supremacist society.

Whereas Willis pins her discussion of self-esteem to her experiences of growing up in the Jim Crow South, hooks opens up her consideration of the affliction of low self-esteem to the wider population. "Low self-esteem is a national epidemic and victimization is the flip side of domination," she asserts.[75] Her statement can be read from the perspective of the oppressor and the oppressed. The constant onslaught of domination that is foundational to this country results in low self-esteem on the part of those who are the victims of that domination—marginalized people, women, the disenfranchised. On the other hand, people feel the need to dominate others because they suffer from low self-esteem themselves.[76]

hooks connects the topic of African Americans' low self-esteem or sense of unworthiness to those who wish to follow the dharma path, suggesting that their inclination to "stay in their place" is in large part responsible for their silence about their spiritual practice. "That silence is often imposed," she writes, "a response to fears that we may not know enough, that we will be looked down upon, especially by whites."[77] Even though at the time the article was published she was already a well-respected scholar, she confesses, "I have always been reluctant to speak about Buddhism, for fear I will mispronounce words, not have all the details and information that will prove me a card-carrying Buddhist and not just a dharma voyeur."[78] This reluctance to claim Buddhism with authority is not something with which she witnessed white people grapple. Beyond even the question of public authority, she notes that many people of color fear not being worthy of claiming their Buddhist practice, another issue that does not plague their white counterparts.

At the same time, hooks points to a kind of nobility in African American Buddhists' relationship to the practice. While our reluctance to claim Buddhism relates, in part, to our conditioning to "stay in their place," it also relates to the African American tradition of humility, rooted in Christianity. For instance, she references the book of Psalms, wherein the seeker marvels at the wisdom of the teacher, completely open to the possibility that "such knowledge is high, I cannot attain it."[79] hooks posits that the African American fear of not being worthy "has to do with the practice of humility, not being presumptuous, not assuming rights, and/or the experience of being in awe."[80] This humility is a gift, then, that allows Black Buddhists to maintain a receptivity to Buddhist teachings that eludes those white Buddhists who claim authority or dominion over the teachings. What hooks describes with regard to Black humility strikes me as akin, in Buddhist terms, to beginner's mind—a state that keeps us open to the wisdom in the teachings; something that is foreclosed when someone believes they "know."

I am always taken by surprise when, if I mention Buddhist teachings in conversation, the person I'm talking with interrupts to ask if I'm Buddhist. Sometimes I will tell them directly that that's not the point. Often I tell them that I *try* to follow the Buddha's teachings. My reasoning for attempting to reposition the question is to refocus the attention from "me" and "mine" to the lessons to be had for us all. In emphasizing the "trying," I hope to tap into the humility that hooks talks about, thereby uplifting my sense of awe and wonder at the Buddha's wisdom and insight and reaffirming the aspiration to wake up. I also acknowledge my flawed humanness. At the same time, I would say that the personal trouble that I have with declaring myself a Buddhist is just that: personal. Ultimately my hope is that my reluctance to label myself Buddhist enables me to mindfully resist my ego's desire to stand in for the real work of practice, that I can remain vigilant against becoming so enthralled by what the label represents that I lose track of the liberation the practice offers me.

hooks was a pioneering voice in the call for white convert Buddhists to wake up to the way that they perpetuate white supremacy in the sangha. When she published "Waking Up to Racism" in 1994, the work of other pioneers, Jan Willis and Faith Adiele, would not be published for another seven and ten years respectively. But a lot has changed in the almost thirty years since hooks published her article. hooks lived to witness the proliferation of BIPOC-dedicated dharma spaces and the emergence of Black people in positions of leadership as dharma teachers and producers of knowledge. As such, people of color can now choose not to be assaulted by the suspicion and questioning that hooks and the other women about whom I write had to endure. Their writing about their experiences, in tandem with the actions of visionaries such as Marlene Jones, Konda Mason, Larry Yang, Gina Sharpe, and Mushim Ikeda means that the landscape of American convert Buddhism truly is changing. White Buddhist convert practitioners are waking up to their complicity in upholding a culture of domination and exclusion. Sadly, it took the murder of George Floyd in the summer of 2020 to meaningfully disturb many a white person who had, until then, been comfortably wrapped in the cocoon of "oneness." This was not just true in Buddhist circles. In fact, if you google the article title "Waking Up to Racism," you will find hooks's article sandwiched between several articles from the past few years with similar names. There has also been an explosion of Buddhist classes, courses, discussion groups, and retreats offered under some variation of the title "Waking Up to Whiteness." This, to me, signals progress.

Gesshin Greenwood, a white American Buddhist practitioner, writes of the difficulty and pain that she felt while reading hooks's essay. She felt that something she cared about deeply was implicated in "the destructive, colonial rampage" about which hooks spoke.[81] Greenwood confesses that seeing herself in the seeker that hooks was talking about did not feel good, especially since she had been oblivious to it. "But this is what bell hooks does," continues Greenwood; "she is an axe to that annoying frozen sea within us we don't want to acknowledge."[82] Greenwood initially felt strong resistance to hooks's message in the article, but while railing about the essay with a former student, Greenwood came to see that the locus of hooks's argument was not in criticizing "spiritual seeking itself (or white people practicing Buddhism, for that matter)" but rather concerned itself with "the attitude which privileges and respects certain kinds of methods and practices over other ones."[83] Greenwood eventually came to the conclusion that, by posing the question "Will the real Buddhist please stand up?" hooks exposes the fact that "this very human impulse to seek what is true can get tangled up in the impulse to want to designate who is the 'real Buddhist' and who is the hack—the devotional Buddhist, the material Buddhist, etc."[84]

I, for one, have no idea what a "real Buddhist" is. I don't think it is a question that is to be answered as it is not the label that matters but a way of being in the world. Being *with* the challenges that this life brings is my understanding of the path of liberation.

Finally, in "Waking Up to Racism" hooks mentions that she was writing fragments of a book, "Buddha Belly," about the meaning of Buddhism in her life. The title refers to the Buddha that she had been carrying in her belly for more than twenty years at that time. She describes the writings as often funny, witty takes on her experiences with Buddhism as a Black female. She remarks on feeling lucky because Buddhism had come to her from so many different directions that even when she was not seeking, she was always found.[85] I don't know why hooks never published that book—perhaps she was too busy with all her other writing and teaching commitments. Or perhaps her fear of not "getting it right" proved too much to overcome. Whatever the case, the fact that she was working on a book about her experience as a Black female Buddhist and was courageous enough to declare it publicly feels affirming of Buddhism's importance to her personal evolution.

While I would not say that Buddhism found me, I will say that my teachers and I have found each other. Sometimes they offered themselves, sometimes I sought them out, and sometimes it was just clear that it was time. Sometimes they waited patiently in the wings until I was ready. I feel like my experience with hooks falls into that last camp. Again, at the time that I was introduced to hooks as an eighteen-year-old Black girl from Queens, New York, I was not ready to receive her offering. In fact, I didn't seriously take up hooks's writing until a couple of years before her passing. I didn't read *Belonging* until after her passing, following a sharing session organized by a colleague in women's and gender studies. During that session, another colleague shared the quote in the opening pages of this chapter about the role of mindfulness in one's choice of a place to live as well as to die.

Finding Home and Belonging

hooks returned to Kentucky when she was in her early fifties, at around the age I am now. Reading about her decision to do so has raised the question for me about whether I could ever see myself returning to my own childhood home of Queens. For me, the answer is a hard no. While I recognize that her return to Kentucky was in many ways about *place*, I also see her sense of belonging as most deeply about a feeling that was facilitated by her proximity to nature.

In *Belonging*, she writes that her girlhood was divided into neat lines demarcating a time before and after. Her "life in nature was the Before and the After was life in the city where money and status determined everything."[86] She wrote of, in the backwoods of Kentucky, learning "to trust only the spirit, to follow where the spirit moved." She continued: "Ultimately, no matter what was said or done, the spirit called to us from beyond words, from a place beyond man-made law, the wild spirit of unspoiled nature worked its way into the folk of the backwoods, an ancestral legacy, handed down from generation to generation." hooks wrote that nature's "fundamental gift was the cherishing of that which is most precious, freedom." She added that "to be fully free one had to embrace the organic rights of the earth."[87] This was a stripped-down bell hooks who was committed to finding freedom as inextricable from others and that of the earth from a place of wildness that was guided by a deep and profound love.

If Thich Nhat Hanh was right—and I believe he was—then as he taught was true of the cloud, bell hooks will never really die. Her ashes traveling on the wind from atop that Kentucky hill have much work to do.

3

OSHO ZENJU
EARTHLYN MANUEL

Embodying the Self, Walking with the Ancestors

I FIRST "MET" Zenju Earthlyn Manuel—Osho to her students—in the pages of a magazine.[1] One of my relaxation strategies as a very stressed graduate student was to check out magazines from the undergraduate library. In one of the countless publications I found a short piece on this Black woman Zen Buddhist priest. I remember studying the three-quarter-page photo of a radiantly smiling bald Black woman in flowing brown robes surrounded by lush green foliage. Below the photo was about a paragraph-long description of her, which included the fact that though she is from Los Angeles, her parents were from Louisiana. I squinted, peering a little more closely into her eyes, and saw in them the island nation of Haiti, my soul home.

The article also mentioned that she had her own sangha, so wonderfully named Still Breathing. There was no contact information for her, and when I did an internet search, very little came up. Of course, the demands of my life at the time quickly reclaimed center stage. For at least the next ten years, I tucked that first encounter away in my memory. It wasn't until I began spending more time with my meditation practice, although in isolation in my new home in Michigan in 2015, that I found her again. In that same year, Rev. Zenju published *The Way of Tenderness: Awakening through Race, Sexuality, and Gender*, which, although not her first publication, seems to be the one that widened her audience well beyond the Buddhist community. After my unfortunate experience with my local Zen center where I felt othered, I was searching for a sense of belonging. I found it when I stumbled upon *The Way of Tenderness*.

Though of a different generation, raised on the East Coast, and very much a novice with no Buddhist home, I found that Rev. Zenju's tracing of her movement from a wounded tenderness to one of open-heartedness spoke to my struggle to step into a liberated life. As I am wont to do, I began devouring everything I could find by her. One of her offerings at the time was her *Black Angel Cards: 36 Oracles and Messages for Divining Your Life*, which included a divination session with her. I jumped at the opportunity. Causes and conditions that I was introduced to during that hour-long conversation continue, more than seven years later, to unfold.

Prior to the COVID pandemic, I followed her teachings through her online courses and listened to the occasional Buddhist summit interview. During COVID, my relationship with Osho blossomed when I was able to sit with her on remote meditation retreats. Now, as one of her students in Still Breathing, I have felt welcomed home to a sangha that heeds the Black femme acapella group Sweet Honey in the Rock's advice to listen more often to things than to beings.[2]

Sitting with Still Breathing following a white supremacist's massacre of shoppers in a supermarket in Buffalo, New York, and then barely a week later, the murder of children and their teachers at an elementary school in Uvalde, Texas, in May 2022, made me fully appreciate the balm of refuge that is to be found in a truly beloved community. There, among my dharma siblings via Zoom, as one of them rang the bell to signal the midpoint of our formal meditation practice, I felt in my bones the field of care and support that we were creating for one another. Tears of grief and gratitude flowed and continued to flow for the hour or so that we sat together. I felt safe to speak my grief into our virtual circle. My tears were met with words of compassion from Osho and nods of understanding and screen hearts from my dharma siblings. I felt seen and fully heard. Most importantly I felt loved despite the fact that I had, at that point, not met anyone except Osho in person. With deliberateness, Osho Zenju has cultivated this sacred container for us to come as our full selves, accepted and loved for all that we are. Indeed, I was able to breathe a little easier that particular morning, to be peace even in the midst of turmoil.

Of course, that peace was fleeting. By week's end I was anxious and slipping into despair as the news cycles kept the horrific stories alive. This pattern has repeated several times. I suffer because I am human. But then I return to the sangha, see myself reflected in my teacher and my dharma siblings, and am reminded of my true name: love.

Sources

Osho Zenju is an ordained Sōtō Zen Buddhist priest and teacher. She also identifies as a "seer, poet, artist, and drum medicine woman."[3] She has authored many texts, including *Seeking Enchantment: A Spiritual Journey of Healing from Oppression; Tell Me Something about Buddhism: Questions and Answers for the Curious Beginner; Be Love: An Exploration of Our Deepest Desire; The Way of Tenderness: Awakening through Race, Sexuality, and Gender; Sanctuary: A Meditation on Home, Homelessness, and Belonging; The Deepest Peace: Contemplations from a Season of Stillness; The Shamanic Bones of Zen: Revealing the Ancestral Spirit and Mystical Heart of a Sacred Tradition,* and

Opening to Darkness: Eight Gateways to Being with the Absence of Light in Unsettling Times, with other works on the way. She is also a contributor to several collections, a blogger, the host of her own poetry podcast, and a facilitator of Buddhist teachings through webinars and in-person offerings.

Osho Zenju expresses herself through music, dance, poetry, prose, prophecy, visual art, and more. Rather than defining herself by her many accomplishments (her *doing*), however, she reflects on her way of *being* and becoming in the world. "Over the years," she once wrote on the home page of her website, "I have conjured up a life of reverence, peace, poetry, tea, esoteric teachings, painting, and sacred conversations with others about life, being born, being a daughter, and living in a dark body."[4] Her website as the place where many first learn about her work reflects her personal evolution and has changed several times since I began this project. My favorite description is her latest:

> I have gone through many gateways. But I am neither monk,
> nor nun, nor priest. I am neither Zen or Buddhist. I am neither
> teacher nor guide, nor author. I am a dark seed of lineage that
> has resisted annihilation for thousands of years. I am a voice of
> the great darkness of transformation, grace, and constant birth
> and death. I am a collective voice that weeps and protests. I
> am the ever-abundant blackness and darkness that has given
> birth to everything. I am life from the first source of life. I am
> because we are.[5]

This description reflects two principles that I find to be at the heart of much of Osho's teaching. One is that we can find all that we need when we empty ourselves of static notions of identity and allow ourselves to be vessels for liberation. Relatedly, she combines a Buddhist understanding of interrelatedness *and* an African worldview known as *ubuntu*: there is no "I" without "we." The two principles are indicative of the way that Osho Zenju approaches her spiritual practice, which, as she has said, is also her social justice practice.[6]

What Osho Zenju offers to date are wisdom teachings that draw heavily on her lived experience. Her way of writing echoes her way of teaching in other settings—replete with stories about her life and wisdom teachings with which her students are invited to sit. Indeed, I see her offerings as invitations for us to sit in zazen, which is as she describes, "a Zen Buddhist way of sitting still, receiving, and releasing."[7] They are gestures of ceremony that, when carried out in an awakened state, are gateways to liberation.

In this chapter I explore several of Osho Zenju's offerings as they relate to her commitment to pointing the way to collective liberation as inextricable from her own. I explore her writings and teachings through the lens of trauma and the possibility of easing suffering that Buddhism, infused with traditional ancestral reverence, represents for African Americans.

Origins

Osho was born in Los Angeles, California, to Alvesta Pierre Manuel and Lawrence Manuel Jr., immigrants from Creole Louisiana. She is the middle of three girls, raised in the Church of Christ. Always attracted to spirituality, she loved attending church. As someone who "adored the true teachings on Christ's path well into adulthood," she was an avid reader of the Bible.[8]

As an adult, she explored spiritual traditions, expanding beyond Christianity. She began participating in indigenous spiritual traditions in her early twenties, briefly attending ceremonies with Ifa diviners from Dahomey, West Africa, and taking part in Lakota sun dance prayer ceremonies.[9] In her thirties, she began her journey into Buddhism in the way many people of color have: with the chanting tradition of Nichiren Daishonin Buddhism (Soka Gakkai), a Japanese school named after its thirteenth-century founder and based on the Lotus Sutra. Soka Gakkai, a lay branch of the school, is the Buddhist group that has historically attracted the greatest numbers of African Americans in the West, including well-known devotees such as Tina Turner and Herbie Hancock. Nichiren is unique in its dedication to bringing Buddhism to communities in despair; it is known for its tradition of proselytizing (*shakubuku*) and for the diversity of its practitioners.[10]

Although she took up Nichiren in adulthood, Osho has talked about being "shakubukued" while walking in a shopping mall when she was eleven years old. Like I did with her photo in the magazine, she tucked the experience away until it could resurface at a time when she needed it. She says, "I was hungry when I attended my first Nichiren Buddhist meeting in 1988. I mean that literally. I wanted to go out to dinner with two friends of mine, but they insisted that I first attend a Buddhist meeting with them that evening before we ate."[11] Coaxed into embarking on a thirty-day trial of chanting at that first meeting, she ended up staying with the practice for fifteen years, serving as a teacher for seven of those years.[12]

In 2002 she started on the path of Sōtō Zen and was ordained as a priest in the Shunryu Suzuki Roshi lineage in 2008. She served as *shuso* (head student) at City Center, a practice community of the San Francisco Zen Center, in 2012 and founded Still Breathing in 2014. She is the dharma heir of the late Zenkei Blanche Hartman, whom she references often in her teachings, having begun her dharma transmission with her and completing it with Shosan Victoria Austin in 2017. Shortly before her teacher's passing in 2016, she edited a collection of Zenkei Roshi's dharma talks, *Seeds for a Boundless Life: Zen Teachings from the Heart*. Osho Zenju also holds a master's degree from the University of California, Los Angeles, and a doctorate in transformative learning from the California Institute of Integral Studies. Beyond but related to her spiritual path, she has been an activist in the Black civil rights movement, a dedicated Pan-Africanist, a social science researcher, a development director for nonprofit organizations serving women and girls' cultural arts and mental health, and a grant maker for many private and public philanthropic foundations.

Going Back to Go Forward

The vast majority of us come to meditation and Buddhism because we are suffering. As I discussed in the preface, this was definitely true for me. I was not happy with where I was or who I had become; I felt trapped. Meditation helped me sit still long enough to get clear on where I needed to be. As my meditation practice continues to deepen, I understand that what brought me to the practice and started me on my journey of inquiry was just the tip of the iceberg. The pain I'm holding is not only wide and deep; it goes well beyond this body that I'm in now. It extends back generations and cannot be separated from the suffering of the earth.

Osho Zenju is forthcoming about the fact that it was suffering that brought her to meditation. As she says, "The need to understand and heal such suffering led me through Christianity and Yoruba to Buddhism."[13] She was already a Zen practitioner by the time she wrote her moving essay "Bearing Up in the Wild Winds," but in it she credits chanting in the Nichiren tradition with her ability to heal from a profound trauma that she had experienced eleven years prior. The essay is only a few pages long, but it's rich in its serving as an opening to the reader to healing from our own traumas—but not without passing through the fire.

The essay's form points us to the inextricability of our individual suffering from that of the collective, particularly of people of African descent. It begins with a discussion of the collective suffering of "people of color." It continues with Osho Zenju calling in the "loud voices of anguish among descendants of African slaves" heard over centuries, followed by an acknowledgment of the suffering of her parents, who "worked against dehumanization" on behalf of their daughters. Finally she arrives at a discussion of her singular experience of suffering and subsequent healing. Her way of approaching her suffering as inextricable from that of the collective allows the power of meditation in the surfacing and subsequent healing of deep intergenerational wounds to come through.

She writes of being kidnapped at gunpoint from a street in Los Angeles and raped. She writes about the experience of depression and having thoughts of suicide, an understandable consequence of being forced to live with personal trauma and suffering. Through meditation and chanting she woke up to living in "a world that thrives on individualism, making social intimacy among us seem impossible."[14] With that awareness, her relationship to the rape does not remain confined to her personal experience of suffering but is situated communally in the context of her family's internalization and processing of her pain, an outsider's seeming disregard for her suffering, and Buddhism's role in her healing.[15] She says,

> The women in my family, my mother and sisters, were afraid to have any in-depth conversation with me about my tragedy. They feared for their own lives. My father had murder in his eyes when he heard what had happened to me. My father had lost a leg to arteriosclerosis and he was in a wheelchair. His rage quickly dwindled into great sadness. A psychotherapist assigned to me fell asleep while I was telling her the gruesome story of my rape. I kept the experience buried for years, waiting for someone to save me. Chanting helped it all resurface and provided a path to healing.[16]

My initial reaction to the essay was one of shock. By the time I came upon it, I had already read several of Osho's other books and listened to some of her podcast interviews. Never do I remember her mentioning that she had been *raped*! I wept, sensing into the pain and humiliation that she suffered during and in the aftermath of such a profound violation of her personhood. And then, as I am trained to do as an academic, I went to work trying to understand what her singular story revealed about larger sociopolitical structures. I researched statistics around sexual assaults perpetrated against women of color and Black women in particular. I thought about how her violation spoke to the sickness of a society that hates women and the double yoke of fear and hatred and the concomitant violence to which Black women are regularly subjected in a racist, sexist society built on their labor. I thought about the fact that her essay addresses the deep and long history of Black female vulnerability and Black male impotence that was endemic to slavery and that continues today as part of its legacy. I reflected on the fact that the fear that her mother and sisters felt upon learning about the rape was not only for their daughter and sister. It also reminded them of their own vulnerability to such violence as a continuation of that to which countless African and African diasporic women were subjected from the slave ship to the plantation and beyond. They were reminded yet again that they were not loved. Such knowing, and the fear that goes along with it, is visceral—deep in our cells, etched into our bones.

My thoughts then turned to her father, whom Osho Zenju often speaks of with love and reverence. He was a Louisiana sharecropper before he migrated to the Northwest. I was reminded that well beyond slavery, Black men were powerless to protect their families from the countless violations to which they were subjected. While Osho Zenju's father's rage at hearing of his daughter's rape was expected, as a Black man from rural Louisiana, he was very aware of this history. His inability to redress the violation of his daughter's body and spirit, a duty and a right of a man in a patriarchal society, broke his spirit. I also read his physical disability, while real and personal, as a metaphor for African American men's collective social, political, economic impotence both historically and contemporarily.

Finally, I thought about the way that both mothers and fathers were powerless to protect their children from those who wielded power over them, whether as masters, mistresses, or overseers during slavery or as gatekeepers of white supremacy afterward. Thus, while Rev. Zenju's mother's reaction seemingly stemmed from one place and her father's from another, both shared the sense of powerlessness to protect their children from the fear and hatred of the Black body that circumscribes Black American life and threatens to extinguish it at any moment.

In reflecting on the legacy of the historical disregard for Black pain and death, I read the fact that Rev. Zenju's psychotherapist—a Black woman—fell asleep as Rev. Zenju told her story as evidence of a widespread (and internalized) disregard for Black women's pain, even our own. In a society built on upholding white power structures, we have all been trained not to see Black pain. Such training makes it possible for someone who is paid to listen deeply in order to hear another's pain and help them through it to actually fall asleep.

I was in awe of Rev. Zenju's courage to write about her trauma, to put it out there for the world to witness. Her vulnerability—what really slapped me in the face as I began reading—is what has stayed with me. It reminded me of what I have been taught both directly and through modeling: I must not speak my pain. I have to keep it close—protect it, keep it hidden—so that I can be safe in a place where I am never allowed to feel safe.

But mostly I was and remain grateful for the way that her essay reminded me that I am not alone in my suffering. Because there is no separation between me and all other living beings, my suffering is not for me to bear alone. This intellectual knowing, of course, does nothing for me when I want to jump out of my skin as memories of past traumas threaten to overwhelm me. I have to know it in my bones and not turn away from the suffering precisely because I understand that if I do not deal with it, it will deal with me and then I will never know freedom. Invited by Osho Zenju to do so, I reflect on my ancestors who for centuries gave everything they had for their freedom so that I might have mine. As such, to continue along this path in the many twists and turns that it takes is not up for debate.

Osho Zenju implies that she buried the memory of the rape until she began chanting with Soka Gakkai. Contrary to what she expected, chanting did not help dissipate the pain. Rather, the pain increased. She says, "Chanting brought memories of the rape and every other dehumanizing act I had experienced."[17] Such is the gift of meditation, which resurfaced the memory of the initial unassimilated traumas that she experienced because of the body that she was born into and that returned to haunt her. This second wounding (the memory of the traumas), however, also provided the path to Rev. Zenju's healing and awakening.

Osho's story is evidence of the mind's desire to protect the traumatized victim and a testament to meditation's ability to dislodge those memories that, though suppressed by the mind, are held in the body. The original trauma resurfaces in perhaps inappropriate ways until it is confronted through the stillness of meditation. To put it another way, the original arrow—the accumulated assaults against her personhood, which were the source of her suffering—was healed through the wisdom that the stillness of meditation presented. It cut through the separation and isolation that held her in their grip for years after her initial wounding. The dharma helped to liberate her from the second arrow—the suffering that ensued. Through her dharma practice, Osho Zenju was able to come to the awareness that her "suffering over [her] rape and past hurts was tightly woven into a larger world of suffering."[18] She became aware of how she suffered, feeling isolated in her own dark body, and was awakened to the innate wisdom that there was no separation between her and all other living beings. She, like any other life, was worthy of a place in the world.[19] With her newfound wisdom she was able to declare, "I would not be an accomplice to my own disappearance."[20]

Osho Zenju's teaching that trauma transcends individual experience is something that the psychotherapist Resmaa Menakem also addresses in his writing about historical and contemporary collective trauma. He writes, "Many African Americans know trauma intimately—from their own nervous systems, from the experience of people they love, and most often, from both."[21] The avoidance, blame, and denial of the trauma cause people to perpetuate cruelty and violence that persists alive and well in the individual bodies of the vast majority of Americans as part of the American collective body.

Osho Zenju traces the somatic nature of trauma related to her immediate family to that of her ancestors and herself in talking about the gifts and limitations of her Christian upbringing to help relieve her suffering. She says, "Although Christianity offered God as a liberator and a community to ease the pain of isolation felt by displaced Africans, we had not learned how to eliminate a sense of inferiority that *pervaded our bodies.*"[22] One major difference between Christianity and Buddhism is in Christianity's emphasis on salvation of the soul. A common belief in the Black church is that believers will be rewarded for their earthly sacrifices in heaven. Buddhism, on the other hand, posits that the body is the vessel of our liberation. Our salvation lies in our being present to our suffering. Only then can we confront it and work to heal it. What Osho Zenju realized in the first two years of chanting was that she was not the "absolute being"; her suffering was woven into that of a larger world.[23] This realization is a major victory in a society that is dependent on us buying into the illusion of separateness.

Sankofa: Go Back and Get It

Shortly after a visit to Tamil Nadu, India, while still a practitioner of Nichiren Buddhism, Osho Zenju received a transmission that resulted in an offering that changed her life—and mine. It was a transmission of oracular wisdom, which she went on to offer to others as the *Black Angel Cards*. She writes,

> The *Black Angel Cards* serve as an oracle and way to inspire
> and affirm, to access your own intuitive nature and guide you
> in unfolding the true essence of your life. A black angel is the
> essence, the symbol of clear seeing inside the mysterious dark-
> ness of our lives. It is an ancient symbol of sacred darkness
> filled with light and wisdom. She is within all of us.[24]

Osho has said that while she was still practicing Nichiren Buddhism, she had a spiritual lucid dream in which she was given some messages that she interpreted as medicine for the world. In the dream she heard the phrase "Black angels." She wasn't sure what it meant, as angels were not something that she was interested in at the time. Nonetheless, she wrote down the dream, which eventually turned into the "Black Angel Card Project."[25]

Osho Zenju understood the cards to be a response to her prayers and meditations to reveal her true nature. She intends for the cards to help others access *their* true nature. She talks about the fact that we are closer to our true nature as children, but that gift is taken from us as we go to school and have different encounters as we grow. The cards are meant "to help stimulate not just past experience but past essence."[26] As such, "the dream symbols such as *The Braider, The Mother Soul, The Drummer, The Moon Child*, surface a profound sense of inner beauty and worthiness for those who want to walk in wellness. They have been used by psychotherapists, life coaches, diviners, educators, work-shop and group facilitators, and with family and friends."[27]

While oracles are very much a part of the African tradition, Osho Zenju is clear that her manifestation of the cards also "came out of Buddhism . . . out of Dharma."[28] When someone bought the cards, they had the option of scheduling a telephone conference with her for "transmissions," as she calls them.[29] I decided to schedule a phone meeting with her. During our time together, following an invocation and an entreaty to the ancestors for guidance and wisdom, Osho Zenju offered insight into the meanings of the images and the text in the accompanying booklet that I pulled from the shuffled deck. The work that she does, the way that she does it, is inspired by the dharma but also grounded in other ancient traditions. The way that she names what she does speaks to the uniqueness of African American women's relationship with Buddhism. More broadly, it speaks to the way that members of the African diaspora, continuing ancient African traditions, incorporate spiritual beliefs that support our liberation into our worldviews.

Rev. Zenju's focus on the dharma as a pluralistic path to wisdom puts her in the company of other Black Buddhists. As the African American writer and Buddhist practitioner Charles Johnson writes, "The dharma is simply wisdom. It can be found anywhere and everywhere. No religion or philosophy, Eastern or Western, has a monopoly on wisdom."[30] Since this is true, one who follows the dharma does not have to relinquish the other aspects of themselves that contribute to their being whole. Thus, Jan Willis is free to declare herself Baptist and Buddhist; bell hooks was free to incorporate Sufism, Buddhism, and Christianity into her way of being and doing her work; Osho Zenju is free to call in her global ancestors and make her meditations on race, gender, and sexuality through the dharma without ever identifying them as Buddhist.[31]

Rev. Zenju's divinations are done in a way that recalls the traditional roles that priests or priestesses, seers, prophets, oracles, mediums, and diviners play in African societies: making sacrifices, offerings, and prayers; conducting rites and ceremonies; giving advice; and serving as intermediaries between God, the ancestors, and the living.[32] According to the philosopher John S. Mbiti, seers and prophets "primarily act as ritual elders, to give advice on religious matters . . . receive messages from divinities and spirits through possession and dreams and . . . pass on the information to their communities,"[33] while mediums (usually women) and diviners make connections between the living dead and humans.[34] In fact, Osho Zenju sees the *Black Angel Cards* as oracles delivering "messages for divining your life."[35] Her guidance for the cards point squarely to her African heritage in this regard and is continued in the accompanying booklet's dedication "to those known and unknown ancestors, ancient ones, who have guided me thus far."[36] Clear that she does not walk her Buddhist path alone, she continues, "I carry your spirits in the highest honor."[37] Also clear about her connection to seen and unseen worlds, worldly and otherworldly forces, she thanks "all teachers, young and old, seen and unseen."[38] Her final inclusive gesture is the deep bows that she offers to her family and spiritual communities. She brings all of her evolving self to her practice.

My divination session with Osho in 2016 revealed some of what I already knew: I do not walk alone. My ancestors walk with me, guiding my path, definitely keeping me out of a lot of trouble. Our conversation sent me on a jaunt to an aunt who lives in the South. I hoped in taking the trip that I would glean some information about my maternal grandmother, who had passed long before I was born. During my visit I was saddened to know that not even a photo of her existed. One thing I did learn was that my grandmother, Beulah Mae Myers, had been a washwoman. A single mother of six children in the early twentieth century, she scrimped and saved enough to buy her own house when she was sixty-five years old. One year later she was dead from cancer. Sitting with that fact from time to time, I am reminded of how people like my grandmother worked this land for centuries for free. Once slavery ended, they were forced to become sharecroppers because they were not bestowed the land that was owed to them. Those who managed to acquire a patch of earth were much too often swindled out of it or run off of it by threats or acts of violence. For my grandmother to have worked her whole life in order to buy her own piece of property only to enjoy it for less than a year seems a real injustice. I wonder what she would think of the life I've chosen, the places I've traveled to, the things I've done; my own reticence about buying land in this country. I don't have answers. But I am grateful that I asked the questions and that with the support of Spirit, Osho Zenju was there to usher me into that opening that is still unfolding.

Another question I had was about an uncle, Edward Clinton Myers, for whom one of my brothers is named. The family story goes that when he was very young, in his early twenties, my grandmother committed a great wrong against him. He, in his anger and hurt, packed his bags and vowed never again to set eyes on anyone in the family. True to his word, he cut off all communication, and no one in the family knew what became of him. Eventually we would all know.

In 2018 I attended my first retreat at Spirit Rock Meditation Center. On the last day of the retreat I came across a flyer for "Deep Time Liberation," a retreat offered by dharma teachers of African descent. The image on the flyer of an underwater sculpture of human figures holding hands, standing in a circle formation, spoke to me. As soon as I got home, I sent a message to the email address on the flyer—and got no response. Never one to give up once I decide that something is for me, I persisted until, almost a year later, I got a message from the organizers announcing that a new Deep Time Liberation retreat was in the works. I immediately registered, and by March 2020 I was set to go when the pandemic hit. The retreat was moved online and I began, fortified by my intention to embark on some intergenerational healing. By the third day of the retreat I was defeated, envious of those who told stories and shared memories and testified to finding long-lost ancestors. When I looked at my own genealogical chart, I found looking back at me a lot of blank spaces. I had almost no names, no dates, no locations. What I did have was plenty of anger, grief, and resentment.

But this is how Spirit works. About a year before the retreat, I received a letter from a law office informing me that my uncle, the one who had renounced his family over sixty years ago, had passed. He had been living in the same city where a cousin of mine lives. My cousin had no idea. Though we don't have the details of his life, we know that my uncle joined the military, and by the time he passed at the age of eighty, he was a wealthy man. While some of my cousins are trying to learn more about his life, I now have gone ahead and included him on my once-sparse genealogical chart and count him as an ancestor who walks my path with me.

My uncle's troubled relationship with his family raises the issue of who we embrace as our ancestors, a question that arises often when Osho Zenju is teaching. Her answer, one that feels true to me, expands beyond our conventional limited understanding of ancestors. She counsels us to embrace not only the difficult ones but also the trees and the frogs beneath them. For she knows that they have all gone into making us who we are. They are a part of us. To reject them would be to reject ourselves.

What's Buddhism Got to Do with It?

In "Bearing Up in the Wild Winds" Osho Zenju remarks that her sister once asked her, "What does Buddhism have to do with black people anyway?"[39] Although she offers a cursory response in the essay, she expanded on the question and her answer in one of her earliest texts, *Tell Me Something about Buddhism*. She extrapolates from the question posed to her by a loved one and makes the Buddha's teachings accessible to a wider audience: the curious. *Tell Me Something about Buddhism* meets people where they are—someone perhaps browsing the self-help section of their local bookstore—and invites them to explore the teachings. Bright red, compact, and thin, with its question-and-answer format, and punctuated with Rev. Zenju's charcoal drawings, the book calls out to the seeker. Although she had several other publications prior to *Tell Me Something about Buddhism*, the book is the one that "announced" her as a Buddhist teacher outside of San Francisco Zen Center. With a foreword by Thich Nhat Hanh, it was well received.

Opening the book, "the curious" finds the author paying homage not only to well-known figures in the Buddhist tradition but also to native peoples of the United States and all of the ancestors who have led her to "the path." She ends with a dedication to her ancestors, both known and unknown.[40] For someone like me, a visual artist, a seeker, someone who strives daily to honor the original inhabitants of this land and is ever-conscious of the ancestors known and unknown who walk with me and guide me on my many paths, this book was a balm to my soul. Picking it up, I felt seen, affirmed. I knew that I was not the only one. I also knew that I wanted her to be my teacher, not because of any burning interest in Zen Buddhism but because I knew in my heart that I had finally found a safe place to land—a place where I could bring my full, evolving self.

As with "Bearing Up in the Wild Winds," reading the book, I found myself in awe of her willingness to lay bare her life for the benefit of others. She includes stories of her difficult relationship with her mother, the trauma of being spat upon by a boy from middle school, and the trauma of her sexual assault. She does so with the understanding that "the initiation into enlightenment begins with our own willingness to not only speak of our suffering, but also to understand it as a condition we share as living beings."[41] Thankfully for those of us who were left hungry for more, Osho Zenju expands on many of the elements she introduces in *Tell Me Something about Buddhism* in several of her other writings, delving more deeply into them, first in *The Way of Tenderness* and then in *Sanctuary*.

Answering her sister's question is a project Osho Zenju has worked on through several of her writings. Even prior to *Tell Me Something about Buddhism*, she published an article using the question as its title—"What Does Buddhism Have to Do with Black People?" In *Sanctuary*, she continued with the theme. One important aspect of this exploration for Osho Zenju is her sense of connection to geographically and culturally diverse black-skinned peoples. In the article, for instance, she invokes an East Indian lineage. And in *Sanctuary*, she writes of feeling a strong connection to the Tamil people of southern India and Sri Lanka. She discusses, in particular, one woman whom she met during a group trip to India and with whom she felt a kinship based on the shared darkness of their skin and the woman's destiny of servitude that was tied to it.[42] She also writes of, during that trip, standing alongside a lake that felt familiar though she had never visited there.[43] The experience helped her reconcile the fact that while she is drawn to retrieve what she sees as her ancestral home, Africa, she is also drawn to India, which she sees as her other ancestral home. In *Black Buddha: Changing the Face of American Buddhism*, Lama Choyin Rangdröl explains such a connection: "DNA studies suggest that the dark-skinned people of India, then and now, are descendants of the original Africans who walked out of Africa 50,000 years ago."[44]

In *Sanctuary*, Osho Zenju discusses finding her sensed embodiment of an unknown African lineage and a known Buddhist lineage when she visited Malaysia for the Sakyadhita Buddhist Conference[45] and overheard Tibetan nuns, exiled from their own homeland, singing "We Shall Overcome," an African American freedom song. She says about the experience, "Tears welled in my eyes." She asked, "What brings such a song of freedom to the heart of an African American woman much older than the young Tibetan nuns?" before guessing, "Perhaps they longed to be in Tibet." Finding solace in recognizing her sorrow in theirs, she concludes, "I longed to know what African country my ancestors came from and what language they spoke. Despite our displacement, we women from forty-five countries arrived together at the home of Buddha's daughters. I slept well."[46]

As people whose ancestors were brought here in chains, we have an ancient, bone-deep sensation of homelessness. Indeed, we will never know where our people come from, no matter how many DNA tests are administered. And if by some miracle we *do* get some notion of our distant heritage, the many centuries that have passed since the "before" time make a "return" to home impossible. In many ways, our only recourse is to find home in our homelessness, a particular kind of exiled status. Our awakeness[47] to our own suffering means that we can also feel into the suffering of others who have been displaced. This awakeness, in turn, allows us to find a sense of home with the Other in community.

As Osho has written, she feels a deep kinship with the people of India. Moreover, she directly explores the history of Black people in India, concluding,

> There is no Dharma gate marked for black people only. But we can acknowledge that there must be some history between the people of the African Diaspora and the teachings of the Buddha. . . . There is awareness on my part that the Buddha's teaching impacted the lives of those who suffered oppression such as the black Tamil Indians, Dalits, and the Untouch-ables—held down by a caste system. Additionally, Nagarjuna, the great scholar of the Mahayana teachings, espoused the freedom of enlightenment to the black Indians of southern ancient India. And because Buddhism spoke of liberation I assume that it did not flourish in a country that through tra-ditions held the caste system in place. . . . While ancient India is where Africans might have connected with the Buddha, it is speculative due to suppressed or lost history, considering Africans as part of the Buddhist movement from its beginning is a crucial and valid historical perspective to unearth.[48]

In her speculations about the deep connections between people of African descent and the Tamil people, Osho Zenju accomplishes two things: First, she echoes what Toni Morrison calls "discredited knowledge" because, as Morrison asserts, "black people were discredited before what they *knew* was 'discredited.'"[49] This fact of suppressed or discredited history is endemic to the American experience as the maintenance of white supremacy relies on erasure, disconnection, and separation to survive and thrive. We see this drive to whitewash or erase history in myriad ways, including the proposed narrative of African diasporic people as "immigrants" coming to "a land of dreams and opportunities" rather than as enslaved laborers.[50] Osho declares, "Enslaved Africans did not *immigrate* to America."[51] In fact, it is in part the way that the majority of Africans were introduced to the New World that is responsible for what Charles Johnson calls "the predetermined story for black people"[52] and the racism and discrimination that are slavery's legacy. Osho Zenju speaks to that attempted erasure in not only refusing to be "an accomplice to [her] own disappearance," as she declares in "Bearing Up in the Wild Winds," but just as powerfully rejecting the delusion of separation that keeps us isolated with our suffering. In calling out the oppression of the Black people of India, Osho Zenju is in turn calling out the caste system to which people of African descent are subjected in this context. In affirming the truth of our interconnectedness Osho Zenju addresses the question that not only her sister asked but also that which was posed to other Black Buddhists like bell hooks and Jan Willis.

From Wounded to Liberated

I came across *The Way of Tenderness* shortly after I made the decision to not return to my local Zen temple in Michigan. Instead, I went on Amazon.com, bought a vibrant purple zafu and a deep blue pillow for my knees, and designated a corner of my bedroom for my solitary meditation practice with the support of the Insight Timer app. For months I was secure in the thought that, as the app assured me, I was meditating with hundreds of thousands of other people at the same time, creating a field of oneness. In short, I had resigned myself to my solitary practice. But Spirit had other plans.

The Way of Tenderness was actually how I re-found Osho Zenju all those years after my first encounter. I remember receiving in the mail a small, relatively thin paperback. On the cover was a sculpture of a woman with a wide nose and a slight smile to her full lips, her eyes downcast. Where her chest was expected, there was an opening with its edges gently folded back. Inside the book, Osho Zenju traces her movement from a wounded tenderness to one of openheartedness through identities that have been used to marginalize and oppress. The book spoke to my struggle to step into a liberated life. Even now, as I reread the opening chapter "Not What You Think," which begins with how she came to Nichiren, I chuckle and shake my head at the marvelousness of the text. Indeed, for me the book was not what I thought it would be: one *about* race, gender, and sexuality. For the longest time it felt like each word was so full of meaning that I couldn't possibly grasp it all. And yet she was telling my story. I saw myself in her pain, in her awareness that the suffering she was experiencing existed long before her birth. I understood her sense of isolation.

Like her, I have never felt like I belonged anywhere. That sense of alienation from my nation of birth, from my family, from the communities I found myself in as a child and young adult is what prompted me to buy a one-way ticket to Haiti as soon as I finished college. I wanted to live in a Black country, one where I would see myself reflected. The Jesuit priest Jean-Bertrand Aristide had recently been elected president of Haiti and I wanted to help build a new democratic nation. Only when I arrived, I was "*blan*" (lit., "white"; foreign). I didn't speak the language. I didn't understand the culture. I wasn't quite poor but I didn't have enough money or resources to be part of the bourgeoisie. I also shunned the ex-patriot community, which consisted mostly of white Christian missionaries. I didn't belong.

When a coup d'état deposed President Aristide only nine months after his election, I stayed in the country. By then I was married and expecting my son. After living all of my life until that point under the boot of white supremacy, I decided to hedge my bets. I wanted my son to grow up in a place where he would see himself reflected. But after two years, discouraged from living for months without electricity, gas, or running water, and feeling a profound sense of isolation, I knew I had to return to the US where I was again confronted with that old familiar sense of nonbelonging. Fast-forward almost twenty years later to a book I held in my hands. I was finally seeing myself reflected back to me. She had been here all along.

Emptiness and Everything

At the beginning of *The Way of Tenderness*, Osho Zenju uses the Buddhist concept of no self to address the dehumanization and sense of isolation that she has experienced, labeling these as the source of her wounded, tender heart. She acknowledges the fundamental emptiness—the interdependence and impermanence—of labels related to identity and selfhood while also considering how problematic it is to deploy "no self" as a teaching in the face of African Americans living and dying with the violence of racism in the United States. "If we were to simply walk past the fires of racism, sexism, and so on because illusions of separation exist within them," she writes, "we may well be walking past one of the widest gateways to enlightenment."[53] Rather than ignoring the social constituents of the self, she engages with the possibility of awakening *through* the self, signified as it is by the body. In fact, the privilege of spiritually bypassing race, sexuality, and gender to get to "oneness" is not available to those of us who are oppressed based on these identities. Rather, as Osho Zenju proposes, "identity is to be explored on the path to awakening."[54] *The Way of Tenderness* points the way to awakening through identity.

Embedded in her exploration—or perhaps more appropriately,

meditation—on the self and the body is her engagement with the question of relative and absolute truth and the concept of nonduality. There is no either/or but rather a both/and that lives in the bodies of people of African descent. Osho Zenju makes the need to address both of these truths—the relative and the absolute—abundantly clear in the opening pages of *The Way of Tenderness* when she states,

> Relatively speaking, I have experienced being "colored,"
> "Negro," "black," "African American," "descendant of Africans,"
> "straight," "bi-sexual," "two-spirited (masculine and feminine),"
> "tomboy," "lesbian," "dyke," and "poor." . . . I have subscribed
> to these labels over time to acknowledge my particular lived
> experience shaped by its particular suffering. Yes, my bones
> know the absolute life, unencumbered by labels, fixed percep-
> tions, and appearances. But the absolute life has never been
> the problem I have to face in the world.[55]

While she knows that many of the labels that have been attributed to her and that she internalizes are socially constructed illusions, she also understands that knowing this fact "does nothing to change the mind saturated with hatred."[56] She is also painfully aware that the body houses the mind that is saturated with hatred and regularly commits acts of violence on people to whom such labels are ascribed.

Several pages later, she lists a few of the myriad ways we witness hatred's workings in the hearts of those who act out of hatred for and fear of the Other. She says,

> We see hatred working in the heart of our society when a
> sixteen-year-old black male is shot to death—with eleven
> rounds fired by six police officers—because the police say he
> was adjusting the waistband of his pants in a "suspicious way."
> We see hatred working in the heart of our society when a gang

of black males murder a black transgender rapper and dump
the body in a landfill. We see hatred working in the heart of
our society when women are gang raped simply because they
are women. We see hatred working in the heart of our society
when the homeless are stabbed on the street because they
are ugly, destitute and unpleasant to look at. Fear of particular
bodies breeds hatred, and hatred breeds monstrous acts. This
is the kind of society that breeds hatred.[57]

As someone who, because of her embodiment, could have been victimized in several of the ways that she lists, Osho Zenju has intimate
knowledge of the visceral hatred that drives people to perpetuate such
violence against others and the equally visceral trauma that haunts the
victimized.

The visceral nature of Rev. Zenju's own trauma is clear in her description of her path to awakening, or "liberated tenderness."[58] When she
began to explore tenderness, she became aware of the fact that she had
been "*hardened* by the physical violence leveled against [her] as a young
child and by the poverty with which [her] parents had to struggle."[59] As
she grew older and chose a woman as her lover and partner, she "lived
in fear of being annihilated." She writes of holding her "life tight in [her]
chest, and [her] *body ach*[*ing*] with its pain for many years."[60] While her
description of her fear and pain points to the somatic nature of her suffering prior to her awakening, she also points to the body as the path
to healing and awakening. In fact, as she says repeatedly in *The Way of
Tenderness*, the way to awakening is *through* our bodies.

Her belief in the possibility of awakening in and through the body
is grounded in a multitude of ancient teachings that have nothing to
do with Buddhism, Christianity, or the Yoruba tradition. She calls it
"Mother Wisdom," a deep innate wisdom that results from reconnecting "with our ancestors and Earth as our common mother."[61] Addressing the somatic route to healing and the equanimity of wisdom, she

says, "Ancient wisdom teachings reside within us. Our minds have forgotten, but our bones know the way. If we let the intelligence of our bodies lead us, as we were led into this world at birth, we will remember the mother's milk of transcendent luminosity, the wisdom that comes from no one and is directed toward no one."[62]

The other half of Rev. Zenju's exploration of the role that race, sex, and gender play in the experience of marginalized groups who seek out the dharma is in her pointing to the importance of accounting for the body as a site of not only suffering but also awakening. It is only through the body that one gets to experience awakening. Refuting many Buddhist practitioners' belief that blindness to one's embodiment is a spiritual path, she says, "But the wisdom of my bones says that we need this particular body, with its unique color, shape, and sex for liberation to unfold."[63] A couple of pages later she asserts, "Still, I feel compelled to speak of what is in my bones for the sake of bringing back the connectedness we were all born with."[64] These are just a few examples of many in *The Way of Tenderness* that highlight the felt nature of suffering as well as the path to true healing. They track her evolution from the tenderness that she begins with as bruised and sore to soft and effortlessly aware of the interrelatedness of all beings. The liberated tenderness that she awakens to is apparent in her use of "monsters" as a motif in *The Way of Tenderness*. An early chapter is titled "Tracking the Footprints of Invisible Monsters," while in the last chapter she declares, "There are no monsters." This liberated state is the source of her heart that is tenderly opened by the end of the text, reflected in the sculpture on the book's cover.

Finding Home in the Ancestors

Ancestor veneration is present throughout Rev. Zenju's work. Her insistence on this practice in particular draws me again and again to her teachings. The expansive way that she conceives of the ancestors—

again, listening more often to things than to beings—has validated my own propensity for listening to the rustling of the trees' leaves as a welcoming gesture to their daughter returned.

In "Sweeping My Heart," one of my favorite essays by her, she seeks counsel from her ancestors to deal with her resistance to the Zen practice of mindful work or service as part of her training. She discusses coming face-to-face with her feelings about being the descendant of people who had historically served "as slaves, sharecroppers, wet-nurses, and maids" in an environment in which many of the work leaders were white. It felt difficult to square her desire to be on the path of enlightenment through the dharma with taking orders to perform manual labor from young white men. She says, "For me, a dark-skinned person of African descent, cleaning the temple as Zen practice felt inappropriate and uncomfortable when I was at the beginning of my training."[65] Her resistance to performing such labor stemmed from her knowledge of slavery, including the menial forms of labor to which African descendants have been traditionally (and often remain) relegated. "The memory of my black ancestors and slavery was visceral," she writes.[66] She relates how through her conversation with her ancestors about the menial tasks that she was to perform, her eyes were opened to the consciousness of hatred. She was made aware of the "isms" that she, as the descendant of enslaved people, carried in her body. In that awareness she was released from the delusions that she has already suffered and freed from the need to suffer them again.

From that awakening the act of scrubbing became a ritualized remembrance of her ancestors. She says, "I felt my ancestors moving my body back and forth."[67] Her action was not only a ritualized invocation of their wisdom but also an invitation for them to help facilitate her well-being. Her remembrance and acknowledgment of her ancestors allowed them to bring her to the point where she was able to use the broom as a ritual tool connecting her life and those of her ancestors. With those tools of awakening (remembrance and acknowledgment) she realized that rather than replicating their lives as enslaved beings, her ancestors had brought her to the moment when she could see the ways that she suffered. What followed was a seamless opening to seeing "the ascendance from enslaved Africans as a sanctioned and gifted walk toward the very liberation the Buddha spoke of, and what the ancestors saw for [her] and everyone else."[68]

I'm pretty sure the reason I love that essay so much is because I can see myself having a similar conversation with my own ancestors. As I've mentioned, I was the only one in my immediate family to attend college, let alone earn a PhD. My identification with those three letters at the end of my name has everything to do with my painful awareness of the history of the prohibition against teaching enslaved people to read and write, something I've always found joy in. I often shiver with the knowledge that there were brilliant writers, artists, scientists, and mathematicians who, because of racism and sexism, were forced to let their talents die on the vine. That knowing makes me work harder at what I am privileged to do. Moreover, in my mind, all that I've accomplished has been on their behalf—an honoring of the sacrifices they made so that I could have the opportunities that I do. How can I go back?

The essay also takes me back to that first retreat at Spirit Rock in my late forties when, during check-in, retreatants chose jobs to do during the retreat. Since I'm an early riser, I volunteered to light the candles in the meditation hall and ring the bell to call the retreatants to first meditation. A couple of times I also volunteered to clean up after breakfast. These were tasks that were, in my mind, noble. I felt special making my way to the meditation hall in the dark chilly morning and having a bit of solitude in the soft glow of the candles. The couple of times I helped clean up after breakfast, I was proud of myself for "being willing to help out." I could imagine what my mother would've said had she seen me wiping down counters with such dedication and thoroughness; what my maternal grandmother who washed clothes for her white neighbors would have thought. I also wondered how the young

Black woman, another retreatant, had been assigned her task of cleaning the bathroom. I was grateful that it wasn't my job and hoped that the people who were using the bathrooms were properly cleaning up after themselves. Even though she didn't seem to have a problem with her job, I was offended for her. When we were allowed to talk after our closing ceremony, I learned that she had been attending retreats since she was a teenager and was in her early twenties when we met. Although I didn't ask her directly about the job she took on during the retreat, I thought I recognized the kind of release from suffering that Osho Zenju speaks of in her essay.

This does not mean that I will seek out those tasks that I find difficult to reconcile as a person of African descent. Rather, like Osho Zenju comes to, in everything I do, I need to know that I am not replicating what my ancestors did as enslaved people. I need to recognize their role in my arrival at this moment. Indeed, as she asks, "How else would I appear in such a temple?"[69] And as the great educator Marian Wright Edelman so eloquently stated, "Service is the rent we pay for being. It is the very purpose of life, and not something you do in your spare time."[70]

I, too, will need to climb down from who I think I have become, "to move beyond easily-accessed, well-served black pride into seeing the ways I suffer."[71] In short, I will need to take the mud that I bring with me into my practice, including the history that drives me, to nourish the lotus that is my awakening. I'm not sure at this point what that will look like.

In *Sanctuary*, Osho Zenju delves more deeply into the importance of welcoming in her ancestors. She describes, for instance, an important ceremony that she participated in as part of her dharma transmission, started with Zenkei Blanche Hartman but completed with Shosan Victoria Austin. The transmission entailed Osho embarking on a twenty-one-day ceremony that began in her home and in which she combined

African diasporic and Buddhist traditions that spoke to her; setting up ten altars, three of which "included Haitian Vodoun [sic] deities that matched in role to Zen's gatekeepers, protectors and Bodhisattvas." As she lit a candle at each altar, she "called forth the Haitian spirits with their chants along with hymns to the Zen deities."[72] Rev. Zenju's incorporating these different indigenous and African elements into her spiritual practice is evidence of what the literary scholar Elizabeth J. West asserts in *African Spirituality in Black Women's Fiction: Threaded Visions of Memory, Community, Nature, and Being*. African American women's writing—and I would add in the case of Osho Zenju, their lives—is informed by spiritual traditions of continental Africa and the African diaspora. Similar to teachings that we find in Buddhism, there are core ethical and philosophical values based in the belief that all world entities emanate from a "cosmic oneness" or interconnectedness of all beings.[73] Furthermore, Rev. Zenju's integration of Buddhist, traditional African and African diasporic, and pre-European indigenous teachings into her spiritual practice demonstrates an understanding of "spirit as formless yet manifested in form and the belief that all entities—formed and formless—interconnect."[74] Although she felt like she might be admonished for altering a Zen tradition that can appear set in stone, she writes, "Incorporating Vodoun [sic] deities into the Zen ceremony created a familiarity that I found deeply resonant with home and therefore my heart."[75] Later, clearer about the importance—even necessity—of creating new rituals and ceremonies that would incorporate spiritual traditions of continental Africa and the African diaspora, she embarked on an African-style vision quest led by a South African *sangoma*.[76] There, she set African fabric and a Lakota prayer shawl that had been gifted her on the forest floor and created shrines of cowrie shells, a beaded white necklace, and elements from the earth alongside a statue of the Buddha, before sitting down and "slipping easily into an ancestral memory of being barefoot on [her] homeland."[77] Mindful of her bodily "manifestation,"[78] as she calls it, her understanding and honoring of her interconnectedness speak to and shape her varied converging experiences and emanations in the material world.

Reflecting a long tradition of African American women who have drawn "on the physical and experiential to explore matters of spirituality,"[79] Osho Zenju has talked and written extensively about how acknowledging her bodily manifestation as different is crucial to her teachings. As she argues, "If our bodies are sources of suffering, then we ignore them at our peril."[80] Reflecting a "multiplicity of oneness" belief held by a number of African American Buddhist teachers, she asserts, "When I have held and embraced who I am, how I am embodied, it has become a source of enlightenment, of freedom." This belief in "multiplicity of oneness" has been controversial in Buddhist traditions that stress the belief in moving beyond the physical to find the spiritual, [81] advising practitioners to "drop the labels."[82] However, as several of the Buddhist practitioners that I discuss here counsel, acknowledgment and engagement with our embodiment in a racialized, sexualized, and gendered society is the way to true freedom. It cannot be bypassed.

Rev. Zenju's teachings on difference and oneness bear clear connections to the writings of other African and African American women. Elizabeth J. West points to four principles central to pre–Middle Passage African cosmology as guiding the "tradition of spiritual musings" that we find in African American women's writing: "(1) the value of memory to both individual and group well-being; (2) the belief that community represents the essence of human existence and being; (3) the view that nature—both animate and inanimate—represents divineness; and (4) belief in the interconnectedness of worldly and otherworldly beings."[83] These principles, West argues, "are integral to black epistemological and ontological thought pre- and post–Middle Passage and are central to shaping a tradition of spiritual exploration in black women's writing."[84] Osho Zenju reflects an adherence to these principles in her writings. Tapping into African and African diasporic people's ability to take various spiritual

belief systems and shape them into something that is more represen-
tative of their culture, she also infuses African cosmology, her Christian background, and, at times, pre-settler indigenous traditions into
the Buddhist tradition to create something authentic—something
that speaks to her embodiment as an elder Black bisexual Buddhist
woman in the United States. She is committed to the work of creation and evolution. As she says, "I feel it is crucial to support other
kinds of Buddhist communities that will be created by folks from different cultures."[85] She advises, "Instead of reshaping what has already
been done, allow for something new to be constructed and not worry
about whether it is too far from the root or not. We have already gone
a long way from Buddha's days. If new relations look and sound different, existing Western Buddhist communities must be willing to open
to that difference rather than say, 'This is how we do it.' If not, what
is different will disappear and what is left is the same."[86] Rather that
viewing her African belief systems and Buddhism as irreconcilable,
she has found a way to harmonize the two, embracing the notion that
"the practice is to make companions of difference and harmony, see
them both as oneness itself."[87]

The Mirror of Zazen

Inspired by a circa thirteenth-century Japanese koan as she approached
her fifty-ninth birthday, Osho embarked on a journey of self-inquiry by
looking in the mirror for five minutes while asking herself the questions, "Am I old? What is old?" She did this for seven days, a challenge
that most of us could never undertake and another testament to her
embodiment as a bodhisattva. Following the weeklong self-inquiry,
Osho Zenju concluded that there are several mirrors: physical mirrors,
which reveal the looks on our faces; and zazen, which "allows us to
look into the heart-and-body mirror."[88] She writes,

> When I look in the mirror I see a black face. In the past I have responded to being black with painful emotions. However, through zazen, when I see my black face I am awake to the suffering that arises. I see the old pain arising in the moment of looking in the mirror. I wait for my response to pass (as it is guaranteed to do), and in that passing I see more of who I am and not so much how I appear.[89]

Here again, she finds relief from the second arrow.[90]

In *Tell Me Something about Buddhism*, she writes of another kind of practice by which, in meditating on our external lives, we are able to see what is manifest as reflections of our inner lives. She relates two initiations into this revelation. The first was during a stay in a monastery where she experienced the great pain of several fellow practitioners not appearing to accept her invisible physical disability, which, we can surmise from her later writings, is arthritis. She experienced their rejection when she was unable to kneel to serve the meals or stand in the kitchen for very long. In meditation and reflection, she realized that her pain, as her teacher told her, was from the past.[91] She says, "Although the incidents that occurred at the monastery were new events to my life, the emotions were clearly from events long gone. I understood those events of the past to be what shaped the suffering for me at the zendo. I allowed the tears to continue for days. For three months, we sat anywhere from five to six hours a day. I had plenty of time to look into the infinite mirror of zazen and see the life renamed Zenju."[92] The mirror that others provided in her practice allowed her to awaken to her suffering and, again, be released from that second arrow.

The second mirror was in the form of a roommate with whom she had a dispute that sent her to seek the counsel of the teacher who instructed her to look to herself for the source of her suffering. When she did so, she came to realize that, first, everything in our lives and in the world is "a mirror reflection of our inner lives," but also that "we can only study our own life in the mirror that we polish with our spiritual work."[93] Again, release.

Osho's wisdom teachings illustrate how in looking and deep seeing we are able to move beyond our physical characteristics, which are used to label us and that we internalize to label ourselves, often to our detriment in its limiting of our full evolving selves. The practice of zazen awakens us to the fact that we are more than those labels. As she has done consistently, Osho Zenju testifies to becoming fulfilled in her own spirit when she is awakened to her connection to her ancestors, to those who came before her, and to a life larger than her own. The limitless possibilities become clear to her. Through facing her self, she is brought to the truth of the Western Buddhist misreadings of "no self." She recognizes that the limitlessness of her self is her "original home,"[94] not blackness or old age. Ultimately she reminds the reader of the value of no self in the way that Thich Nhat Hanh defines it: interrelationship with everyone and everything;[95] that like the heart unclouded or unobstructed, our bodies with all of their labels and changes are nonetheless interconnected.

I am in my early fifties. After reading Rev. Zenju's commentary on the koan, I gazed at myself in my bathroom mirror, noticing some changes in my own visage. As someone who has always been mistaken for a much younger woman, I reflected on what the new and interesting textures of my face revealed about the life I've lived thus far. I remembered how, when I first arrived in Haiti in my early twenties, after living in upstate New York for the previous four years, I actively sought out the sun. I examined the gray that was taking over my scalp and remembered when I began coloring it in my thirties after a friend pointed out the white patch that sat in the middle of my head. I pondered how the high cheekbones that used to draw others' admiration and that I detested because of the way my eyes disappeared into them when I smiled began to be not so high in my forties. And I wondered how the no-longer-taut skin on my neck, which I began to notice about a year ago, would be received by others. I became grateful for the over-fifty years I've been gifted on this earth, the many glorious sunrises and sunsets I've witnessed, the joys and challenges that I've been blessed to experience. This gratitude has become more pronounced in the age of COVID. In a state of gratitude, I was released from societal constrictions that try to tell me that I'm not white enough or male enough or young enough to be valued. I, instead, become attuned to my oneness with the earth and look forward to one day returning to her. And then I remember that I don't have to wait. I pull on my sandals and head out to be among the trees, which I am reminded, are also the ancestors.

4

REV. ANGEL KYODO WILLIAMS

Waking Up, Staying Woke

OF THE WOMEN whose work I discuss in these pages, Rev. angel Kyodo williams, Sensei, aligns herself most explicitly with warriorship. She is an ordained Zen Buddhist priest and the second Black woman to be recognized as a teacher in her lineage, White Plum Asanga, a school associated with the late Japanese teacher Taizan Maezumi Roshi and known for its commitment to socially engaged Buddhism.[1] Rev. angel, like Osho Zenju, makes a clear connection between her spirituality and her commitment to social justice.[2] And, like many Black leaders, she has been subjected to racial reductionism. When I read *Library Journal*'s description of her as "the most vocal and intriguing African American Buddhist in America,"[3] I was reminded of the writer and critic James Baldwin's eloquent response to being labeled a "Negro writer" in his BBC interview with Peter Duval Smith in 1963:

I'm an American Negro in the eyes of the American Republic.
Now, later on, of course, I had to become an American Negro
in my own eyes, which is a very different matter. But I don't
think that anyone can be labeled, ultimately, in this way. When
I say I'm not a Negro writer I don't mean that I'm ashamed of
being a Negro or afraid of being a Negro or any of that. I mean
there's a level of experience beneath that which in turn oper-
ates to obliterate.[4]

In the mid-twentieth century, Baldwin rejected white America's desire
to reduce Black humanity, in all of its complexity, to that narrow and
diminished capacity encapsulated in the designation "Negro." During
Baldwin's lifetime, such reductionism was rampant. Qualifiers that
were regularly inserted into the biographies of artists, intellectuals, and
athletes of African descent sought to "obliterate," in Baldwin's words,
not only the level of experience *behind* the person being qualified but
also the talent and hard work that they contributed to the American
tapestry. It seems clear to me that this propensity for reducing Black
people's contributions to the world through the myopia of race is still
very much alive and well in *Library Journal's* qualifier for Rev. angel.
She is all this and more, evolving and ever-striving to meet the needs
of her community.

I *do* agree with National Public Radio's Krista Tippett's description
of her as "one of our wisest voices on social evolution and the spiritual
aspect of social healing."[5] She is also prolific. In addition to authoring
many articles, she makes countless public-speaking appearances, facilitates teach-ins, and grants interviews widely. She has multiple internet as well as in-person offerings and a strong social media presence,
including Instagram and Twitter under the hashtags #getintheconver-
sation and #radicaldharma. In addition to being the author of *Being
Black: Zen and Art of Living with Fearlessness and Grace*, Rev. angel is
part of a collaborative activist project that grew from the book that she

coauthored with Dr. Jasmine Syedullah and Lama Rod Owens, *Radical Dharma: Talking Race, Love, and Liberation.* She is also the founder and senior fellow of the Center for Transformative Change, an organization "dedicated to bridging the inner and outer lives of social change agents, activists and allies to support a more effective, more sustainable movement of justice for all."[6] In addition, she is the founder of Liberated Life Network, a community of people who are committed to realizing their individual and collective freedom.

This chapter explores Rev. angel's first book, *Being Black,* as a kind of love letter to Black people and as an integral part of her larger body of work that is focused on facilitating liberation for those who seek it. The chapter also looks through the lens of Black radicalism at her work in and around *Radical Dharma* as well as several of her other offerings. Hers is a kind of "by any means necessary" approach in which she translates the teachings of the dharma so that it is accessible to the majority or does away completely with the language of Buddhism, instead focusing in her activist work on communicating the ancient wisdom *behind* the teachings. All of this I read as part of her commitment to spiritual warriorship.

I first encountered Rev. angel during my second year of grad school in 2002. I was living in Madison, Wisconsin, full of an anxiety that had taken hold of me one year before, after I witnessed on TV the bombing of the World Trade Center's Twin Towers and the Pentagon, quickly followed by countless Americans across the country getting whipped into a frenzy to "annihilate," in the words of President George W. Bush, "the evildoers."[7] A native New Yorker, I had moved with my son to the Midwest just a couple of months before the events of September 11, 2001. On the morning of the bombing, I spent fruitless hours trying to get through to my mother by telephone. I finally came to learn that, thankfully, she and all of our friends and family members were physically fine. Nonetheless, it was startlingly clear that the individual and collective trauma that we had experienced in those initial moments was irreversible.

Because I lived in an international community of graduate students in a relatively progressive city, I did not witness firsthand the anti-Islamic vitriol that quickly descended on most of the nation. But I was horrified to read in the news that some of that hatred and blame emerged from African American and Caribbean communities in New York, my home city. Descendants of those who had been brought to this country in chains, as well as more recent immigrants who came in search of a better life for themselves and their families, chose to believe the narrative of "swarthy Islamic terrorists" who all meant to do the United States harm. They believed the lie that othering equally maligned Black and brown-skinned people would somehow shield them from the hatred directed at *those* others. While I could identify the workings of white supremacy, I didn't know what to do with the fear, anger, and grief that permeated my body as a result of what I witnessed. I looked where I had always sought answers: books.

I was lucky to have a Borders bookstore within walking distance of my apartment. There I found *Being Black*, along with Thich Nhat Hanh's *Peace Is Every Step*, and Charles Johnson's *Turning the Wheel: Essays on Buddhism and Writing*. Those texts enabled my first tentative foray into Buddhist philosophy, and they introduced me to Buddhism as a way of alleviating some of my personal suffering following the 9/11 bombings. I read the books as if my life depended on it. Eventually, though, as with my first encounter with Osho Zenju, the responsibilities of single motherhood and graduate school called. I tucked *Being Black* with its yellowing pages onto my bookshelf and into my subconscious for many years. Pulling it out again and flipping through it many years later, I noted the passages that I underlined:

Never being afraid is not what fearlessness is about. What fearlessness is really about is knowing that you are afraid . . .

and acting anyway. When you cultivate fearlessness, you are making true bravery a part of your life. You are claiming your warrior spirit.[8]

Transcending something doesn't make it go away, it just means that you get on the other side of it. You get on the other side that doesn't let the fear keep you from moving forward anyway.[9]

My homing in on those two passages speaks to how gripped by fear I had been. It brought into focus the fact that the fear was still very much there. I recognized it as a monster holding me in its gnarled claws—and doing so to the vast majority of African Americans, as such fear stems not simply from individual events (even those that make national or international headlines) but also from the simple fact of being Black in America. For as the MacArthur Fellow and writer Claudia Rankine reminds us,

Anti-black racism is in the culture. It's in our laws, in our advertisements, in our friendships, in our segregated cities, in our schools, in our Congress, in our scientific experiments, in our language, on the Internet, in our bodies no matter our race, in our communities and, perhaps most devastatingly, in our justice system. The unarmed, slain Black bodies in public spaces turn grief into our everyday feeling that something is wrong everywhere and all the time, even if locally things appear normal.[10]

As such, Black life is one of constant grieving over the inevitable death of our fullness as human beings within a society that was built on our death and continues to profit from it. Rev. angel's *Being Black* offered an alternative to the suffering, a path of flow into a stream of consciousness that was liberatory and life-giving.

The Molding of a Warrior-Spirit

Like me, Rev. angel is a native New Yorker. Her characteristically New York directness and no-nonsense approach feel familiar. Even though I don't have a personal relationship with her, I agree with Jasmine Syedullah, one of Rev. angel's coauthors and her student, calling her teacher's practice "all fiery, full-on gangster compassion, unapologetically Black."[11]

Rev. angel spent her young childhood in Lefrak City, Queens, with her firefighter father, before moving to Flatbush, Brooklyn. When her parents separated, she and her father became "thick as thieves" until she turned eight and he married a woman who already had a daughter and together they had a son. With her father's attention divided between the demands of his new family and his work, Rev. angel felt like she "had to make do with the painfully little individual attention" she received; a childhood trauma that stayed with her until her practice of *oryoki* (the Zen tradition of ritualized mindful eating) helped surface it.[12]

Rev. angel's early experience attending a Black Baptist church affected her. Following her parents' separation, her father's new girlfriend and then wife, who doubled as Rev. angel's caretaker, took her to church with her on Sundays. There, the young williams sang "in the hand-clapping, foot-stomping choir" and witnessed women and men catch "the Holy Ghost." Behind the public show of loving inclusion, in the privacy of their home, williams suffered abuse from her caretaker. Though there are hints of the abuse she suffered in that relationship in *Being Black*, in *Radical Dharma* she describes it more fully, identifying it as "the most poignant reminder of the gross conflict between the life we lived in full view of everyone and the one that went on behind closed doors where the yelling, head-thrust-into-the-flushing-toilet scenes were performed alongside the rehearsal of stories that obscured the truth."[13] When her father learned of the abuse, he left the woman. But rather than feeling relief for her escape from her stepmother's sadistic behavior, williams felt a sense of loss, writing that with the woman went the "only motherly love" she could remember.[14]

Her father's relationship with his next girlfriend was responsible for their move to Flatbush, where williams spent years in a kind of hiding.[15] Her new stepmother and her daughter were from Jamaica and fair-skinned, both identities that came with a sense of superiority to African Americans who were darker than them. In Brooklyn, williams began attending the more reserved Protestant church where, feeling "a connection to both the compassion that He must have felt to allow himself to be sacrificed for us, and to the depth of pain He suffered as He sought insight into His father's wisdom," she became an admitted fan of "the long-haired, blue-eyed Jesus."[16] Feeling out of place in her new environment with her proper speech, lighter skin, longish hair, and sharp mind, she "passed the years becoming invisible behind comic books, walking to and from school, and slinking in hallways" to avoid being noticed.[17] By the time she was twelve, she declared herself an agnostic. This was also around the time that she began to feel that she didn't fit in, a sense that remained with her into early adulthood.

In her teenage years she went to live with her mother in the Tribeca neighborhood of Manhattan, where she attended a Chinatown school that was largely Chinese populated. There her world opened up and she began cutting school to immerse herself in the life of the Chelsea neighborhood that was undergoing gentrification by gay white men. From there she began immersing herself in queer culture in the West Village in the '80s. About that time, she says, "We tested the boundaries of our boldness and practiced holding hands, kissing, loving, fighting, and fucking where everyone could see."[18] Honestly, I feel like I would've seen Rev. angel, probably in Washington Square Park, where I spent a lot of time during my high school years. It was the place to be, where artists and writers, freethinkers and misfits hung out, trying on personalities. As a shy, nerdy kid living with my older sister because my mother didn't have a place for me, I relished being someplace where it seemed no one belonged. It also seemed that our not belonging was where we found community. Indeed, as Rev. angel says, "It wasn't always safe, but it was ours."[19] While she attributes her ability to stay relatively safe to her aversion to drugs and alcohol, I can only attribute my ability to stay relatively safe to the spirits and ancestors that walked with me, guiding me when I had no idea who I was or where I was going.

Stepping into Zen

Rev. angel took her first meditation instruction at San Francisco Zen Center while she was visiting the West Coast, and for the next couple of years she continued to check out different meditation centers in both San Francisco and New York. When she got serious about making Zen practice a much larger part of her life, she decided to embark on a weekend retreat at a monastery just outside New York City. Despite feeling like an outsider for a couple of reasons—her blackness and her lack of monk's clothing—she decided then that she wanted to be a monk.[20]

Her childhood experience of loneliness and sadness had produced in her a tendency to be by herself and do things alone. As a result, her first two years as a Zen student were spent meditating alone. The way she describes learning all she could from books and magazines, signing up for newsletters, and designating a small space for practicing meditation resonates with me, as this is precisely how I began my practice. Eventually, wanting to go deeper, she sought out a teacher. She found her in Sensei Pat Enkyo O'Hara, the head of Village Zendo in lower Manhattan, who was ordained by Maezumi Roshi and given dharma transmission by the innovative Zen teacher and socially engaged Buddhist Bernie Glassman. About a year after joining the sangha, Rev. angel came to a difficult time in her life. A business that she had put all of her heart into failed, she moved from the city to an isolated area in upstate New York, and was betrayed by a close and trusted friend. Finally, her "first adult relationship" fell apart.[21]

Though she had no money, she felt too depressed to find a job. She spent three weeks not eating, not really feeling alive anymore. Her loneliness and misery were disrupted when she received a calendar from the Village Zendo announcing an upcoming weeklong *sesshin*, or retreat. The retreat proved to be a turning point for her. She describes it as the beginning of not just healing the pain she was dealing with at that moment but of opening her heart wider, expanding her vision farther than she ever realized was possible. While she had been taking refuge in the Buddha and the teachings for a number of years, it was during the retreat that she finally learned what it meant to take refuge in her teacher and sangha. Even though she never spoke with the majority of the thirty other retreatants with whom she shared space during the retreat, she writes, "By being silently supportive and allowing me the space I needed to both acknowledge my sadness and not be isolated, they collectively taught me that healing begins at home, and that home is wherever you make it."[22] While she was the only Black person in the group, she became aware that the thing to focus on in sangha is not whether people are the same. Rather, what is important is an agreement to be mutually respectful and supportive no matter who you are. In that way, all sangha members contribute to serving the community and everyone benefits.[23] For years after that retreat, she focused on developing her Zen practice at the Village Zendo and in the White Plum Asanga, eventually receiving an offer from Penguin to write *Being Black*. She was later invited by Francisco "Paco" Lugoviña Roshi, another dharma heir of Bernie Glassman, to receive dharma transmission from him and thus become a Zen teacher in her own right.

Being Black, in its description of that first sesshin as well as elsewhere in the book, addresses the experience of suffering as universal to the human experience and the possibility of awakening as available to everyone. Yet it also very pointedly addresses the particular suffering of people of African descent. For her efforts, Rev. angel has been embraced by the hip-hop generation, who recognize the call-and-response style that she often deploys in her work—for instance, in the way that she uses "us" and "we" in *Being Black* to invoke a collective experience and invites her audience to nod their heads to and—even in the solitude of their homes—say "Yes" and "Amen." It is in her later creation of a number of highly participatory retreats and trainings. According to Tracy Curtis, the author of "Born Into This Body: Black Women's Use of Buddhism in Autobiographical Narratives," African Americans' appreciation of and support for Rev. angel's teaching style is evidenced by the capacity crowd that turned out for her appearance at a Black-centered bookstore in Los Angeles, bought her book, and waited in line for hours to have it signed. In turn, Rev. angel produced a musical compilation, also called *Being Black*, in what Curtis calls a kind of reciprocal gesture.[24] We find this affinity for call-and-response—an embodiment of her belief in the inextricability of the "me" from the "we"—in the dynamic way that she builds community, going beyond simply publishing texts to building whole programs around serving the community and having everyone benefit.

Loving Blackness

Although *Being Black* is not a traditional autobiography or memoir, Rev. angel narrates events from her life to help illustrate Zen lessons. As Curtis observes, "The text primarily provides instruction in Buddhist practices alongside ways one might connect them to a variety of common black experiences."[25] This is why I think the book can be read as a kind of love letter to Black people. Rev. angel acknowledges the particular difficulties that African Americans face given the history of this country and uses "we" and "us" to draw Black readers into the text and thus help them, in Curtis's words, "understand her statements as sympathetic and empathetic rather than accusatory."[26]

Rev. angel injects elements of encouragement for the spiritual and social evolution of African American people throughout the book. For example, in reference to teachings on the innateness of our "Buddha nature," she deploys a passage from Alice Walker's novel *Possessing the Secret of Joy*: "Black people are natural, they possess the secret of joy. . . . They are alive physically and emotionally, which makes them easier to live with."[27] Referring to the quote, Rev. angel says, "I fully believe this to be true. How powerful it would be if we all, blacks and non-blacks alike, recognized this truth, even if only for an instant? What if we as black folks were to make a practice of touching such a reality every day? A radical transformation would begin."[28] In her interview with Tippett on *On Being*, she comments on the use of "grace" in the subtitle of her book, reiterating her position, saying,

> I just want to say that I think black America, as non-monolithic as it is, has persisted in an amazing grace throughout the history of this country that is phenomenal; that if any of us were willing to be just a little bit sane and look, we would recognize, "Oh, my goodness. How extraordinary that black people, in particular—indigenous people, as well—could live the lives of dignity that they have chosen for themselves in the face of the onslaught of what this country's history has been and continues to be and continues to put upon them. So grace, I think, is a gift that black peoples have inhabited for a great deal of time.[29]

Her statements echo the words of bell hooks, who told the audience during a public dialogue with Cornel West, "I always say black people are some of the most forgiving people in the world."[30] Indeed, we are. For me, Rev. angel's encouragement also summons Toni Morrison's character Baby Suggs, the "unchurched" preacher from *Beloved*. In a forest clearing, Baby Suggs reminds her formerly enslaved congregants about the importance of African American people loving themselves in the face of constant white violence. She counsels those gathered about the importance of loving their bodies, their flesh, their eyes, their hands, their livers, their mouths, their necks, and most of all, their hearts, "For this is the prize."[31]

Being Black is all about Black people leaning into loving these bodies that we were born into and seeing them as the source of our liberation. The book holds a place within the long history of loving words and gestures by Black women for other African Americans.

"From Fear to Fearlessness: Facing Slavery's Legacy"

There are several junctures in *Being Black* in which Rev. angel refers directly to the impact of slavery and its legacy on the African American psyche and spirit. One of the effects is that Black people too often are not able to see ourselves outside of the images that have been fed to us in the media.

> Each of our spirits suffers from the guilt of every negative image, idea, and stereotype about black people ever conceived. And there are many to choose from. When a news announcer says, "The rapist is described as a black man, about five foot eight inches . . ." I believe every black person that hears it feels a momentary sagging of their heart. Huge numbers of us continue to be plagued by an enormous fear of failure, and our failures somehow seem more monumental, more impossible to recover from because not only do we not have as many safety nets to catch us, but there is always the danger of systematic racism lurking nearby to keep us down as well.[32]

The long history of anti-Black racism in this country means that African Americans carry an enormous burden of being judged collectively based on negative stereotypes, or the "nigger image" that Baldwin has rightly attributed to the white imagination.[33] Many African Americans, in an attempt to escape this "monstrous being,"[34] have not sought out love as the solution but are rather steeped in self-hatred. We have internalized "the nigger" and thus become our own worst enemy.

Discussing the effects of internalized racism on the Black psyche, Rev. angel states, "It has been said many times for many years that it is the racist-minded white people that hold black people back and keep us from moving forward. In many ways this is still true. But it is also true that we have lived so long with so much fear deep within us that we may not be able to tell if we do not move forward because we cannot or because we *will not*."[35] We can again hear in her words an echo of Baldwin who, in a 1971 conversation with the poet Nikki Giovanni, pointed to the source and repercussions of internalized hatred that plagued Black America then:

> It was not the world that was my oppressor only, because what the world does to you, if it does it to you long enough and effectively enough, you begin to do it to yourself. You become a collaborator, an accomplice of your own murderers because you believe the same things they do. They think it's important to be white and *you* think it's important to be white. They think it is shameful to be black and you think it is shameful to be black. And you have no corroboration around you of any other sense of life. All those corroborations, which are around you are in terms of the white majority standards, so deplorable they frighten you to death. You don't eat watermelon, you get so rigid you can't dance. You can hardly move by the time you're fourteen.[36]

This fear of being associated with any of the myriad negative stereotypes attributed to blackness is in part the source of the sagging heart that afflicts many African Americans when we hear the perpetrator of a crime described as Black. While Baldwin refers to Black people's rejection of eating watermelon and dancing as a consequence of being steeped in and submitting to the white imaginary, it is easy to make the leap to what is viewed as inherently antisocial and depraved behavior: committing crimes (also in the white imagination associated with blackness) as a reason not only for self-hatred but also for fear of ourselves. "Black people are some of the most scared people in the world," says Cornel West on this topic. "That's what it is to be 'nigger-ized.' See, when you're 'niggerized,' you're told you are less beautiful, less intelligent, less moral and you will have fear at the center of who you are because of the terror that will come at you."[37]

The fear that Rev. angel, Baldwin, and West talk about is real and justified given the history of Black people in this country. It is also something that is largely unaddressed in the African American community. Talking with Tippett about using the word *fearlessness* in her book's subtitle, Rev. angel makes the point that "fearlessness is the really bold statement, because we (Black people) are expected to not be fearless. And, in fact, our fearlessness is dangerous and threatening. And so having people of African descent, people that identify as Black, to choose fearlessness is a very, very bold statement of defiance."[38] This defiance in the face of white violence and aggression is what puts a target on Black people's backs. At the same time, it is the awareness and concomitant fear of that same target that has made Black people as a whole shy away from expressing the fullness of our humanity.

Rev. angel argues in *Being Black* that "the fear that lives within us is like a dirty little secret that we carry in our pockets everywhere we go." She continues, "Some of us are aware of the fear and carry it inward, sheepishly struggling to keep it to ourselves."[39] Curtis has commented on Rev. angel's use of the word *sheepish*, proposing that she uses it to undermine commonly held beliefs that hostile actions or attitudes are spurred primarily by responses to the outside world. But given West's comments and Rev. angel's summarizing comments, that some "are less aware and direct it outward, sometimes in the form of aggression,"[40]

I would disagree with Curtis's assessment. African American men in particular are deathly afraid of being seen as weak by their peers and community members. In addition, especially for poor Black men who live in a country in which they hold no real power, their anger and the bravado that accompanies it are a way for them to mask their fear.

Rev. angel's comments reflect sentiments expressed by Lama Rangdröl, who states, "When I discovered that it was possible to avoid becoming ensnared in the mentality of an angry black man by applying Buddhism, I found that I had found a great treasure, not just for me but also for my people. I could immediately see the potential for resonance in millions of black people's minds. I could see how it could reverberate down to the core of the hurt so many of us carry; that one could emerge from Buddhist study and practice healed."[41] The hurt that Lama Rangdröl speaks about is inherited from generations past and is a result of the myriad ways that we feel racism pressing on us in our everyday lives. This hurt, we know, lives not only in the mind. It sets up shop in our bodies, our cells, such that we see the world through it and pass that narrow and diminishing viewpoint on to future generations. For Rev. angel, as for Lama Rangdröl, the dharma represents a practice path to a different way of being.

Baldwin posits that the way for Black people to relieve ourselves of the burden of living through the lens of whiteness is to "break out of all of that and try to become yourself." He continues, "It's hard for anybody, but it's very hard if you're born black in a white society. Hard because you've got to divorce yourself from the standards of that society."[42] I see Rev. angel's work as an ongoing effort to use the dharma—not in a narrow sectarian sense but in the broad sense of embodying and applying wisdom teachings—to help Black people divorce ourselves from the self-annihilating standards of the society into which we were born. She is an exemplar of someone who has found a way to become, and go on becoming, herself.

Waking Up, Truly Woke

Rev. angel devotes the whole middle section of *Being Black* to the Buddhist concept of wakefulness. In a gesture that echoes those of other Black Buddhists, she addresses the usefulness of Buddhism, saying, "In the long run, there's really no point to any spiritual or secular path or training that doesn't show you that the way to freedom is to surrender your ideas and concepts and wake up to the life you have now."[43] This idea of waking up to the life that one has is very different from the way most people live their lives, which is spent either dwelling in the past or hoping for something better in the future. But only when we wake up to our life as it is can we begin to take responsibility for it and stop looking outside of ourselves for the answers to our suffering.

Rev. angel reminds the reader that, contrary to the common belief at the time that he lived, the Buddha taught that becoming awake to one's life was possible for anyone. In short, anyone could be a bodhisattva, an awakening being. Bodhisattvas do not have to be fully awake themselves. Rather, they are "awakening warriors that give up floating through life aimlessly and being concerned only with themselves. Awakening warriors live in a way that is of benefit to all."[44] And they do their work here in this world, not in some imagined heaven (as is taught in a number of religious traditions, including many Black churches).

In *Being Black*, Rev. angel introduces the concept of warrior-spirit, breaking down the two words as a way of defining the term: "'Spirit' refers to that which gives life. 'Warriors' live a life of action and clear direction."[45] She advises that "we can bring a warrior-spirit to the cause of peace and harmonious connection because it is about life and living, not power and aggression."[46] Rather than attributing the warrior-spirit to any particular religious tradition, Rev. angel advises that it "is a frame of mind that lets us make a habit of cultivating the qualities and skills" that already live inside of us.[47] While she contextualizes warrior-spirit through the lens of the bodhisattva vows—a traditional set of vows found across Mahayana Buddhist schools—she explains each vow via everyday lived experience, at points addressing the particularity of the Black experience. For example, in her explanation of a vow that she phrases as "The truths are without limit, I make a promise to master them," she discusses the importance for Black people and other people of color to actively analyze our individual situations as inextricable from those of our communities. Given the racist history of this country and its contemporary reality of aggression and oppression, there is too much at stake for us to be "lazy thinkers" who accept what we are taught about our innate beauty, intelligence, and potential. We must be vigilant in our analysis of the causes of violence and oppression. Moreover, she argues that Black people's history of suffering in this country makes us sharply sensitive to the suffering of others. Calling for us to remember our "Buddha nature" as Black people, she also echoes Thich Nhat Hanh's declaration, "Once there is seeing there must be acting."[48]

On the whole, *Being Black* does a lot of work to make seemingly foreign Buddhist concepts pertinent for African Americans, acknowledging and addressing our history of suffering as well as our activism based in care for the collective. In the book, Rev. angel introduces Black freedom fighters such as Sojourner Truth, Muhammad Ali, Pierre Toussaint,[49] and Malcolm X as examples of warrior-spirits, "a fine legacy of people" who "were awakening warriors in their own time."[50] By considering these figures alongside internationally celebrated activists such as Mahatma Gandhi, she makes a move that Adeana McNicholl highlights in "Being Buddha, Staying Woke: Racial Formation in Black Buddhist Writing"—the effort by Black Buddhists to "situate themselves as racialized subjects within an imagined international community situated in a Buddhist worldview."[51] By including these people of color who were visionaries in their own time as part of her vision for Buddhist lineage, Rev. angel brings Buddhism to ordinary African Americans who aspire to achieve our individual freedom as well as contribute to the freedom of the disfranchised collective. She thus opens the door for us to summon to memory other people from our own lives and communities as examples of awakening warriors and to see ourselves doing the same.[52]

Rev. angel's Love Ethic

I see Rev. angel's work as an enactment of what hooks would call a love ethic, with "love" serving as a source and site of individual and collective liberation. But the sentiment is not enough. Love, as hooks reminds us, is a verb and must be enacted. As she counsels, "When we are loving we openly and honestly express care, affection, responsibility, respect, commitment, and trust."[53]

Rev. angel has been deeply influenced by hooks. In her interview with Tippett, she says,

> bell—and reading bell, and getting an opportunity to meet bell, also—gave me a lens into the possibility of love being something that I could—not only "could," I want to say—that I *had* to bring into the language of my perception of the world. And that love was not to be limited to my bedroom or my family and just people that I thought that I liked. That what I was doing in the past and what we often do and what our culture calls us to do is to use love to be a quantifier of "Do I have a preference for you?"

She continues by stating that the conditions that people place on love—for instance, ideas about enlightenment, affinity, or reflecting back to people what they want to see as a way of enhancing their ideas of themselves and thus being worthy of love—make for a very limited way of understanding love. Rev. angel has come to think of love most often as space.[54] By "space" she means developing one's own capacity for internal spaciousness to allow others to be as they are.

And that doesn't mean that we don't have hopes or wishes that things are changed or shifted, but that to come from a place of love is to be in acceptance of what is, even in the face of moving it towards something that is more whole, more just, more spacious for all of us. It's bigness. It's allowance. It's flexibility. It's saying . . . "Oh, those police officers are trapped inside of a system, as well. They are subject to an enormous amount of suffering, as well."

I think that those things are missed when we shortcut talking about King, or we shortcut talking about Gandhi, or we shortcut talking about what Aung San Suu Kyi was doing at some point. We leave out the aspects of their underlying motivation for moving things, and we make it about policies and advocacy, when really it is about expanding our capacity for love, as a species.[55]

Rev. angel's words invoke the principle of interbeing. We gain spaciousness when we are able to step back and see the interconnectedness of all beings; that the victim, the victimizer, and the witness are one in the same, driven by systems steeped in violence. What does it truly mean to offer lovingkindness, not only to the victims of racial violence but also the victimizers?

"Lovingkindness is like true friendliness," writes Rev. angel. "Not fake smile-in-your-face, cheesy friendliness. And definitely not the kind that's about accepting anything anyone decides to lay on us." Rather, it is about being able to accept people for who they are with all of their foibles and flaws. It is about opening our hearts to others. She reminds the reader that, contrary to what most people are taught, it is important to cultivate "lovingkindness of our own selves before we can really accept anyone else."[56] This need to love and show love for one's self is particularly true for Black women who, because of familial and societal pressures, tend to put ourselves last on the list of those who need tending to. The necessity for Black people to love ourselves is urgent, especially in a country that devalues and directs hatred toward us on a daily basis. In this context, self-love and self-care is a revolutionary act. To paraphrase James Baldwin, it allows one to become oneself. The deep work of radical self-acceptance entails rejecting negative images projected upon the Black body. Rev. angel advises the reader, "Whatever your doubts and beliefs about who you are, you have to learn how to be at ease and make friends with yourself before you can truly be at ease with the rest of the world."[57] Rev. angel extends a version of this view of self-love to social justice work as well, saying that activists must learn to take care of themselves.[58]

The radical self-acceptance that Rev. angel advocates is the key to African Americans gaining a sense of wholeness, which enables us to open our hearts to "accept the whole world with open arms, not because you have been told you should, but because you realize in your heart that we are all ultimately deserving of love and compassion."[59]

From *Being Black* to *Radical Dharma*

In the years after *Being Black* was published, Rev. angel came to feel ambivalent about the book. She stated in an interview with Kerri Kelly, for instance, that she considers it her "bastard child." She says, "I did a book that I thought it was time for. That was in the year 2000. I thought people of color were going to be interested in Buddhism, and they were, and that they needed an invitation; they needed an explicit invitation."[60] She continues,

> The degree of rejection that I was confronted with in terms
> of the Buddhist community, in terms of the white bookstore-
> owning community, in terms of even media and media opportu-
> nities was crushing. First of all, I was much younger. I was thirty,

and so we get more easily crushed, but . . . I was confronted with the distinction between what people said about what it meant to be Buddhist or yogis or practitioners or spiritual and who they really were and how they could really show up. I just wanted to get away from *Being Black* for the longest time.[61]

The white Buddhist community's cool reception of *Being Black* is sad but not surprising. She was challenging the status quo. She was also correct in her belief that the time was right and that people of color would be interested in Buddhism. I and the hundreds of people who waited for hours at her book signings to meet her are a testament to that.

Again, *Being Black* came into my life at a time when I was having an existential crisis; I was fragmented and trying to put myself together. For several years I had flitted around, never putting down roots anywhere. When asked about it, I was inclined to respond that my son was my home. This was true. But my sense of homelessness also came from a deep sense of dissatisfaction with wherever I found myself. Six months before moving to Wisconsin, my son and I had spent about six months in Ghana. Again, as I had done in my early twenties, I was looking to see us reflected in those around us. And now here we were in the middle of cheese country. I had committed at least the next eight years of our lives to a graduate program. My spirit had decided that it was time for me to step into my "Waking Path."

Rev. angel was around thirty years old when she published *Being Black*. I was around thirty when I read it. It would take several more years for me to no longer be plagued by a nagging sense of disappointment and dissatisfaction that had been with me for much of my life. Through the practice of meditation—first in solitude, like Rev. angel, and then in community—I have been able to face my suffering and embark on the work of healing. Although *Being Black* was something that Rev. angel wanted to distance herself from, I hope she also knows that it was a balm to people like me. I was one of those who needed an invitation, if only in the form of a text that acknowledged my experience by someone in whom I could see myself.

Unlike *Being Black*, *Radical Dharma: Talking Race, Love, and Liberation,* her collaborative book project that subsequently unfolded into an ongoing series of gatherings and retreats, is something that she feels she can fully own. The book and the activism around it provided a kind of healing for her, making it possible for her to "fully reclaim *Being Black* as well."[62] The book has been hailed as "the book for right now" by Autostraddle, a "progressively feminist online community."[63] As a woman who claims her multiple intersecting identities, including her queerness, Rev. angel celebrates Autostraddle's recognition of the radical inclusiveness of the text.

I see *Radical Dharma* as conceived of and executed from a Black radical political ideology.[64] As I mentioned at the opening of this chapter, Rev. angel takes a by-any-means-necessary approach to spreading the message of liberation. This approach, of course, is synonymous with the name Malcolm X, who famously pronounced those words and who is considered to have been "radical." But as the Black studies scholar Kehinde Andrews points out, the phrase has been distorted. "Radicalism," he writes, "is not about the means (violence/non-violence), but the ends (reform/revolution)."[65] Even more basically, as Angela Davis explains, the word *radical* simply means "grasping things at the root."[66] "Advocacy of revolutionary transformation was not primarily about violence," Davis writes about the Black power movement, "but about substantive issues like better life conditions for poor people and people of color."[67] The focus on violence serves to detract from revolution's goal, which is to do away with a corrupt society. Radicalism is based on rejecting the fundamental principles that govern a sick society and creating a new paradigm. The West, built as it is on the attempted genocide of the indigenous population, the enslavement of African and African diasporic populations, its warmongering, and its denigration of the feminine, to name a few of its ills, must be uprooted and a new society imagined. Andrews argues that in the radical tradition there is the recognition that "the system *is* the problem. There can be no reform, no adjustments and we as Black people should not waste time daydreaming of equality."[68] It will not be given.

Rev. angel speaks to this conceptualization of radicalism in her discussion of the need for a new and radical dharma. She says, "What is required is a new Dharma, a radical Dharma that deconstructs rather than amplifies the systems of suffering, that starves rather than fertilizes the soil of the conditions that the deep roots of societal suffering grow in."[69] She is drawing upon the Black radical tradition, for instance, when she states that "it is our responsibility to recognize this is the water that we are swimming in and there's no way to *not* swim in the water and *not* be a part of making those waves and moving that energy around and continuing its flow if you don't take the opportunity to lift yourself up out of it and see where you are swimming."[70] She is not interested in accepting a "'kinder, gentler suffering' that does not question the unwholesome roots of systemic suffering and the structures that hold it in place."[71] Rather, she is looking to have us all deal with the discomfort that comes from really confronting our personal and collective suffering and then pulling up that system by the roots.

Radical Roots

The inspiration for *Radical Dharma* originated in late summer 2014 when Rev. angel and Lama Rod were asked by editors at *Buddhadharma* magazine to talk about their practice of radical dharma and discuss the challenges of being teachers of color in predominantly white communities.[72] The half-hour video of their conversation was released online on the day of the no-indictment verdict of the police murder of eighteen-year-old Michael Brown. The Eric Garner verdict, also no-indictment for his murderer, followed shortly thereafter. Rev. angel and Lama Rod's video conversation went viral within Western

Buddhist circles.[73] The impetus to turn that initial conversation into a "talking book" came from the Black oral tradition that Cornel West and bell hooks modeled in *Breaking Bread: Insurgent Black Intellectual Life*, a book in which their recorded conversations are interspersed with personal essays.

Rev. angel, Lama Rod, and Jasmine Syedullah took their conversations on the road, inviting community participation. (Syedullah could not be present for all of the conversations, but her voice is included in the text when she was, and her essays are very much part of the project.) They chose to have those conversations in places where they each were already rooted: Brooklyn, Atlanta, Boston, and Berkeley. In Atlanta, at Charis Books, the oldest feminist bookstore in the South, Dr. Jan Willis was in the audience. By the time they held their conversation in Berkeley on June 19, 2015—Juneteenth—a white supremacist had massacred nine Black church goers in Charleston, South Carolina, again pointing to the urgency of their work. Syedullah remarked about the experience, "As we were traveling, an incredible amount of violence, anti-black violence, persisted and really fueled a different kind of conversation about the negative impacts of race." The organizers noticed a disconnect between the conversations about race that focused on those most impacted; those who needed support and help and bystanders who were saying, "I don't know what my place is in this conversation." They were keen to start a conversation about how everyone is impacted by violence.[74] Those that they facilitated became a practice of healing in places where diverse populations had never sat down together and been in conversation with each other. Those eye-opening conversations were given life through the text as well as beyond it in those communities, and they continue to unfold.

Radical Dharma was published in 2016, a political moment that created a heightened sense of anxiety for those of us who are always already in an anxious state. Rev. angel addresses the timing in her preface: "We

. . . pressed for the publication of the book to happen well before the 2016 presidential election rather than right in the thick of it. We foresee an increasing anxiety about transitioning from the first Black U.S. president." Perhaps she envisioned the text as a kind of road map for navigating the moment as well as an opportunity for those who read it to uproot our societal suffering that is based in "the racialization of people and its underlying supposition—the superiority of white people."[75] Donald Trump was simply a new facade on the original edifice of this country.

Following the no-indictment verdicts for both Brown's and Garner's killers, national attention was being given to the systemic state-sanctioned violence and oppression that have persisted in various and evolving forms against Black people since the slave era. *Radical Dharma*'s "Editor's Note" states, "Their deaths set in motion a new iteration of a Black-centered movement for liberation, the achievement of which we believe must be articulated by and inextricably linked to an embodied personal liberation."[76] Indeed, that was a pivotal moment for a Black-led movement. And yet since then, many people of African descent have died as a result of state-sanctioned violence, both by police officers and private citizens operating on behalf of the state.

The May 25, 2020 murder of forty-six-year-old George Floyd in the streets of Minneapolis, Minnesota, brought this racial violence to light for many white people who had before then been able to distract themselves. In lock-down the nation had no choice but to pay more attention to something that Black people had been aware of for centuries. This time the whole world took to the streets to protest the murder. In places where there was a sizable population, many of the protests were Black-led, with the Black Lives Matter movement being responsible for many instances of mobilization. Riots ensued, some of them instigated by law enforcement sent in to preserve property. Murals bearing Floyd's likeness appeared across the globe, and multinational companies proclaimed that "Black Lives Matter." All of the police officers involved were convicted in varying degrees of Floyd's murder. And yet by May 25, 2021, one year after Floyd's murder, at least 229 Black people had been killed by police.[77] After Floyd's death, Democratic lawmakers vowed to address systemic racism and the "George Floyd Justice in Policing Act" was introduced to Congress. The bill passed the House of Representatives but stalled in the Senate. As of this writing, it has not been resurrected.

In May 2022, a white supremacist traveled over two hours to massacre as many Black people as he could in Buffalo, New York. Like the man who massacred the South Carolina parishioners, the killer in New York was called "an extremist." But it seems facile to me for the news media to call the man who carried out the murders "a violent, racist extremist." Such labels obscure the fact that he emerges from within a society that is built on his right to violent action as a means of enforcing and preserving his superiority; that he is but indicative of a system of violence.[78]

Radical Dharma was conceived "as a call to transform sanghas and communities so that queer folk, people of color, and members of other marginalized groups could achieve the healing needed to recover from centuries of social injustice." It is also "an exploration of what it is to practice Buddhism in a society where African Americans are routinely killed by police and incarcerated in vast numbers."[79] This is a good and important undertaking. In truth, however, I feel an inability to connect deeply to *Radical Dharma*. The reality of living as a Black woman in this country is at the heart of my feeling. For all of the truth-telling, the community involvement, the appeals to get uncomfortable—in short, the loftiness of *Radical Dharma*—I find myself over and over again frustrated with the text as I don't see myself as part of the Black collective it presents in the way that I saw myself in *Being Black*. For all of its community engagement, it also feels very abstract. The majority of us "out here in the streets" cannot hold these truths while being steeped in the waters of white supremacy. We're just trying to live. And we all know that there will be another George Floyd, another Elijah McClain, another Breonna Taylor, another Walter Scott, another Jayland Walker . . .

Even though I don't connect with this piece of Rev. angel's writing, I admire her persistence.

And Yet . . .

She continues the work.

One section of *Radical Dharma* was excerpted in a 2017 issue of *Lion's Roar* magazine and titled "Where Will You Stand?" In it, Rev. angel issues a challenge to white Buddhists by invoking the history of racial oppression and terrorism of the Jim Crow era and the activism of their ancestors—some of whom may have stood shoulder to shoulder with Martin Luther King Jr. She calls on them to live up to their ancestors' legacy at this critical time. Referring to the election of Donald Trump to the US presidency in 2016, she writes,

> We are at a critical moment in the history of the nation as well as within the Buddhist teaching and tradition in America. This is the "back of the bus" moment of our time. Fifty years after civil rights laws were laid down, it is clear that these laws were enshrined within a structure that continues to profit from anti-Black racism. The necessary bias that the system requires in order to perpetuate itself has permeated our sanghas, and in this very moment, Buddhists are called upon to put aside business as usual.[80]

Rev. angel appeals to this generation of Buddhists who consider themselves activists, addressing them directly, when she says, "If you have ever wondered how you would have shown up in the face of the challenge put before white America when Rosa Parks refused to give up her seat, upending the accepted social order, now is when you will find out." She also invokes the Buddha's commitment to social justice in asking, "Will we actually embody our practice and teachings—or not?" Similarly she states, "It is a clarifying moment about who we are as individuals and who we have been thus far as a collective of people laying claim to the teachings of the Buddha, waving the flag of wisdom and compassion all the while."[81]

We can see how much Rev. angel's outlook changed in the intervening years by contrasting *Being Black* to "Where Will You Stand?" It would seem that at the time of her writing *Being Black*, she was more hopeful of the future of Black America. This is evidenced by her invocation of Martin Luther King Jr.'s dream, which comes immediately after the book's opening sentence: "Black folks have arrived."[82] In the ensuing years, her position shifted, becoming more "radical" in its orientation as a result of what she has witnessed unfold politically. Having seen supporters of white supremacy witness the progress that African diasporic people had made in this country and try to turn back the clock or remind us of "our place," by 2016 Rev. angel was much more clearly drawing from the radicalism of the Black activist tradition.

In the article, she also shines a light on the country's history of the genocide of indigenous populations as well as the enslavement of African and African diasporic peoples. "Our inability as a nation to atone for the theft of these lands and the building of wealth, power, and privilege on the countless backs and graves of Black people," she writes, "is our most significant obstacle to being at peace with ourselves, and thus with the world."[83] Like the other Black Buddhist women whose work I discuss here, Rev. angel consistently links this distant history of oppression to the present moment. Acknowledging those ancestors who succumbed to their subjugation, dehumanization, and exploitation, yet also highlighting the collective resistance, resilience, and survival of her ancestors, she points us in the direction of a healed, liberated future.

The Revolution Continues, or Staying Woke

The Black revolutionary thinker Kwame Ture (Stokely Carmichael) once said, "A true revolutionary must provide an alternative, not just rhetoric condemning the existing system."[84] Rev. angel provides an alternative in the many ways that she shows up in community in the world—co-imagining and cocreating liberatory spaces as part of the cultural, intellectual, action-oriented, and spiritual labor for which Black radicalism is known.

In its second year of publication, the coauthors of *Radical Dharma* organized "conversation circles" and their first "summer camp" to bring people together to "get in the conversation" about the impact of white supremacy on their lives and in their communities, using the lens of the dharma. In the book's third year, the coauthors organized a second "summer camp." They released an audio book of *Radical Dharma* in their own voices in June 2019 in time for Juneteenth. The timing of the release was auspicious, as it marked the four hundredth anniversary of the disembarkation of "twenty and odd" enslaved Africans on the shores of Point Comfort, South Carolina. It was also the fiftieth anniversary of the call for Black reparations.[85] As such, Rev. angel remarked that

> it is particularly poignant that the Radical Dharma Move-
> ment project is launched in this year to take radical dharma
> to the next level of bringing it beyond just Buddhist circles as
> it has been always emerging and revealing itself to certainly
> be beyond that, into the activist and social justice communi-
> ties. But even going beyond that into yoga communities, into
> different *faiths* . . . and it's our commitment to really recog-
> nize and move forward in such a way that we make race and
> the . . . abolition of white supremacy, *the* conversation for this
> time.[86]

Highlighting the overdue nature of the conversation, she continued:

> It occurred to me that really we've never had a conversation
> ... about race in this country. We've had movements for sure
> that were about laws, that were about policies, but we haven't
> had a conversation, a practice, a heart-to-heart, a revealing
> ourselves, a willingness to step into vulnerability around the
> ways in which racialization has impacted all of us. Our con-
> versations have tended towards conversations reifying power
> and centering power with white power by focusing on race as
> something that is "a black people or a people of color problem"
> and we really wanted to undo that.[87]

To facilitate the conversation and begin the work of dismantling the paradigm that posits that racism is people of color's problem, the coauthors organized camps around what they call "the Radical Dharma Five (RD5): A Framework for Liberation."[88] The RD5 uses accessible language that appeals to common people.[89] For example, in a letter that Rev. angel published about RD5 directed to those who might be interested in the program, she quotes the truism, "Once you see it, you can't unsee it." She references "real talk" and draws the reader's attention at the end of the letter to the absence of "a sales page" and "hype." For those who seek liberation but feel alienated from the stoic religious or academic jargon that surrounds most invitations, Rev. angel's message feels like cool water on a parched throat. This is a continuation of the way that she has deployed the dharma in the past, such as her use of the term *woke* as a play on dharmic wakefulness and the Black vernacular expression "stay woke." The term, featured on her personal Facebook page in the days following the 2016 election, read simply, "Staying woke. Literally."[90]

In making the post, Rev. angel was moving beyond the formal Buddhist term *wakefulness* to the African American colloquialism "woke" to make a connection "between herself, Buddhism, and the idea of being 'awake.'"[91] Her use of the term *woke* taps into her love of hip-hop culture and is congruent with her desire to reach and connect with people within the Black community who do not necessarily read much of anything, let alone Buddhist philosophy.

Her followers—most of whom were probably familiar with her work on Buddhism, blackness, race, and embodiment—seemed perfectly attuned to the connection that she was making between herself, Buddhism, and the idea of being "awake."[92] As McNicholl asserts, in her post, "williams was purposely playing with the relationship between the Buddhist concept of 'awakening' and the modern word 'woke' to frame her awareness of the operation of institutionalized racial, gender, and sexual inequalities within a Buddhist worldview."[93] Her use of "hip" language is a deliberate appeal to the generation that will follow her—an effort to give them the language and the tools to realize not only their spiritual liberation but also their physical freedom from the labels and assumptions that seek to diminish and disempower them. Thus, she enacts the commitment that other Black women Buddhists such as Roshi Merle Kodo Boyd and hooks have made in their own way: to give hope to the next generation.

Rev. angel also remains clear about the need to focus on "white supremacy" as an institution rather than on the *agents* of white supremacy. Pointing to the importance of identifying *systems* of oppression, she explains the Radical Dharma summer camp's approach to white supremacy by stating, "Racism is a symptom and an outcome of the ideology of white supremacy. By white supremacy, I don't mean formal white *supremacists* . . . but I'm talking about run-of-the-mill, the basic cultural water of which American culture is, of white supremacy and those practices and protocols that uphold white supremacy which are known as *whiteness*."[94] In a webinar I attended, she reminded the attendees that contrary to popular belief, "whiteness can be inhabited and practiced by people of any skin color, people inhabiting any body and upholding . . . maintaining white supremacy can also happen as a result of internalized racism and internalized oppression that people in black bodies, yellow bodies, indigenous bodies, all the colors, all the peoples, all the heritages, all the faiths can all uphold and maintain."[95] Finally, clarifying the difference between not being racist and being an antiracist, she stressed the importance of active participation in resistance to white supremacy, arguing that silence equals complicity. Furthermore, identifying the contagion that is white supremacy, she observed that "those who arrive on this soil from some other land, some other place, immediately the culture induces us to participate in the advancing of white supremacy from every possible corner."[96] In a clear reference to the necessity of ridding ourselves of the contagion by "awakening" or "staying woke," during the webinar, Rev. angel insisted that the waters that we collectively swim in, white supremacy, must be recognized as the disease and all of the "isms" that preoccupy us as waves in the ocean, as symptoms of the disease. She contends that those isms are actually distractions that water the roots' continued proliferation, largely under the surface. While I see Rev. angel's point—indeed, slavery as the exploitation and denigration of Black bodies for the profit of white bodies is the original sin of this nation—we should also remember that whiteness emerged from wealthy white men convincing poor white men of their difference from Black people as a tool of capitalism. As such, I find bell hooks's phrase "Imperialist white supremacist capitalist heteropatriarchy" to characterize the interlocking nature of oppression to be more salient.

Awakening to the Whole

Rev. angel's ever-growing and evolving body of work seeks to facilitate individual and collective freedom by transcending suffering. Above all, it takes us to a deeper understanding of the nature of our suffering. Seeing suffering in what john a. powell, the director of the Othering and

Belonging Institute at the University of California, Berkeley, calls "individualistic terms" imposes a limit on our understanding. Rev. angel's work instead implores us to take seriously the systemic operations that we witness in our interpersonal relationships. In her interview with Sharon Salzberg, Salzberg observes that she believes that meditation by itself will produce a kind of good-heartedness and compassion. However, it is not directed at systems. Rev. angel responds that looking at underlying systems of oppression is a necessity for the marginalized and disenfranchised.[97]

Although one would think that meditation and mindfulness practice could be of service to people in recognizing structural oppression, that process has been impeded by the fact that these practices have by and large landed in communities of relative privilege that are not adversely affected by structural inequality—or indeed, that benefit from it, at least in an economic sense. Rev. angel is driven by the question of how we resist the tendency to let our current circumstance be the only direction from which we choose to organize the *lens of attention* of our meditation. She argues that if our compassion only extends through the lens of our privilege, then we only turn our attention to things that are personal or interpersonal and very rarely outward to social systems and structures because the need does not exist in us. She goes on to explain that in the course of her work, she has moved from the contemplative practitioners' "camp" to the activist side because they looked at larger systems. However, she insists that we need to close the gap between the two approaches because we cannot let such a powerful tool be limited by someone's current circumstances.[98] "We do not have the numbers to move this country towards greater justice," she says, "if the only driving force is whether or not people are actually feeling the pain of that particular thing."[99] It has long been an insight of the Black radical tradition that limiting the scope of our attention to personal and interpersonal relationships of domination or oppression leaves systemic oppression in place to perpetuate itself.

Wakefulness/Wokeness

Rev. angel has been known to refer to Siddhartha Gautama, the Buddha, as "a brother." I find that indicative of how, throughout her career, she has sought to connect the historical and contemporary African American experience to the wisdom teachings of Buddhism. She continues to draw from Buddhism, other spiritual wisdom traditions, and the Black radical tradition in her teaching and activism. Her seemingly endless granting of interviews, online and in-person offerings, and taking the conversation around *Radical Dharma* across the country, sometimes under very difficult circumstances, are all evidence of her tireless commitment to spirit-warriorhood. She is trying to reach as many people who could benefit from her message as possible, reaching back as she climbs.

As far as she has traveled in the world and in her personal development, she has never wavered from her commitment to staying grounded in her community. In *Being Black*, she writes that during her first retreat she heard Zen monks referred to as "home-leavers," and she was clear that that was not an acceptable path for her. This is a point that she reiterates in her conversation with Salzberg, stating that she was determined to serve *her* community, and she refused to make her "newfound Zen community" *her* community. She felt tethered to the realities of the people she was connected to: those who were in unjust circumstances, some of whom did not even know they were in unjust circumstances.[100] Rather than taking her out of her community, she found that taking up the priest path made her better equipped to return to those she felt committed to serve. "Rather than renounce the world of politics, political engagement, and activism," observes John Demont, Rev. angel "has chosen instead to interweave them into her path as a bodhisattva."[101]

About her work as a politically engaged Buddhist priest, she says, "You make an actual vow to hear the cries of the world . . . to step into the experience of awakening to the suffering of the world, and the desire to bring an end to that suffering."[102] The path that Rev. angel has chosen of pulling from various positionalities to do political and social justice work is the very meaning of being awakened (in Buddhist terms) or "wokeness" (in hip-hop terms). She has shown up again and again on the front lines, working to bridge the disconnect, in Demont's words, "at some of our country's most intractable and comprehensively impacting intersections including race, the environment, economic disparity, and a host of other intertwined issues that she feels prevent people from reconnecting with themselves, each other, and the planet."[103] As such, she exemplifies what it means to truly "stay woke."

To date, my connection to Rev. angel is through her offerings with Liberated Life Network, an inclusive community of people where all are invited to come as we are, leave as we must, and mind our own business. The network holds meditation practice most days of the week via Zoom, where basic meditation instruction is given. These are BIPOC-centered spaces where people are held accountable to themselves and to one another as part of our larger human community. Once a month Rev. angel offers half-day or full-day sits with BIPOC breakout rooms to help facilitate people's ability to access their liberation. For me, these spaces have been transformative in large part because of the radical honesty that I've found there. During COVID, wanting to bring in the New Year engaging in rigorous soul work rather than the mindless revelry that constituted too many of my younger years, I began attending Rev. angel's New Year's Eve gatherings. I look forward to those gatherings that incorporate sitting and walking meditation, for the opportunity to be in a mindful, loving, and respect-filled community, and for Rev. angel's dharma talks that remind me that awake/woke is the only way to live. The practice extends well into the wee hours of the new year. After them I always rest well and open my eyes the next day ready and grateful to begin again, truly a gift.

5

SPRING WASHAM

A Lotus in the Mud

I FIRST MET Spring Washam in 2018 when, as a birthday present to myself, I flew to California to attend my first weeklong silent retreat at Spirit Rock Meditation Center. For a few years I had hoped to visit that sacred place, where people such as Alice Walker, Jan Willis, Osho Zenju, and Jack Kornfield have spent time. The retreat was for self-identified women and featured as head teachers two women of color—JoAnna Hardy and Spring—and another woman of color, Kate Johnson, as student teacher. Even though I knew we would not be allowed to read once the retreat started, I brought along Spring's recently published *A Fierce Heart: Finding Strength, Courage, and Wisdom in Any Moment* and read it on the plane ride from Michigan. By the time I touched down in Oakland, I had a fierce fangirl crush.

I felt honored when a few days into the retreat I spotted my name on the list of those scheduled for an interview with her. In the day leading up to the interview, I went over all the things I wanted to talk with her about. I was prepared to blow her away with my intellectual prowess and the profundity of my thinking. But my body had other plans. Sitting in a tiny room with several other retreatants, I burst into tears as soon as she looked at me and called my name. I babbled about my sensing of indigenous ancestors on the land. Spring graciously handed me tissues, listened intently, and then at a break in my gasps, assured me that the spirits of my ancestors were there as well. At the time, I thought she'd missed my point and I was terribly disappointed. The answer to my deep grief could not be summarized in "Your ancestors are here too." Upon reflection, I realized that under my "confession" was a desire to be seen and heard for who my ego self thought I truly was. In the space of a few days I had worked myself up into an impossible expectation of this woman who I believed would utter the magic words to make go away all of the pain that I had brought with me into that tiny room. I came to realize that my disappointment had nothing to do with her. Over the next few days I was able to release her from the pedestal that I had put her on and truly hear her.

It took returning to *A Fierce Heart* several years later and many hours of sitting with her in retreats and listening to her dharma talks and interviews for me to *get* Spring. Something about the way that she approaches teaching the dharma made it seem initially like she didn't "get it." But once I really sat with her words, whether on the page, in her presence, or via recorded interviews, the deep wisdom that she imparts in the midst of a laugh (she is *very* funny) or as she smiles placidly sank in and I got it. *A Fierce Heart*, as part of her many offerings, reflects and echoes her centeredness in the Buddhist teaching of equanimity that I heard in her dharma talks and in her response to my overwhelm during my interview.

When I decided to shift my approach to writing this book from a solo endeavor to one done in community, I emailed Spring and, once I heard back from her, sent along her chapter. Within a few days she responded, inviting me to a Zoom meeting. Our time together was brief, and I appreciated that she had taken time out of her busy schedule to speak with me. She assured me that the chapter I sent her was fine and invited me to get in touch if I needed anything else. I left the call feeling affirmed and went back to my reading, writing, teaching, painting, taking walks in nature, living my life.

It was in the midst of living that I remembered something that I had tucked away in my memory: my interest in participating in an ayahuasca ceremony to heal some of my deep wounding that left me always feeling unsatisfied, grieving, and angry. I had been told in consultation with an *oungan* (Vodou priest) many years before that those feelings came out of my *marasa*-ness, or twinness, haunting me. My mother had told me many times that I was born a twin, but while I had been born a healthy nine pounds, my twin brother was a mere two pounds—too tiny to survive in 1968 at a public hospital serving mostly poor people of color. According to the oungan, the loss of my twin left me feeling incomplete. When my son was born, I felt in my bones that he was my brother returned to me, and I have often called him my marasa. Still, the sense that there was something more remained, nagging at me. I also knew that much of my anger stemmed from being born in a Black female body in the United States. The many assaults—physical, verbal, and spiritual—had left me pissed off but unable to express it for fear of exposing myself to further wounding and trauma. So I seethed. And drank wine. And I pushed myself to excel academically. And I continued the cycle of generational wounding with my own son in subtle and not-so-subtle ways.

I don't remember when I first heard about ayahuasca, but back in 2011 I watched the film *The Sacred Science* about eight people with various medical conditions who traveled to the Amazon in Peru and, as part of a thirty-day healing journey, participated in several ayahuasca ceremonies. I decided that because of my need to feel safe, I would not push to insert myself into a ceremony. Rather, I would put the intention out into the universe and let Spirit guide me to what was meant for me.

In February 2022, my call was answered with news in my inbox that Spring was offering a BIPOC retreat in Costa Rica through her organization, Lotus Vine Journeys. I emailed the organization expressing my interest and heard back from Spring's assistant, Janeth, with, first, an intake form and then an invitation to an interview. During the interview somehow it came up that I had watched *The Sacred Science*, to which Janeth enthused, "I was there!" That and our larger conversation that resonated deeply made me know that I was doing what I was meant to be doing. Janeth assured me that the time would fly by until the December retreat, but the weeks and months crawled by. In the meantime, I continued to read, write, teach, paint, take walks in nature, live my life.

I also got to spend a bit of time with Spring in a consultation shortly after realizing that I was ready to embrace this incarnation—through willful fugitivity. Let me explain why: Years ago, my mentor, a Black woman professor, had in passing referred to the university where she taught as "the Plantation." That reference has stuck with me for the past thirty years because it was a source of dissonance for me. At the time, in my mind, teaching at the university level seemed like finally arriving in "the promised land." Looking at it from the outside, professors seemed to me to have the ultimate freedom, only needing to be somewhere a few days a week with the rest of their time open to do the research they loved, to shape young lives through advising and informal conversation over coffee, to travel. Over the years I have come to understand what my mentor meant. Today, as one of very few women of color at a predominantly white institution, I have often felt pulled between serving my students and taking care of my needs as a full human being. My decision to embark on a fugitive journey came out of a realization that, in the words of Ruth King, too many of us were "dying on the vine." I finally began to internalize the fact that I didn't need to choose between myself and my students. Rather, as the women whose work I am discussing here teach, my freedom is inextricable from theirs. Modeling self-care is also a service to them. So, by "willful fugitivity," I mean an attitude that prioritizes personal and interpersonal care even when it means becoming a fugitive from institutional pressures and values. But my sense of that possibility was still somewhat unclear. I articulated my inchoate notions of fugitivity to Spring during our consultation and watched her eyes light up as she let me know that her book on Harriet Tubman, the ultimate fugitive, was due for publication in January 2023.

Spring's book *The Spirit of Harriet Tubman* had taken flight during the COVID-19 pandemic. Beginning in the summer of 2020, she embarked on a project about Harriet Tubman, the great Underground Railroad conductor, Civil War nurse, spy, and military strategist. The project began with a five-week course, "The Dharma of Harriet Tubman," offered through East Bay Meditation Center. People were obviously hungry for Tubman's inspirational message of liberation as the course sold almost seven hundred tickets and was at capacity by the time I found out about it. Wanting to make sure that those who needed Tubman's wisdom but perhaps needed to access it in a space away from the white gaze, she also offered another class, "The Dharma of Harriet Tubman for People of Color." Finally, from July until November 29, 2020, she opened the Church of Harriet Tubman and the Underground Crew to anyone who was interested. During "church," held every Sunday over Zoom, she would share with "members" the story of how she had been visited by the spirit of Harriet Tubman and was charged with writing her biography.

I learned about the church as it neared its end and was able to attend a few sessions. One of the things I noticed was how Spring, inspired by the spirit of Tubman, had fostered and nurtured an inclusive community where people from diverse backgrounds testified, sang, and cheered one another on. She mentioned during one of the sessions that the vice president of her publishing house had attended some services and was interested in working with her on a book project. I was delighted when during our consultation she mentioned that her book would be out in the world soon. A few days later, while walking in the woods near my home, the thought occurred to me to ask if I could access an advance copy of the book. When I got home I did just that. Spring, with true openheartedness, immediately emailed me back with the manuscript proofs. Reading it, I saw not only Tubman's fierce heart but also that of Spring. It made perfect sense to me that Tubman would choose her to help communicate the message of freedom to the world today, for Spring has shown herself to be able and willing to wade into the muddiest waters in order to find and bring back the jewel of the lotus. Reading the manuscript, with its provocative claim that what the reader is getting is a direct message of liberation from Tubman through Spring, has been impactful, affirming my deeply held knowing that Spirit, the universe, uses those who are open to it as vessels.

In December 2022 I traveled to Costa Rica and, with several extraordinary people of color from different walks of life, participated in four ayahuasca ceremonies. The process of integrating the experience will take time. I am being patient and compassionate with myself, with my newfound community holding space for me. While I offer glimpses into the experience at different points in this book, this chapter focuses on the liberator message of Spring's book, *A Fierce Heart*.

A Fierce Heart

In the opening pages of *A Fierce Heart*, Spring states that she hopes to show the reader "how to use the mud and the muck of our lives to wake up and grow."[1] Her sentiment is clearly reminiscent of Thich Nhat Hanh's teachings. "We must remember that suffering is a kind of mud that we need in order to generate joy and happiness," he writes.[2] Spring undertakes the task of showing the reader how to use their suffering as a path to liberation by testifying, bearing witness to her own individual suffering and liberation, and elucidating the continued bondage of the collective through the lens of spirituality. This approach places her squarely within the African American autobiographical tradition.

The memoir shares much in common with the writings of the other women whose work I discuss in this book. For example, Spring makes clear in the opening pages of *A Fierce Heart* that it was deep suffering that brought her to the dharma. She shares her story from birth through adulthood as a way of illustrating ancient wisdom teachings that transcend Buddhism. She also includes the stories of others to show the universality of the teachings that she discusses.

Spring frames her narrative as a rites-of-passage tale that is steeped in the hero/heroine archetype, allowing her to connect to her readers on a universal level. Though not all the details of her story will be relatable to everyone, she allows all an entryway to the Buddha's teachings by presenting the universality of the human experience of movement from birth to childhood to adulthood—or stated differently: birth, death, and rebirth. In addition, she appeals to human beings' desire to see themselves as the hero or heroine of their own stories.[3]

Through an exploration of some of the details of her life that she recounts in *A Fierce Heart*, this chapter reads Spring's simultaneous deployment of the rites-of-passage motif and the heroine's archetype as pathways to the spiritual awakening and liberation that she works to facilitate in both her Buddhist teachings and her healing practice. The way that she organizes the text, interweaving her personal narrative with universal truths, allows the reader to view Spring in a manner that is illustrative of the way that Joseph Goldstein, one of the founders of the Western Insight Meditation tradition, proposes that the Buddha can be read: as both a historical figure and an archetype. Her approach to the memoir through the lens of a rites-of-passage motif is clear in her decision to begin with her early childhood and continue to adulthood with periods of exile in which she underwent several trials on her ongoing path to enlightenment. The rites of passage, a practice and motif that has long been a critical aspect of traditional cultures marking the transition of a member of a society from childhood to adulthood, is seen as necessary for the health of the individual as well as the collective mind, spirit, and physical body.

The form of *A Fierce Heart* is as important as its contents. Quotations from various leaders precede each chapter in a way that foretells and echoes Spring's teachings. And the book features grayscale drawings by Anna Oneglia, a California-based multimedia artist. The combination of text and image makes for a dual sensory experience that reinforces the overall message of the path to liberation and wholeness.

"This Is Gonna Be a Tough Life"

Spring was born on December 26, 1973, in Long Beach, California, to a white mother and an African American father. Her parents met in Long Beach in the 1960s while sleeping in the living room of their mutual friend Billie, a prostitute and drug dealer whom her mother described as having "a beautiful heart."[4] When they met, Spring's mother had just left her first husband whom she had married in Tijuana and her father had just been released from prison after serving a year for check forgery. Spring describes them as "young, homeless, and completely down on their luck. Neither had family and both were looking for someone or someplace to call home."[5] Within days of meeting they had fallen in love and set off to start a new life together, before the old Cadillac they were driving broke down in Reno, Nevada. There, they decided to get married. After being turned away by several ministers because of racism, they finally found one to marry them in a small Nevada chapel.

Ongoing racism, the couple's lack of formal education, and their difficulty finding work and housing all proved tough challenges for their relationship. Not only did their constant struggle to make ends meet take a toll on their relationship but their unresolved personal traumas of childhood neglect and physical abuse from their fathers continued to haunt them. Convinced that she needed a child to keep them together, and against her husband's wishes, Spring's mother gave birth first to Spring's sister, Hope, and then to Spring. A couple of days after Spring's birth the family moved into a tiny apartment in Bellflower, California, a low income neighborhood riddled with gang violence. Rather than bring her parents closer, she and her sister's births increased the tension between them. As Spring says, "My birth was not the celebrated magical moment we all hope for."[6] After her birth, Spring's father became increasingly erratic and unstable. He got lost in drug addictions, the pursuit of money, and life in the streets, staying away for longer and longer periods of time. By the time Spring was three years old he disappeared completely. Her mother, meanwhile, underemployed and dependent on government support, got lost in food. By the time Spring was five years old, she understood that she was on her own and remembers thinking, "This is gonna be a tough life."[7] She would not see her father again until she was twenty-four years old. Rather than setting her on a path of self-destruction, Spring identifies her father's abandonment as the initial trauma that set her on her path to healing and freedom.

Over the next few years the family moved in and out of different houses and apartments until Spring's mother eventually fell in love. Hoping to give her daughters a better life, she and her new boyfriend moved them from their mostly Black and brown community to an apartment in the suburbs. He was so abusive that by the time Spring was fifteen, she felt compelled to leave home to live with a family friend in Los Angeles. The arrangement didn't work out, so a year later Spring found herself living in a small apartment in South Central Los Angeles, with a friend. As a way to get by, she started buying marijuana to sell, from her neighbor André, a young man in his early twenties who was a lifelong gangbanger and who grew up in the streets.

Despite having a gut feeling about André's dangerousness, Spring had no choice but to continue working with him in order to survive living on her own. Eventually cornering her in a friend's apartment, André raped Spring for the first time. After that he stalked her for months before kidnapping her from outside her house, forcing her into his car. She says about the kidnapping that she "endured a night of hell" before he drove her home the next morning.[8] Deeply traumatized and knowing that her life was in danger, she packed her bags and moved away two days later. As would be expected, the experience with André changed her. She says it made her turn her away from her innate free spirit—someone who trusted everyone. From my own experience with Spring, however, I would say that either that fire of her free spirit was never completely extinguished or the work that she has done to heal over the years has brought it back. I find her to be incredibly generous of heart, a trait that speaks to my own heart.

Spring includes the story in "Free Your Heart," a chapter that she states was one of the most difficult to write and in which she discusses the importance of radical forgiveness. It is preceded by her asserting that her life has been blessed by her encounters with both saints and "powerful demons."[9] Able to see the opportunity to awaken that suffering offers—or in the words of DaRa Williams, the wisdom in the wounds[10]—she asserts that "in whatever manifestation or form they take, what they offer us is the bitterest medicine and the hardest lessons. Like a metal sword being crafted in hot coals, our own strength is also forged through the fires of hell. Inevitably what we learn from all demons is how to love, how to forgive, and how to reclaim our power."[11] Spring's demon—her violation by André—brought her face-to-face with her commitment to love and to reclaim her power. It also challenged her ability to forgive those who have wronged her.

She was able to feel compassion for André when she learned years after she escaped him that he was serving a twenty-five-year prison term for drug-related charges. She also shares that despite moving away and blocking out the whole ordeal, it didn't leave her. It all resurfaced much later in her life when she embarked on an intense meditation retreat.[12] In an example of her body "keeping the score," she relates that during the retreat she woke one morning unable to move. She says, "It felt as if I were being stabbed again and again. As I lay there, memories of abuse began flooding my mind, and the sharp pain moved from my lower abdomen down into my vagina. I was sweating profusely, and the images, sensations, and feelings just kept coming."[13] When it was safe to do so, and when the tamping down that may have been necessary for her to get through life was no longer an option, her body vomited up the trauma. In order for her to be truly free, she needed to work through the pain, grief, and anger that her body had been holding. Spring bravely tells her story as a way of testifying to the power of being present with one's pain through meditation while being honest about the reality of the psychological, spiritual, and bodily pain that she suffered. The passage is powerful in its raw honesty and for its insight into the process of moving trauma through the body and gently ushering it out.

I am in awe of how kind the mind and spirit are to the traumatized, in their shielding us until we are ready and safe to face it. I have read the story of Spring's kidnapping and rape several times over the past few years. I have edited this chapter several times over the past couple of years. It is only now as I sit with it on this new moon in September, my birth month, that I am able to recognize my own story in hers. I had my own André. His name really was André, and he was my adopted cousin, several years older than I. During a particularly difficult time in my mother's life when she was homeless, she sent me to live with my aunt and uncle. I want to say I was eleven at the time but, again, everything seems to have happened when I was eleven, so I can't be sure. At eighteen, André was the youngest of my aunt and uncle's children, and he was living at home. They gave me their older daughters' vacated room, which was on the second floor in the front of the house, while

André's was in the back. We shared a bathroom. My aunt and uncle slept on the first floor.

Shortly after I moved in, I began to see a sinister side of André. As a way of coping with the instability in my life, I had developed a nervous habit of giggling at most everything that someone said. André pounced on what was essentially a nervous tick, berating me just quietly enough so that no one else could hear him. Every time we locked eyes I could see the arrows of hatred that he shot in my direction, so I kept my head down while in his presence. Eventually his abuse escalated from the verbal and visual to the physical. I had no lock on the door for the room I slept in. Within a few weeks of my living with my relatives, almost on a nightly basis, André would take the opportunity to tiptoe into my room, get under the covers, and run his hands over my body while whispering all the things I felt to be true: that there was no one I could tell because no one would believe me, and my aunt and uncle would choose him over me; I would be on the street with no place to go. I say he did this *almost* every night. I think he deliberately skipped some nights as a way of keeping me off-balance, in a state of terror. As a result, I developed body dysmorphia that manifested in some pretty horrific ways and lasted for years after.

In my memory, it all came to a head one night after my aunt and uncle left the house to food shop. André decided to make his big move. For what seems like hours he stalked me from the top of the house to the bottom, chasing me around as I hid in closets and corners, under furniture. At one point, in my desperation to evade his claws, I knocked over a planter in "my" room. My aunt was a very particular housekeeper, and we both knew we'd have to explain ourselves. I took the opportunity of his momentary distraction to dart past him and run downstairs. Emotionally and physically exhausted by that time, I just gave up. André caught me and pinned me under him. As I lay on my back on the floor between the tiny kitchen and dining area, trapped under his massive weight, I went limp. Then looking into his malice-filled eyes I realized that the thrill for him was gone. What he craved was the chase. He enjoyed feeling my terror.

I do not doubt for a moment that he would've raped me if he thought he could've gotten away with it. But he had no idea when my aunt and uncle would return and the physical damage that he would've done to me would've been too much to hide. I also know in my bones that my guardian spirits, Ogun the Warrior and Erzulie the Mother, were standing watch over me that night. They were the ones who said no when I didn't have the strength to do so myself. André stood up and walked away. He never came for me again. When my aunt and uncle returned, André made sure to tell them I had broken the planter. It was technically true, so when my aunt asked me about it, I hung my head and nodded. But something strange happened. Where normally she would've been angry about my carelessness, she shrugged her shoulders and asked me to help her put the groceries away.

Years later, after I had moved to Haiti, I returned to my aunt's house with my son for the Christmas holiday (my uncle had passed). André was there with his wife, and he handed me a card with a fifty-dollar bill in it, saying that he figured I could use it. Indeed, since my then-husband had lost his job, I could. But when I returned to Haiti a few days later with my baby boy, I left the card with the money inside on the dresser in the room where I had been so terrorized as a young, vulnerable girl. We never talked again.

In 2016 I learned from another cousin that André had died several years before of a heart attack. When he realized that I was quietly weeping into the phone, he said he thought I knew. I did not. But it seemed appropriate that that was how André should pass away. He was several years older than I was and, as with most families, many things are never discussed. Therefore I have no idea who André's biological parents were nor what he experienced before my aunt and uncle adopted him and his sister when they were toddlers. I have no idea what growing up with my exacting aunt was like for him. I *do* know that his heart was hardened. I also know that his treatment of me stemmed from his own trauma and pain. Hurt people hurt. It is with this realization that I commit to including him in my lovingkindness practice starting now.

From Mental Prison to Full Freedom

Spring has said about her path that even in her worst moments she knew she was destined for more: "I knew somehow that my life wouldn't stay that way. I was all alone, yet I had this incredibly strong desire to live a spiritually based life and to help others, and it grew with me every passing day."[14] Today she is a well-known meditation teacher, leading workshops, classes, and retreats worldwide.

In *A Fierce Heart*, Spring states unequivocally that she always knew she was guided. That guiding light led her in her late teens to join the self-help movement and in an attempt to understand the workings of her mind, study psychology. At nineteen she was able to overcome a debilitating period of depression by reading spiritual books and putting what she read into practice. Similar to the way that I began my own spiritual journey, Spring's journey began in the Hindu tradition with the writings of Paramahansa Yogananda and the Self-Realization Fellowship.[15]

In her early twenties that light led her away from a dysfunctional relationship, a dead-end job selling timeshares to people who couldn't afford it, and the dangerous neighborhood in which she was living. Things came to a head when in the course of one day she got fired from her job for calling in sick, her relationship with her boyfriend began collapsing, and her car was scheduled to be repossessed. After laying on her couch for a straight week eating cookies and praying for help, the answer to her prayers came when she learned about a ten-day Buddhist retreat. She says,

On the day the retreat was going to start, I made the nine-hour drive from Oakland to the Southern California desert, crying hysterically, chain-smoking cigarettes and drinking Diet Mountain Dew by the gallon. My boyfriend and I had had an extremely dramatic final break up the night before and I had all my belongings in the car, my last $25, and nowhere to go after the retreat was over. I didn't care; I knew if I could just get myself to the retreat, everything would make sense.[16]

During that retreat she met her beloved teacher and mentor Jack Kornfield, whom she credits with helping transform her life. In her acknowledgments in *The Spirit of Harriet Tubman*, she thanks Kornfield for believing in her when others didn't and when she didn't even believe in herself. Nonetheless, the retreats that she, a young woman of color, attended early on were not without complications.

While she loved the dharma teachings and the practices, she "always felt like an outsider" in groups that were "almost a hundred percent white and consisted mostly of middle-aged people or seniors" and in which "all the teachers were white, mostly from upper middleclass backgrounds." She recalls consistently walking into a room and being "the youngest practitioner and the only person of color." The experience was a trigger for her, reminding her of her youth when her mother, in a desperate attempt to give her children a better life, took them from their mostly African American community and moved them to a predominantly white community where Spring and her sister, Hope, were bullied. Spring reflects, "The racism and pain I had experienced growing up would arise in me constantly during that time."[17]

Unable to find the sanctuary she sought in those majority white spaces, Spring joined with other teachers of color to found East Bay Meditation Center (EBMC) in 2001. As its mission statement announces, EBMC has been committed to fostering "liberation, personal, and interpersonal healing, social action, and inclusive community building."[18] About the process Spring says,

It felt like the medicine my heart had been needing, and sure enough, through the process of co-creating the East Bay Meditation Center, so much healing has happened. Gathering with people who look like me, I can allow in both the pain and the support of others who know the experience of racism as well as sexism and homophobia. We now have a place for those who feel like outsiders, the voiceless who have never felt safe or truly at home in this world.[19]

For Spring, EBMC is a place of refuge in ways that white sanghas from her younger years could not be. Her setting up such a space means that others do not have to endure the discomfort and isolation that she experienced. Rather, she has been able to provide a supportive space for other refuge seekers.

She links her struggle with the meditation center's organic growth around diversity to that of the Buddha, who, she says, was also challenged by difference in a society that had a deeply ingrained caste system.[20] She shares this view with other Black Buddhist teachers including Rev. angel and Gina Sharpe. In a 2012 interview, for instance, Sharpe identifies the Buddha as a civil rights leader.[21] The Buddha's commitment to equality and equanimity inspires Spring to heal the places of separation within herself as the path to living with compassion. Although she travels around the world leading retreats, facilitating workshops, and visiting communities, Spring has found her "true spiritual home" in EBMC, her heart community to which she returns.[22]

The true gift of the center is brought home in Spring's telling about how, in the days following the election of Donald Trump to the US presidency in 2016, a crowd of over two hundred refuge seekers—"people of all shades of brown skin, Native Americans and people whose ancestors had come, or been brought, to the US from Africa, Central and South America, the Middle East, and Asia"—filled the sangha.[23] While a riot raged outside, the group sat meditating in silence. Over the next few days, while most of the US reeled, unmoored by the election of someone who embodied separation, isolation, and alienation, Spring led meditation circles of almost five hundred people. Rather than succumb to the samsara or collective confusion that gripped the nation, they "sought refuge in their spiritual community."[24] Her story is a testament to not only the power of the dharma but also the exponential power that unfolds when the dharma is practiced in a space where people feel deeply at home.

Although Spring regularly travels away from her community, she returns again and again to contribute to and partake in its healthy evolution. Her repeated movement from and return to her community, a rhythm that began in childhood, can be examined through the lens of the rites-of-passage motif whereby one dies or sheds the past to be reborn stronger, able to contribute to the community. This shedding is not a one-time occurrence. Rather, as Kornfield reminds us, "Just as a snake sheds its skin, we must shed our past over and over again."[25] There is a similar process at work in the heroine's journey whereby one leaves home, experiences adventures, and shares what she learns with her community. As such, Spring's journey to her own enlightenment and her wish to share it with the human family may be read simultaneously through the archetype of the heroine.

Rites of Passage and the Heroine's Journey

In the final chapter of *A Fierce Heart*, Spring breaks down the heroine's journey into three stages: departure, transformation, and return. These rites of passage are commonly divided into birth or childhood, whereby a child is born into the community where she spends her early years; exile, whereby she leaves the community to undergo trials; and return, whereby she comes back with her newly acquired knowledge and is reincorporated as an adult and a contributing member of the community. In *The Rites of Passage*, the ethnographer Arnold van

Gennep labeled the three stages as separation, initiation, and incorporation. He proposed calling the rites of separation from a previous world "preliminal rites"; those executed during the transitional stage "liminal (or threshold) rites"; and the ceremonies of incorporation into the new world "postliminal rites."[26] Before van Gennep, the literary scholar and mythologist Joseph Campbell wrote about the rites of passage, saying, "It becomes apparent that the purpose and actual effect of these was to conduct people across those difficult thresholds of transformation that demand a change in the patterns not only of consciousness but also of unconscious life."[27] It requires dying to one way of being in the world to be reborn to another way. In *A Fierce Heart*, Spring writes about symbolic death: "Everything is always dying and always reborn." Change is always stressful because "any time we make a change, we experience a small death."[28] The death to one way of being in the world can produce a feeling of sorrow because of "the sadness of letting go of an energetic part of ourselves that has died. It's the grief of shifting out of one situation and flowing into another. Sometimes we even have to let go of an old identity or sense of self."[29] Campbell and Spring show these stages or rites of passage to be universal to the human experience and closely tied to the archetype of the hero or heroine and their journey.

In "The Example of the Buddha: Relating the Life of the Buddha to Our Own," Joseph Goldstein, another of Spring's first teachers and mentors, delineates Campbell's hero archetype in relation to the Buddha. He proposes that by looking at the Buddha's life from the perspective of the narrative of a historical figure as well as "a fundamental archetype of humanity," we can "view the Buddha's life not as an abstract, removed story of somebody who lived twenty-five hundred years ago, but as one that reveals the nature of the universal in us all." He continues, "In essence, the same question that motivated the Buddha to leave his home and seek enlightenment is the same one that motivates us: 'What is the true nature of our lives? What is the root cause of our suffering?'"[30]

Like Goldstein, Spring connects the Buddha's status as an archetypal hero to her own spiritual journey. She asserts, "At the end of the story, the hero or heroine returns to their community to bring back the newfound knowledge, wisdom, and medicine they have bravely acquired. Most significant of all, they return transformed and ready to begin a life of service."[31] Indeed, Spring as an awakening spirit or bodhisattva has dedicated her life to liberating not only herself but all beings. As someone who lives in the twenty-first century and travels extensively to teach, in many ways her community is the whole world.

"Archetypes are the patterns, images, and symbols that appear in dreams, myths, and fairy tales," writes Spring. "They represent the instincts shared by all humans toward compassion and the many other qualities that are collective, ancestral, and bigger than any individual." She reiterates the universality of the archetype in stating that "the great myths are our stories." She also points to the accessibility of the archetype to everyone by reminding the reader that "as we grow in the practice, we start to move in the direction of heroism."[32] She challenges the reader to rise to the occasion similar to those heroes who are ancient and well known.

Finding Refuge in the Earth Mother

Although Spring grew up in an urban environment, in her adult life she has spent a good amount of time immersed in nature. These spaces have been sources of some of her greatest awakenings. Her times in the forest may be read in relation to the heroine's journey as it has been associated with the Buddha. It may also be seen in relation to shamanism as an earth practice that honors Spirit. Spring marries the two practices in her life and in her memoir.

In "For the Benefit of All Beings," the final chapter in *A Fierce Heart*, she discusses the Buddha as an example of a bodhisattva, someone who takes the wisdom they have acquired and is "determined to free others from the harmful effects of greed, hatred, and delusion."[33] As Rev. angel puts it, such a person sacrifices "what we consider elements of their personal freedom in the course of remaining true to their commitments of waking up the world."[34] As Spring puts it, "The hero surrenders their life to something bigger than themselves."[35] Connecting this archetype to the story of the Buddha, she writes of his spending six long years in the forest trying to undo the tangle of his mind and then having an epic showdown with the demon Mara, a personification of greed, hatred, and delusion. "As Siddhartha sat under the Bodhi tree," writes Spring, "Mara's armies ferociously attacked him over and over. In the end he was able to conquer them all and discover the great truth he had sought for so long."[36] Spring notes that in conquering Mara, the Buddha "placed his hand on the earth, roared like a lion, and declared his right to be free."[37] Like the Buddha, Spring also finds the earth to be the ultimate source of inspiration and sanctuary for her own heroine's journey. This is evidenced by the fact that she has accessed some of her most profound revelations in forested areas, surrounded and supported by Earth wisdom.

Alice Walker, Spring's good friend, also reminds us of the Earth Mother witnessing Siddhartha's victory, drawing on the story for her own victory over her "unbearable suffering" following the assassinations and betrayals of the civil rights movement. She says, like Siddhartha,

> I too sat down upon the Earth and asked its permission to posit a different way from that in which I was raised. Just as the Buddha did, when Mara, the king of delusion, asked what gave him the right to think he could direct humankind away from the suffering they had always endured. *When Mara queried him, the Buddha touched the Earth.* This is the single most important act, to my mind, of the Buddha. Because it acknowledges where he came from. It is a humble recognition of his true lineage. Though Buddhist monks would spend millennia

pretending all wisdom evolves from the masculine and would
consequently treat Buddhist nuns abominably, Buddha clearly
placed himself in the lap of the Earth Mother, and affirmed
Her wisdom and Her support.[38]

Walker notes that the traumas to which she refers are not only those
that are suffered in this lifetime but also those of her ancestors, which
she says, "are also carried in our unconscious files, hidden from view."[39]
Spring makes it clear that without the support of the Earth Mother,
she would not have been able to access those deep traumas and subsequently transform them into sources of wisdom as she has done.

There are several other examples that she gives where the earth is
both a conduit for and witness to the release of her deeply embedded
traumas. One is, years after she was raped and kidnapped, suffering
the bodily flashback of the abuse that I discuss above. Nestled in the
safety of retreat, she finally felt safe enough to release the pain that it
had been holding on to for all those years, unprocessed and thus possessing her.

Spring continues exploring the healing power of the Earth Mother in
the chapter that follows, "The Great Chief," where she relates embarking on a five-month retreat in Crestone, Colorado, in an area sacred to
indigenous communities. There she was able to access her ancestral
trauma. As soon as she was alone, she became consumed physically,
mentally, and spiritually for hours by what she calls "African grief."[40]
In those woods, the purification and release of not only her personal
trauma as an African American woman but also that of her ancestors
took the form of wailing that turned into gospel hymns, screaming
that lasted for hours, and "unimaginable" bodily contortions, all calling up aspects of the African and African diasporic experience from
the moment of capture, throughout their enslavement, and beyond
into the contemporary moment.[41] While there, she became intimately

aware of her vulnerability as a woman of African descent in a predominantly white town on a secluded mountain. The only way she was able to fall asleep was by seeking shelter in the Earth Mother's embrace. She writes of stuffing pillows behind her, sinking down, and imagining "these big Black arms reaching around me as if I were being held in the arms of the Great Mother."[42] Her doing so helped her realize the power inherent in her ability to visualize the Great Mother, which she used to evoke compassion, a great force, and protection. She also came to understand that "letting go of ancestral sorrows," purifying ourselves, is a process of dying and being reborn.[43] The Earth Mother, which as Thich Nhat Hanh affirms, we always carry within us,[44] facilitates and bears witness to the transformation that is a critical component of our spiritual awakening and liberation.

Evolution into Healing

Spring's founding of Lotus Vine Journeys began in 2007 when, feeling like something was wrong, she decided to do an intensive three-month meditation retreat. During the retreat, some deeply suppressed traumas surfaced that she thought she had already worked through. Something deep inside her cracked open and she realized that she "needed a new approach and a way to go much deeper."[45] At the suggestion of a friend, in 2008 she traveled to Peru to begin working with indigenous Shipibo healers in the upper Amazon region of Peru. After spending months at a time there, she discovered that she had found a place where she felt at home.

She also discovered that she had a capacity for navigating between worlds and dimensions. When some of the local Peruvian healers began referring to her as "*Maestra*" and "*Curandera*" (healer or doctor), she initially laughed it off, but slowly began to understand that she was able to see and interact with the entire plant-spirit world and help people to heal.[46] By the time she wrote *A Fierce Heart* in 2016 she had founded Lotus Vine Journeys and begun bringing groups of people to the jungle to do healing work.

One of Spring's most powerful chapters in *A Fierce Heart*, "The White Condor," blends her Buddhist practice with shamanism at a time when she felt her life was falling apart, nothing made sense, and she contemplated suicide. There, during a solo retreat in the mountains of Northern California, after losing to a younger woman a man whom she loved deeply and who she dreamed of starting Lotus Vine Journeys with, then getting into a car accident, followed by having her uterus removed when doctors found a massive tumor, she spent days imploring God to take her so that she could be relieved of her suffering. Instead, she was not only visited by but shape-shifted into a female white condor and underwent a profound breaking open of her heart. In the chapter she includes the story of Siddhartha's renunciation of or death to his old identity to be reborn awakened and free, invoking her own rites of passage. She died to her old attachments to samsara, or suffering, to be reborn as one who also realizes true freedom, symbolized by the feminine wisdom of the condor and embodied in the Earth Mother, as Walker suggests. Spring concludes that her own death and rebirth also birthed Lotus Vine Journeys, which combines Buddhist wisdom with plant-spirit medicine as an essential component of her commitment to using her gifts to alleviate her suffering as inextricable from the suffering of the world.[47] In an interview with ABC reporter-turned-meditation podcaster Dan Harris, she explains that plant medicine has been part of Buddhist traditions for centuries, so the healing work that she is doing is part of that tradition.[48]

Taking Up Moses's Mantle

In her interview with Harris, she tells him that she had been on a long retreat at Insight Meditation Society (IMS) when COVID hit. Once she left, she went to spend time with Alice Walker at her home in the California mountains and while there she found several books on Tubman among Walker's extensive library. Shortly after, she had a "visionary" dream in which she was running and holding on to the back of Tubman's jacket. It was so dark she could hardly see, but Tubman could. She had a very clear sense that they were being chased. In the dream Spring said, "Get me out of here," to which Tubman responded, "I will." She became obsessed, watched the 2019 biopic *Harriet*, and then began to talk about Tubman as a great ancestor.

During her interview with Harris, Spring made an important connection between the Underground Railroad and the eightfold Buddhist path, declaring that the eightfold path is like a road that we are being encouraged to get on. Seamlessly bringing the struggle for justice in Tubman's time to today, she says that she started the class because she wanted access to the kind of power and courage that Tubman had in order to undertake the struggle for liberation that is still so needed. Positing Tubman as a bodhisattva, Spring talks about Tubman deciding that she would return to slavery to get others out. In defining the bodhisattva, she discusses the archetype of the enlightened hero, explaining that in the Mahayana tradition, one practice is to become awakened so that one can be of help to others. Tubman had that spirit: "May I get free so that I can help other people, so that I can teach freedom."[49] Many on the Buddhist path aspire to be bodhisattvas; to alleviate suffering and to help others find freedom. Tubman was that for Black Americans, which is why they referred to her as Moses. Spring considers Tubman to be a great bodhisattva and sees her energy coming through today to organize modern-day abolitionists.

The announcement for the Church of Harriet Tubman and the Underground Crew reads:

> All beings are welcome to join our Soulful Sunday class in
> which we will explore the life, spiritual message, and legacy

of Harriet Tubman and other great freedom fighters throughout time. We will call forth her spirit so that we can honor
and embody her incredible strength and unwavering courage. Every week we will reflect on the Buddha's teachings
on freedom alongside Harriet's journey as one of the world's
greatest conductors on the underground railroad. Just like
young Siddhartha, Harriett too was also guiding people toward
liberation.[50]

During services she would recount moments from Tubman's life
and discuss some of the insights that she gained from what she saw
as visitations from her. This is, again, a testament to Spring's Buddha
nature. She is willing to be used as a vessel for ancient wisdom to come
through in the face of "this perilous political moment,"[51] to lead all who
are willing to set out with her to liberation.

Moreover, in calling on the energy of Tubman, Spring invoked the
qualities of deep truth and courage that she wants to cultivate in herself. She understands that our ancestors are part of our deep collective healing. In recent years, the US has in fits and starts attempted to
reconcile its demons that have surfaced in ways that we have never
seen before, sparked as they were by the videotaped murder of George
Floyd by police officer Derek Chauvin on May 25, 2020. For Spring,
Tubman is more relevant now than in any other time as we try to
escape from the greed, hatred, and delusion that keeps us all enslaved.
She has returned to help guide us all to freedom.

Spring's inheritance of the African American narrative tradition as
well as her dharma-inspired teachings and writings, steeped as they are
in a love ethic, perfectly position her to write the biography that she says
Harriet Tubman has wanted to write for centuries. As a warrior-spirit in
her own right, Spring is providing a fierce and strong light on the path to
us all awakening to freedom. Her light shines brighter every day.

6

FAITH ADIELE

Finding Faith

A FEW YEARS INTO my graduate career, one of my professors of African literature recommended to me Faith Adiele's *Meeting Faith: The Forest Journals of a Black Buddhist Nun*. When it arrived in the mail, I took one look at the cover, which featured a bald-headed light-skinned woman seated with her back to the camera, read the description as the narrative of someone who had gone to the forest to meditate, and promptly put it away. Her experience was the furthest thing from my daily concerns and felt unrelatable.

Picking the book up again years later was a struggle. Since its publication, the United States has devolved into a jumbled mass of divisive and hate-filled speech and action driven by fear of those labeled Other. Perhaps even more so, in the fifteen years that had elapsed since its publication, I could not see the value in reading the personal memoir of a biracial woman from rural Washington State. It was only by reflecting on the memoir as an exploration of the very feelings that I experienced in majority-white sanghas and with which I began this text—that of being simultaneously hypervisible and invisible—that I came to appreciate Adiele's story as my own. More recently, reading her second memoir—the short but poignant *The Nigerian-Nordic Girl's Guide to Lady Problems*,[1] about her struggle with uterine fibroids—I felt immensely grateful for the courage that Adiele demonstrates in sharing her personal stories as part of her commitment to social justice.

Adiele mostly writes creative nonfiction, with much of it focusing on the year that she spent as a Thai forest nun, as well as her negotiation of her Scandinavian and Nigerian heritage. She is also the coauthor, with three of her university friends, of the thriller *The Student Body*, based on their experiences at Harvard and published under the pen name Jane Harvard. Shortly after the novel was published, she answered a call for anthologies, "pulled together her writings from the period of her ordination in Thailand," and compiled them into the book-length manuscript that became *Meeting Faith*. In the midst of all of this she earned a master's degree in creative writing from Lesley College and went on to earn two master's of fine arts degrees, in fiction and nonfiction, from the University of Iowa's writing programs.

Today she is a sought-after writer and speaker and hosts a monthly African book club in collaboration with the Museum of the African Diaspora. While she no longer cohosts the BIPOC writing group that she cofounded, she remains an active participant. She is currently working on *Twins: Growing Up Nigerian / Nordic / American*, a book of nonfiction that blends her family's histories and the political and social changes from late-nineteenth-century Sweden and Finland to Nigeria and America in the 1960s that influenced them.[2]

Adiele is the recipient of many awards and grants, including fifteen artist residencies in four countries. *Meeting Faith* won the PEN Beyond Margins Award for Best Memoir in 2004. Despite being published almost twenty years ago, it continues to make "listicles for inspiring travel books."[3] She counts it as one of her favorite pieces of work, which, as she describes it, tells her story of being type A, having a breakdown, and putting herself back together in Thailand.

While she incorporates aspects of both her Nigerian and Nordic heritage in *The Nigerian-Nordic*, the focus of the text is on her changing relationship to her body when fibroids disrupt her life. The work, only thirty-three pages long, is funny, insightful, and resonant, reflecting the experience of countless women—in particular, those of color—in this country.

I will admit that while I was intellectually drawn to *Meeting Faith* and her other short writings because she's a talented writer, *The Nigerian-Nordic* is Adiele's most emotionally compelling piece of writing to me. I, too, have lived with uterine fibroids for at least the past fourteen years. While mine do not cause me nearly the same amount of suffering, much of what Adiele relates experiencing in the American medical system echoes my experience. In fact, there are many ways that our experiences intersect well beyond that with the medical institution.

Following an introduction to Adiele, the person who would grow into the writer, I explore the form and content of *Meeting Faith* as a record of her quest to self-define. I also discuss her experience of hypervisibility and invisibility as a Black woman in the US and abroad. Finally, I discuss *The Nigerian-Nordic*'s resonance in my life. Although there is not one word about the dharma in Adiele's second memoir, it has been an immense gift. In reading it I have felt one of my most intimate long-suffered struggles being brought into the light and have found healing in that.

Meeting Faith, the Writer

Even before Faith Adiele was born, her life was marked by turmoil. Her mother, Holly, became pregnant with a Black man's child in her sophomore year of college.[4] When her parents, Scandinavian immigrants, discovered the pregnancy, they stopped paying their daughter's college tuition and exiled her from the house. She contemplated suicide. Four months into the pregnancy, on October 21, 1962, Holly's mother drove her to a home for unwed mothers in Spokane, Washington, where she stayed until after she gave birth—a fact that Holly kept to herself until just before Faith's sixteenth birthday. The home, part of the Florence Crittenton Association under the auspices of the Salvation Army, was run like a boot camp by a "flinty, pinched-faced woman" whom all the girls called Captain. Its goal, writes Faith, was to turn the wayward girls into "God-fearing young ladies eventually worthy of marriage and legitimate offspring."[5] To that end, the young mothers-to-be were "locked up" far away from everything in a place that "existed as a secret, parallel world alongside polite society."[6] Holly had no interest in attending chapel or learning to perform tasks that were associated with ladylike behavior, so she was always getting into trouble. She also refused to give her baby up for adoption as was expected in the postwar flourishing adoption market of 1963. Interracial adoption had recently been legalized, and the two years of college that Holly had along with the fact that her unborn baby's father, an African student from Nigeria named Magnus, was soon to have a doctorate, made her a very attractive candidate. Despite her own father's fury, Holly refused to relinquish her child.

I find many opportunities for reflection in this story. I consider what the still-forming Faith experienced as chemicals of fear and despair flooded her mother's body as she confronted her father and considered ending her and her unborn baby's lives. I think of the sense of abandonment Holly must have felt as she sat in the family car beside her mother in the predawn hours on her way into exile. As a single mother without a college degree, Holly must have felt intense anxiety about her and her baby's futures. Lastly—and this is what I believe sustained her—I imagine the love she already felt for her unborn child and the hope she experienced as she felt the baby's first kicks against her belly.

Reading Holly's story I was also reminded of my first summer job as a teenager. About fifteen years old at the time, I got a job that was arranged through a citywide summer employment program at a home for unwed mothers in an upper-class neighborhood in New York City. The girls, also around my age, and their children lived together in a brownstone in a residential neighborhood with a headmistress-director who kept them on the straight and narrow. My title was counselor but really I was a glorified babysitter while the young women of various races—some pregnant, others with babies or toddlers—got their lives together. I watched the children while the women earned their GEDs, visited with their baby's fathers, and went to see the families that had sent them to the home. I remember one woman in particular, a Korean American mom and her toddler whose father was an anesthesiologist. I remember them because the little boy had a T-shirt that advertised the father's medical practice. I later learned that the reason that she and her son were in the home was because the man was married. I recall another one, a young white girl, who was interviewing potential parents for her unborn baby. We weren't allowed to socialize with the girls. Nonetheless, to this day I remember those girls and sometimes wonder what became of them. I'm not sure if I, along with the other two Black girls who were my coworkers, was assigned to that home as a kind of "scared straight" tactic. If it was, the maneuver was lost on me. I was not really into boys, happy to spend my days and nights in the company of my sister, Lisa, and my best friend at the time, Debbie.

Faith's parents split before she was born because of religious differences, but they maintained a friendship for her sake. After Faith was born, Holly returned to college, earning her degree from the University of Washington when her daughter was three years old. By then, her father, Magnus, had returned to Nigeria after receiving a letter summoning him home. Four years earlier, in 1960, Nigeria had gained its independence from Britain and was trying to find its way, writes Adiele, from "under the heavy legacy of colonialism and a new, indigenous layer of political corruption."[7] It was Magnus's job to help build the new nation. Shortly after he arrived, the Biafran War broke out.

While living in Igboland, where he was eventually able to secure a position at the University of Nigeria, he wrote to Faith and her mother regularly, keeping them abreast of political developments. After the Biafran War broke out in 1967, he wrote them about the atrocities, including the murders of his own family members. But when Faith was four years old, the letters ceased. Holly, believing him dead, penciled his name in the family Bible. In 1966, having finally earned her college degree, Holly was able to secure a teaching job at a junior high school in Ceres, a small town in California. When she was released from her teaching contract in 1969, she reconciled with her parents and moved with her daughter to a trailer home on her parents' farm in Yakima Valley in Washington State. Miraculously, in fall of 1970, a letter arrived from Magnus. For nearly half a year, writes Adiele, it had "crept and crawled its way from Igboland in the east to the federal government in the west, through US Customs, along the streets of Washington, DC, to Washington State and finally to my grandparents' farm."[8] Her father had survived the war, but Faith would only meet him many years later when as a young adult she traveled to Nigeria.

Holly didn't have more children, so Faith, raised as an only child, spent most of her childhood and teenage years in that farming community populated by white farm families and Mexican migrant workers. The experience, along with participating in a student cultural exchange program to Mexico and Thailand in high school, would shape her life-long commitment to social justice.

In *Meeting Faith*, Adiele describes her experience of both hyper-visibility and invisibility throughout her young life, starting even from birth. Because biracial babies were rare in 1960s Seattle, her birth was heralded by "nurses who oohed and aahed" over her.[9] Then as a young child, strangers would stop her and her mother on the street and ply her with gifts, shiny coins, and candy. At the same time, her white babysitter's mother regularly used the word *nigger* to describe Black people and questioned her daughter's decision to have that "picka-ninny" around her white children. In junior high school, during Faith's preteen years, she tried to imitate the tousled mane of Farah Fawcett by straightening her hair. Unlike the photo on the box, she writes, "my hair poofed around me, thick and unruly as shrubbery," distinguishing her from her white female classmates.[10] Though she was hypervisible as a Black girl, she was also deemed inadequate in the realm of beauty based on white standards. This rendered her invisible, in the sense that she was socially unsuitable to date publicly.

Her experience with invisibility and hypervisibility continued in the study-abroad program to Mexico. She relates two instances back-to-back to illustrate the demeaning experiences that she suffered. In the first instance, she is invisibilized when the group that she was trav-eling with went to a nightclub. All of the American girls (read: white) were besieged by a collective of young men who wanted to dance with them; all except Adiele, who was left sitting with Mrs. Allen, the group's fifty-something chaperone. When the dust cleared from the stampede, the two stared at each other—the "white grandmother and the sixteen-year-old-black-girl who had just learned that her undesir-ability was so wide it spanned the borders of nations."[11] She continues, "What would we say to each other during the two hours the tall, angu-lar white girls and the short, busty white girls spun and shuffled on the dance floor?" Summoning the image of the stereotypical Mammy—Black, nonsexual, undesirable—she asks, "How would we pretend not to see the elephant—ugliness, Blackness, Blackness, ugliness—in the center of the room?"[12]

Her hypervisibility as a Black American female was driven home in the second incident that she relates immediately after the first. As she rode a crowded Metro in Mexico, a man rubbed against her despite her repeated attempts to move away from him. "I felt his belt buckle, cold metal, against my left buttock," she writes, "and got off at our stop to find a circle of liquid, cold and white, soaking through my pants, not a belt buckle at all."[13] Her sexual assault presents a mirror image of the invisibility she felt as the only one not chosen as a dance partner. The assault indicated her hypervisibility as the only Black girl among several whites—an aspect of her hypervisibility that is tied to the history of African Americans in this country, particularly African American women, that gets exported around the world.

During the slave era, Black women's imagined sexual availability and promiscuity was inversely related to that of white women, who were imagined as pure, innocent "white lilies" to be protected.[14] The image of the sexually available Black woman, exemplified in the stereotype of the Jezebel, continued throughout the Jim Crow era and beyond, and it was exported to other countries via American political influence and pop culture. Linking her experience with that of enslaved women, Adiele realizes that her embodiment as a Black woman means that her desirability is not that "of someone you ask to dance" but "of someone you take from behind, standing up, not caring who sees, like a slave."[15] Although her travel mates and Mrs. Allen tried to protect her for the rest of the trip, the damage was already done. She had learned a life lesson that many of her counterparts would never have to learn firsthand.

The Crucible of College

Despite the accumulated trauma of her childhood and teenage years, Adiele excelled academically in high school. Her good grades earned her a scholarship to Harvard College. Matriculating in the early 1980s, she again experienced simultaneously hypervisibility and invisibility. She was considered exotic by white men, who found her "dusky enough" to spark their fantasies "while still behaving and speaking white enough not to scare." The fact that her blackness was not American blackness but "straight from Africa!" added to her allure.[16] At the same time, she experienced rejection from Black students for not being "Black enough," by way of overheard unkind remarks about her hair. "In the freshman dining hall, I'd been overcome by shame and sadness," Adiele remarks. "Shame that I still didn't know how to work my hair, that my own body was foreign to me; and sadness to learn that as a black baby, I had indeed come with an instruction manual—only it was missing!"[17] Those of us who are of African descent know about the heaviness of having Black-textured hair in a white-dominated culture. There is a long tradition of elaborate hair care that reaches back to pre-colonial Africa, when a woman's hair was seen as her crown. However, during slavery, as part and parcel of the denigration of the Black body, our hair was criticized. The legacy of that time persists. As such, Black hair and hair care come with lots of cultural baggage. Amongst African Americans, not knowing how to care for one's hair is seen as more than a personal failing; it is an affront to one's Black heritage.[18]

Being neither Black enough nor white enough condemned Adiele to a liminal state. As biracial, and thus outside of either category, she was made into a spectacle to be pitied on one hand and exoticized or feared on the other. But rather than getting stuck in the lament as "the tragic mulatta," Adiele capitalized on her outsider status by becoming "the traveler, the cultural chameleon, the adventuress, the empath."[19] She did this by finding volunteer work in social service programs, initially attempting to bridge the divides between Southeast Asian refugees and Americans experiencing homelessness in urban Boston. Over time she found she could "interview Latino immigrants, teach English to the illiterate, pass through the inner city unscathed." She discovered belonging in her outsider status as it was what made her able to "pass" or "Go Native."[20] In other words, as a social chameleon, she was able to blend into the culture in which she was immersed at the time.

By her sophomore year, unmotivated, scared, and exhausted—in a word, depressed—she ended up on academic probation. In hopes of salvaging her academic career, she enrolled in a University of Washington–sponsored study-abroad program to Thailand. She planned to study

Buddhist nuns with the goal of perhaps developing a sociology proj-ect. Once there, she made an almost spur-of-the-moment decision to undergo ordination herself. She wanted to experience the nuns' life-style firsthand, hoping that doing so would allow her to "challenge traditional anthropological methodology and understand the women [she] was presuming to write about."[21] As would be expected, the year spent as a Thai forest nun was transformative. Upon her return to Har-vard, she decided to major in Southeast Asian studies, graduating with honors in 1986.

That was the same year I matriculated at a mini-Ivy in upstate New York. Like Adiele, I was a scholarship student. However, I didn't wait until my sophomore year to land myself on academic probation. Dealing very badly with the shock of being one of twenty-five stu-dents of color at an institution populated by overwhelmingly white, mostly wealthy people and biting off a bit more extracurricular activ-ity than I could chew, I received a threatening letter from the dean's office by the end of my first semester. But when winter break arrived and I found myself yet again thrust into the disarray of my home life, I knew that failing out of college was not a choice. By the end of the six-week "vacation," I returned to campus determined to stay. I did so well during the spring semester that I received an award for the greatest academic improvement of the whole student body! There was never a question of whether I *could* do the work. It was a matter of focusing enough on *why* I needed to be there. At the time, my actions weren't driven by any career plans. Rather, it was understanding that despite all of the racist and classist hostility I faced on campus, it was, in its own way, a refuge. There was quiet, there was nature, there was order, there was food, there was shelter. It was my only way out of a dead-end life.

Following graduation, Adiele remained in Cambridge until 1989, when she traveled to her father's "sleepy little village," Okpu Umuobo, in

Nigeria. While there, she got to know her father and her newly discovered family, including her younger siblings—a sister and two brothers. She credits her time as a nun with giving her the courage to make that trip. "I wouldn't have been able to go to Nigeria to meet my family if I hadn't taken that trip first," she says of her time in Thailand.[22] Her 2004 documentary *My Journey Home: Faith's Story*, which she wrote and narrated, is about the sojourn to her father's village that she embarked on in 2002.

Meeting Faith, the Memoir

More than any other work I explore in this book, Adiele's *Meeting Faith* highlights and explores Black female outsiderness. As an only child of mixed heritage and raised in rural Washington State, Adiele spent much of her life acting as a bridge and a translator for opposing sides: whiteness and blackness. She is deeply aware of her status as an outsider and thus as a spectacle in many of the spaces that she occupies. As such, much of her life has been marked by loneliness and a deep desire to establish an identity for herself on her own terms.

This desire is evident in her naming her memoir the way that she does. "Faith" is, of course, her name, but it is also the vehicle by which she embarked on her journey into believing that which she had no models for: being her truest self. The reader meets *her* through the text and is also taken along to her "meeting" or coming to terms with her embodiment through her meditation practice as an ordained nun. Adiele's defining herself on her own terms is an ongoing process, one that invites readers to ask the question that she asks so bravely and publicly of herself in different ways in her writing: Who am I?

Although she was ordained as a Buddhist nun in the Thai forest tradition, Adiele was raised and remains Unitarian.[23] She is considered an *upasika*, a devout laywoman, but has said about herself that the only thing to suggest the otherworldliness of her time as a Buddhist nun in the Thai forest "might be a quaint refusal to smash bugs and an inability to keep shoes on my ringed, painted feet."[24] Everything else about her—her blackness, piercings, addiction to African dance grooves, snacks involving processed flour and sugar, good jewelry, bad television, and her lack of discipline—bespeaks the trappings of an American upbringing and adulthood.[25]

The cover of *Meeting Faith* features Adiele sitting in a white sarong tunic with her back to the camera. The image highlights her status as *farang* (foreigner), singular and unique as the first and, at the time, only Black Buddhist forest nun. I read her lone image against a cream-colored, flower-speckled background seemingly out of time and space as a metaphor for the isolation she felt for much of her life as a consequence of her biracial heritage, intelligence, and the physical environment in which she was raised, as well as that which she experienced in the wat (Buddhist residence). "I think I ordained as a nun as a rejection of all of that external stuff that had been projected on to me," she says in her film. "I had to strip away everything in order to rebuild myself from the inside out."[26]

Meeting Faith consists of both a main narrative and an equally important marginal text that incorporates quotes from Buddhist scholars and several of Adiele's journal entries. The memoir integrates in-depth information about the Buddhist principles and precepts as well as practical aspects of the Theravada tradition. Each chapter is preceded by a photo from different stages of Adiele's preordination and ordination, photos from the wat where she stayed, or Buddhist statues. Together they form a holistic picture of the author's experience of her short tenure as a *maechi*, a Thai nun in the forest tradition. The reader comes away with a clear understanding of the workings of meditation as well as the significance of the Four Noble Truths and the eightfold path as a road map to spiritual freedom.[27] Although Adiele's background and path differ significantly from the other women I explore in this project, her narrative, like theirs, offers insight into the lengths to which Black women go in pursuit of mental, emotional, and spiritual health and freedom.

What most interests me about *Meeting Faith* is Adiele's exploration of her outsider status as a mixed-race Black girl, then woman, born and raised in the US and who travels abroad. In the section of the book that will be the focus of my discussion here, she delves into her Black femaleness in relation to US white women—who, unlike her, are seen as delicate beings to be cherished and protected—and to Thai women, who are characterized in relation to local flowers that have deep meaning in Thailand: the sacred lotus, the profane poppy, and the exotic orchid.

The Buddha said that the way to enlightenment is through the body. Adiele seems to take this first Buddhist tenet to heart, using her embodiment as a Black female to reflect on the mental and spiritual effect of living most of her life in the US where, because of Christianity, women are thought of in dualistic terms, as either saints or sinners. She spends considerable time in the text exploring the status of women, highlighting differences in the chapter titled "Orchids: Half Sacred, Half Profane." In the first section, she begins with the lotus, a flower for which one of the Mahayana Buddhist sutras is named but which occupies a liminal space. Although sacred, it is edible. Although beautiful, it's also bitter to the taste. And though beautiful *and* sacred, it grows out of the profane mud. Women in general in Thailand can be compared to the lotus in their ambivalent status in Thai society.

The particular cultural ambivalence about Thai women in Thailand is seen in the way that they are marketed to Western consumers. To illustrate her point, Adiele includes in the text a website advertisement for Thai women described alternately as sacred: "Shy as a flower" and "Untouched beauty"; and profane: "These girls are not seeking marriage or any similar relationship."[28] She recounts her conversations with Thai people about the Buddha's views on the ordainment of Thai women, all of which leave Adiele dissatisfied. While women may be ordained as monks, they are never the equal of men. As a banana vendor reminds Adiele, "A hundred-year-old *bhikkhuni* was required to bow down before a newly ordained *bhikkhu*, and the conditions of their ordainment were very strict."[29] Adiele later comments on this unequal relationship when she meets a young monk and muses that no matter her chronological or ordination age, her mentor, Maechi Roongdüan, would have "to bow before this child."[30] Even as the head of her own wat, Maechi Roong-düan would be seen as inferior to a man. Not only are women viewed as inferior but at the wat, nuns are viewed as taboo, impure temptations to the monks. Beyond the wat, Buddhist monks are more valued by the lay population, who perceive the giving of alms as a source of improved karma—a value that is not extended to nuns.

Before her time in Thailand, Adiele believed that the female-body problematic was a Western issue. She comes to recognize that it is also a problem halfway around the world, and in doing so, memories of her own life begin to surface. She recalls her vulnerability as female in a culture that denigrates the feminine, and she considers her "own cultural dilemma—two opposing identities residing in a single body."[31] She says,

> I fled the West precisely because of this, because of dichotomous thinking, the crushing pressure to be either-or, to exist in black or white. This pressure has led me, like any respectable American girl, to hate my body a bit. It is, after all, the site of a tiresome external identity: the blackness that will get you tossed before a subway train, the femaleness that will get you felt up or held down. The biracialness, a lack of clarity, which never fails to unsettle.[32]

While she thought that the adherence to nonduality and tolerance of ambivalence for which the East is famous would be her salvation, she is brought face-to-face with her embodiment as a Black woman precisely because of Thai Buddhism's attempt to disappear the body. Ordinees must shave their hair and eyebrows and hide their bodies under multiple robes. Rather than being able to escape her "skin sack,"[33] as Maechi Roongdüan calls the body, she is confronted with the implications of the intersectionality of her femaleness and her blackness, as well as the liminal space that she occupies as a biracial person in a world that demands taking sides. The nondualism that Buddhism teaches forces Adiele to confront the nondualism that she embodies as a biracial person. As she says later in her discussion of the poppy, "Thailand teaches me that the body does matter."[34]

In the section on the "profane poppy"—beautiful but also the source of the drug opium—Adiele continues exploring the ambivalent place that Thai women hold in their society. She remarks that Thais wage a constant battle against the profanity that threatens to overtake their women, believing that the female sexual appetite is uncontrollable (and therefore destructive). As a way to escape the stigma, girls and young women adhere to a long list of acceptable behaviors in order to appear proper. "Before and during my ordination, I spent a great deal of time trying to mimic this proper behavior so that the stereotypes about American and Black women won't put me at the kind of risk from Thai men that Asian stereotypes put Thai women at risk from Western men," she writes. "It doesn't work. There is no safety for any color body."[35]

Whereas Thai women suffer sexual exploitation—such as being chained to beds and pressed to do tricks with their vaginas as part of their lure as both sacred and profane to Western men—African American women's lives are circumscribed by the stereotypes that haunt them alternately as Jezebels, mammies, and sapphires. We have seen how these stereotypes impacted Adiele's life growing up in the US and when she traveled abroad. In Thailand, the triple yoke of American, female, and Black prompts her to try to alter her behavior—a losing battle when patriarchy is built on maintaining stereotypes that circumscribe the lives of women from opposite sides of the world. This realization of the power of male desire—which, Adiele remarks, is at times just another word for hatred—also helps her awaken to the fact that her embodiment matters and that the Thai Buddhist insistence on suppressing it by hiding it in white robes is inextricably related to her later, as she writes, cloaking her body in fat.[36] It comes out of a desire to rid one's self of the marker that is the source of one's oppression and abuse. If one can't rid themselves of the body, they can at least hide their truest self within the folds of cloth, or fat, or at the other extreme, thinness.

In the final section of the chapter, Adiele explores the "exotic orchid"—another beautiful flower, yet one that's also hardy in its ability to grow in seemingly inhospitable environments. The source of Adiele's low self-esteem was growing up as "the only black girl"[37] in rural Washington, where white maleness is valued and white femaleness cherished. The issue of Adiele's liminality, the embodiment of nonduality in a society that insists on it, is raised in her consideration of the esoteric, exotic, and erotic orchid.

In college, Adiele was considered exotic by white men. Summoning the image of the lotus in the mud, she comments about the slipperiness of such a label. "Exotic is a tightrope to walk," she writes. "If you keep moving, eyes toward the sky, you reap admiration from a distance. But if ever you slow down, lock eyes, listen to what someone is telling you, then you tumble into the mud of the erotic. So quick the fall from sacred to the profane!"[38] It is not clear from Adiele's writing whether she is talking about slowing down to listen for the meaning behind the admirer's words or making oneself accessible to the admirer as the source of "the fall from sacred to profane."[39] In other words, the question becomes, is the exotic Black woman always a step away from the mud of the erotic in the minds of white men or does she have the power to remain in the realm of the sacred by holding herself aloof? Can she divorce herself from his fantasies, maintaining her sacred beauty regardless of the vulgarity of his imagination? I don't think there's a ready answer to these questions. It would seem that based on her earlier discussion of stereotypes that haunt the Black female body, there is no way for her to escape the mud of the profane even as she is being constructed as sacred in her exoticism. However, I think a partial answer may be found in the Buddhist principle of nonattachment to outcomes or the opinions or concerns of others; in as much as is possible when one is in the world, to not let one's identity be determined by societal projections. This is not an easy thing to do. As Adiele demonstrates, it is an ongoing process.

In the chapter "American Girls," Adiele explores more extensively the issue of the different imaginary spaces that women occupy in Thailand. "The Thai woman is pale, almost white, but infinitely more touchable," she notes. "Anglo women are white lilies and blushing roses that must be protected (well, at least in terms of rhetoric and literature). Snow White, Rose Red. Peach blossoms and magnolia high above the dark soil." She then brings in the third and the lowest-ranked space, occupied by Black women. She asks rhetorically, "Who are the African flowers?" before answering that "Black women are sweet, I gather," but in the most profane way—one that "makes you lick your lips, rub up against her in public, take that which is not offered, deflower her."[40] Unlike Thai and white women, Black women are to be consumed like food items—"Brown Sugar, Mocha Delight, Chocolate Love"—and then discarded; they are imagined to be wholly in the realm of the profane. She asks, "When do we get to be flowers? Beautiful? Untouched?" We might add "Sacred," like white women? Despite her experience that tells her that the answer is "Never," Adiele seems to hold out hope—represented by the orchid that grows "without soil, in the air"—that Black women's magic, like the hashtag suggests, will one day be recognized.[41]

Adiele's childhood and teenage years were marked by her outsider status, which she learned to use to her advantage. She continued to embrace her outsiderness during her study abroad in Thailand, label-ing herself and her friends "exotic, special birds."[42] She was "extra exotic"—the first foreign and Black woman that many of the Thais she encountered had ever seen, yet someone who read and wrote Thai and was well versed in Thai culture and politics. Despite her accom-plishments, Adiele was unable to get a date. This stands in contrast to Cathy, a white woman who "drops in for a two-month visit" and begins dating "a political intellectual, a principled artist, a kind revolutionary . . . the pick of the crop," and someone Adiele was clearly interested in. Comparing her experience of invisibility in the realm of romance to that of the visibility and desirability of Cathy, she asks rhetorically, "Is life for some women really this simple?"[43] The answer is yes when the world is organized around whiteness as the ideal against which every other racial category is measured and comes up short.

The Heroine's Journey

The scholar Tracy Curtis asserts that the genre of memoir is a concern for women who venture out into the wider world and whose departure from their expected roles destabilizes many people's sense of security. *Meeting Faith*'s emphasis on Adiele's singular experience in a foreign land and as part of a religious tradition with which African Ameri-cans are not usually associated, may indeed be viewed as a betrayal.[44] However, as a text that addresses larger issues of spiritual liberation, *Meeting Faith* can be read, like Washam's memoir, as a rite-of-passage story or a heroine's tale. It is a visual and textual recording of her death to her old self through the trial of her ordainment to be reborn anew, transformed and ready to be reintegrated into her community. Her transformation is signified by the titles of the book's preface, "Strip-ping," which signals her shedding her old identity, and those of the first two chapters: "Killing Faith" signifies her death to her old self, and "Birthing Faith" signals the process of rebirth that makes up the rest of the book before ending with her leaving the womblike environment of the wat to be reintegrated into society. This rite-of-passage motif is deeply steeped in the African tradition and would be familiar to her Igbo father.

Like that of a newborn taking her first breath outside of the womb, her reintegration into the wider Thai society was noise-filled and disorienting. As she remarks shortly after her return to secular life, at her birthday celebration held in a Thai club, "I'm still out of sync."[45] While there, she and all of her friends are robbed. Luckily they are able to retrieve their belongings, but in the midst of trying to explain to a police officer the events of the evening, she is interrupted with the question that drove her to the forest in the first place: "What are you?" It was a simple question prompted by the spectacle of Adiele's shaven head and her wearing pants—as yet uncommon in Thailand—but also makeup and jewelry. It nevertheless haunted her, at first shaking and annoying her and then pleasing her that "for once, identity cannot be recognized, assumed, categorized, explained from outside."[46] She was pleased that she had accomplished her goal of establishing that there is no easy, static answer to the question. With that goal accomplished, Adiele was poised to continue her journey to embracing her multiple identities, this time in Nigeria, her fatherland, and a place she calls "home."

Nigerian-Nordic Woman with Lady Problems

Adiele's *The Nigerian-Nordic Girl's Guide to Lady Problems: A Memoir* is a very different project from *Meeting Faith*. It can easily be overlooked as it seems at first glance like a lighthearted take on a subject that *should* be handled lightly. After all, many people have no idea that there is such a thing as uterine fibroids—benign tumors that grow in and around the uterus—until they interrupt their life or the life of someone they love. They can be quite debilitating and leave some women unable to carry a pregnancy to term.

Much too often, when those who have uterine fibroids approach their doctors for solutions to their condition, they are given one of three options: *Wait & Watch*,[47] undergo an invasive surgery that may or may not permanently alleviate the condition, or have a radical hysterectomy. I suspect most women would agree that none of these options are really *solutions*. Furthermore, the lack of care and attention to this physical—and, I believe, societal and spiritual—disease speaks to the devaluation of the feminine—and in particular, the Black feminine—in this society. As someone who has struggled with uterine fibroids since they announced themselves shortly after I turned forty years old, much of what Adiele explains about her dealings with the American medical institution resonates. I suspect it will resonate with countless women, especially women of African descent, who are among the groups most susceptible to uterine fibroids.[48]

I have mentioned that most of my young life seems to be compressed into one year—the year I turned eleven. It was the year that puberty hit—like a ton of bricks—and kept hitting for several years. I remember the day my period started. There was no rite-of-passage ceremony, no party, not even a heart-to-heart with my mother to mark my entry into womanhood. She had more pressing issues on her mind and heart. At the time, my family was squatting in someone else's house after we'd been evicted from yet another apartment for nonpayment of rent. While I don't remember what I was doing, I have etched in my memory the searing pain that shot through my body, followed by cramping so intense that I was convinced my insides were going to fall out of me. I writhed and groaned until my mother told me to "Hush, girl." That, or similar scenarios, would commence each month for many years. Before that time, I thought girls' bodies were preferable to boys', more elegant as everything was tucked neatly away. This new normal made me despise being born female. Each month I felt my body betrayed me, declaring itself my sworn enemy and winning the battle every time. In high school I would regularly have to leave early, praying that I made it home before the worst of the pain debilitated me.

One particularly overcast afternoon, I had to take a dollar cab because I couldn't wait for the public bus to take me to my sister's apartment.[49] The whole ride I was doubled over in pain. The driver, a young man, read my body language and, rather than drop me along his regular route, followed my finger to my sister's place where he waited, making sure someone was home to take care of me. I never knew his name or saw him again to thank him for his kindness. Years later, when I moved to Haiti in my early twenties, one of my first jobs was teaching English as a second language. One morning, feeling the first twinges of uterine revolt, as soon as my classes were over, I grabbed a *tap tap* to get home before the monster roared. I didn't make it. And like so many times before, sweating profusely, I doubled over in the back seat, near tears, clutching my stomach. Another passenger asked, "*Sa'w genyen?*" (What's wrong?) This time, ignorant of the word for *period* in French or Kreyòl, I could only screw up my face. Finally, one of the other passengers, an older gentleman, reading my body language exclaimed, "*Aah! Bon, se règ li!*" (It's her period.) I could only nod, my eyes squeezed shut against the pain. And gratefully, after moaning out the vague coordinates of my apartment, I found myself safely deposited outside my home by the driver. This was my life almost every month—until I gave birth to my son. While I have never investigated the science behind it, whatever hormones my body manufactured during those nine months shielded me from the torture of the death cramps for the rest of my childbearing years.

In my early forties, during a routine doctor's visit, I mentioned that I felt an occasional ache in my right lower abdomen. The doctor asked me a few questions, including whether I exercised. When I told him that I had recently taken up yoga, he suggested that it was probably a pulled muscle but decided to do a sonogram, "just in case." And there they were: relatively small distensions within my womb, probably the reason for my minor discomfort.[50] I was one of those people who had never heard of fibroids until I learned I had them. My doctor assured me that while annoying, they were not dangerous, so I need not worry. He recommended the *Wait & Watch* approach and sent me on my way. I was lucky. I had already had the one child that I wanted. And my fibroids never got so large as to constantly press on my bladder or obstruct my intestines, as they do for some women.

This was not the case with Adiele, who writes of having four or five tumors inside her womb, including one the size of a grapefruit. She begins the narrative, "One shoves angrily at my back, forcing me to sleep upright against a bank of pillows, like a princess. Another hunkers against my bladder, malicious, sending me constantly loping for the bathroom to strain and strain. Two clutch high, one churning whenever I eat, the other morose as a prisoner, twisting on its stalk and cutting off its own blood supply. The unconfirmed fifth one waits on the bench, ready to go in if any of the first string tires."[51] The rest of *The Nigerian-Nordic* takes the reader through Adiele's struggle to come to terms with her condition, wondering if she is somehow to blame for it while pushing back against the inhumanity and disregard with which she is treated by the medical industry in small-town Iowa, where she was attending graduate school. The question that she asks, whether she is to blame for her tumors, emerges from her Nordic tradition and her Nigerian heritage, both of which suggest that she, as "The Selfish Artist, Independent Woman," is to blame for her condition.[52] As she muses, "The Selfish Artist, Independent Woman. Worse still. I'm my mother's only child. The irony of their presence, the fact that their actions mimic those of a fetus, is not lost on me, the Single Girl Writer. Modern Career Woman gives birth to something other than useful."[53] Interestingly (and this is not a connection that Adiele makes), her fibroids are the size of a four-month pregnancy, the same fetal age she was when her mother was sent away to give birth. Indeed, there is something mystical or otherworldly about fibroids. Having lived with them for over fourteen years, I have become intimately familiar with my own and read lots of theories about their source—from Black women having more collagen than other races to them being unexpressed creative energy that gets lodged in this physical place that is considered a woman's creative center.

According to the surgeon general, there are four factors that predispose a woman to fibroids: heredity, not having experienced pregnancy, being over thirty, and being of African descent. These factors also predispose those who develop fibroids to receive less than the best medical care. Just before Adiele lists the factors, she writes about her grandmother's death from ovarian cancer. Misdiagnosed by her small-town doctor as hysteria, she was sent home with a prescription for valium. Adiele relates, as a child, hearing her grandmother mutter to herself as she grimaced in pain, "All the things I never said, balled up inside me." Again, the esoteric explanation of "lady parts" tumors as unreleased energy. With it comes the common practice of blaming one's self for the tumors' existence: a symptom and consequence of being a women in this society. Another symptom and consequence is the regularity with which the solution to fibroids is the seemingly casual prescription of removal of the offending parts. Adiele writes,

> Hysterectomies are one of the most commonly performed surgeries in the U.S., the country that leads the world in hysterectomies. Many women's health experts believe that a large number—perhaps even most—of hysterectomies are unnecessary. Ten years ago, fibroids would have been enough for many doctors to advise a patient to undergo a hysterectomy. Younger doctors are less likely to recommend hysterectomy than older doctors.[54] (loc. 195)

And yet one of Adiele's doctors, a "youngish" woman, tells her with a shrug, "Obviously you need a hysterectomy."[55]

The second factor that predisposes women to fibroids, not experiencing pregnancy, is an Igbo cultural taboo. Adiele writes, "It's nearly impossible to think about being an African woman and not a mother, with a proverb to express the unthinkability of it: One who has been procreated owes a debt of procreating."[56] While she approaches this belief through an Igbo lens, it is in no way unique to the Igbo, and is, in part, responsible for the overturning of *Roe v. Wade* in the US.[57] The still widely held beliefs that if a woman is going to give birth she should do so early and that career women who decide to have children later in life are the cause of all the world's troubles support Adiele's self-blame for being "The Selfish Artist, Modern Career Woman." The two dispositions, pregnancy experience and having children by the age of thirty, make me wonder if it's necessary, in this way of thinking, to carry the pregnancy to term. If fibroids are some sort of curse for not procreating, as Adiele tells us is a belief among the Igbo, then I would assume that having an abortion would also be seen as opening up one's self to them. Fibroids are seen, then, as women's punishment for not contributing to the continuation of the species.

I, too, wondered for years what I had done to cause my fibroids. Was it the hormone-pumped chicken I grew up eating? The power lines that surrounded my neighborhoods? Pesticides on the fruits and veggies? Some truth I didn't speak? An ancestral wounding coming through me? Retribution for all the years I cursed my womb? How were they my fault? I do think there is something to the belief that fibroids are creative energy that has not been birthed. Eventually, rather than continue to beat myself up for being at war with my body, I decided it would be better to care for my womb. I would stop cursing her for causing me pain for so many years. After all, out of that pain came my son.

Nonetheless, I know that deciding not to have a child should not sentence me to years of excruciating, potentially debilitating pain with the alternative being to have an intimate part of my body pulled out. "With a vaginal hysterectomy, the surgeon approaches the uterus through the vagina, and pulls it out," writes Adiele. "With an abdominal hysterectomy, the surgeon makes an incision in the abdomen and pulls it out."[58] The fact that so many women are without real, viable, dare we say joyful alternatives speaks to how much we are left out of the paradigm of medical advancement. And as Black women, even though we are the very reason that this country is where it is in gynecological advancements, we benefit the least from them.[59]

Not wanting to undergo a myectomy—a "conservative surgery" that cuts off the fibroids' blood supply so as to kill them but that comes with a regrowth rate of between 10 and 80 percent—Adiele advocated for herself and got a referral for an alternative treatment for her fibroids. Although the initial treatment, "healing touch" performed by nurses, was not covered by her student medical plan, Adiele tried it. While on the table, one of the nurses informed her that "creativity is located in two places . . . the belly and the throat." She continued, "The belly is the root, the place of family, of creativity." There it was again, the connection between silencing one's self and a diseased creative center. This connection and others around family that the nurse was able to bring to light brought Adiele to tears, itself a release.

Shortly thereafter, while at an artist colony in Virginia, a massage therapist offered to do a healing touch session with her for free. For the next month and a half following the treatment, Adiele felt her uterus shrinking, returning to a normal size, and she had more energy and regular periods. She was finally a friend to her body.[60] By mid-July, however, her pain returned so strongly that she cried out in a crowded theater during a performance of *For Colored Girls Who Have Considered Suicide When the Rainbow Is Enuf* by the acclaimed Black woman writer Ntozake Shange. The moment that Adiele's womb cries out is at a pivotal scene in the play: the character Crystal, who has two children with an abusive Vietnam vet who is trying to cajole her into marrying him, has been convinced to let the father of her children hold them.

When she refuses to marry him and demands her children back, he drops them out the window of the apartment. Adiele writes, "Crystal collapses to the floor, anticipating her children's crash to the pavement below, and I drop to my knees, wailing as if my own children have been dropped out of my existence."[61] There is a lot in these few words: there is the loss that is being witnessed and the empathic reckoning with that loss. Though unstated, there is also Adiele's recognition that as someone with fibroids, she may never be able to give birth. With it comes a sense of lost potential. She leaves the reader to meditate on the pain that is suffered by both those who give birth to children and lose them and those who have the choice to have them taken away. Both are potently devastating experiences.

Invoking her ever-present sense of hypervisibility, Adiele comments about her crying out, "The polite Midwestern audience of New-World Nordics doesn't quite know where to look." They are torn between looking at the stage at a Korean-born actress adopted by white parents playing a Black woman living in the projects or "a bi-racial black girl squirming between her white mother and black boyfriend." They choose to focus on the stage. Adiele speculates on the audience speculating about her own situation: perhaps having suffered a similar violence, perhaps someone took her children. "Perhaps she's the kind of Frightening Black Woman pain happens to."[62] In writing about the experience in this way, Adiele, as someone who has lived much of her life as an outsider having to read others' thoughts as a tool of survival, reflects on the toll that such an existence takes on the psyche and the body. It wears away at Black women's sense of self, of our right to acknowledge and express our pain. "The Frightening Black Woman" trope is alive and well in the American psyche and enables those who would bear witness to turn away from Black women's mental, spiritual, and physical pain so that it goes unhealed.

The morning after the performance, Adiele went to see a gynecologist who suggested the *Wait & Watch* approach. Seven months later she had to undergo a myectomy. She writes, "And later, like ten to eighty percent of cases, the tumors will return."[63] She ends the text with the reflection that in the month before the myectomy, she spent time naming her unborn children, having imaginary conversations with siblings she hadn't seen in ten years, and trying not to think about the amount of blood her family has had to shed as she bled.

Reading Adiele's text brings to my heart a recent experience that I had with what Spring Washam would call "ancestor grief." Surrounded by a community that knew how to support me one night during a retreat with Spring, I found myself repeatedly throwing my body on the earth, wailing and crying as I released a grief that I knew instinctively was not mine alone. What seems like hours later, I came out on the other side of the experience cold, wet, and filthy with a few scratches and bruises but also joyful. I knew that I had released into the earth not only *my* pain but that of countless women in my lineage who didn't have the space and resources to do so. And in their preoccupation with survival, they pushed it down and stored it in their bodies. It was passed down to and stored in their daughters' and their daughters' daughters' bodies. I also recall a half-day sit that I did with Rev. angel a couple of years ago in which one of the meditators, a Black woman, shared that she had fibroids. Rev. angel responded with something that has stayed with me. I'm paraphrasing: It makes perfect sense that so many Black women suffer with fibroids. Historically our bodies have been used and abused as vessels to bring forth children to be handed over to the plantation system. These womb distortions are yet another aspect of our intergenerational trauma. They are clues to the healing that we must do. We have been bleeding for over four hundred years! And we will continue to bleed as long as our deep soul wounds are unacknowledged and untended to.

I have chosen not to go under the knife to remove my fibroids. Since mine never got to the point where I couldn't handle them (I have a very high pain threshold), I stayed with the *Wait & Watch* approach until menopause kicked in with the promise that, deprived of estrogen, the fibroids would, if not shrink, at least stop growing. At one point, though, a few years ago, when I could feel these lumps of fury through my skin, I sought out a healing touch practitioner, a white woman affiliated with a neighboring university. I made an appointment and on the agreed upon day I went to her home, where I sat on a table while she interviewed me. I was near tears when, after so many years I said out loud to someone else what I had said to myself countless times: "I have fibroids." But something shut the tears down. A little voice inside told me I just needed information from this woman: how to perform the massage on myself and when to take the homemade tincture that she handed me. I gratefully accepted the photocopied cheat sheet she gave me, the tincture that she had formulated especially for uterine maladies, and paid the small fee. For a while I kept up the exercises, ingested the recommended dosage of bitter-tasting fluid with my morning water, and applied castor oil packs and a hot water bottle to my abdomen as I laid on my futon and read novels. And then life got in the way. I stopped the self-care practice and never returned to the healing touch practitioner.

A couple of years later, I booked a massage with Sharonda, a Black woman who owns her own healing space in my area. It was supposed to be a routine "lay back and relax" massage with a foot reflexology add-on. What happened was anything but routine. About a half hour into the session when she began gently kneading the area just below my navel, I released a flood of tears, grieving. And then I grieved some more—loud, ugly sobs not just for me and the difficult relationship that I had had for so many years with my womb but for all the joy that I missed out on in rejecting that part of me. I grieved also for all of the women who came before me, whose wombs were used as labor-making machines against their will and without their consent. Sharonda, a gifted healer, stilled. She then bent down and whispered into my ear three magic words. I went home, spent and grateful to have found her, and I sat with this painting that I had done a few years before:

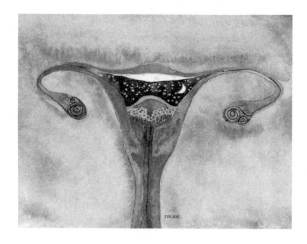

In *A Burst of Light and Other Essays*, writings that she penned after she learned that she was dying of liver cancer, the Black feminist revolutionary poet Audre Lorde declares that for Black women, caring for one's self is an act of self-preservation. In a capitalist sexist heteropatriarchal system that is built on our labor, it is an act of political warfare.[64] Indeed it is. After half a century on this earth, I have finally come to understand that I do not take care of myself *only* for myself. I do so with the knowledge that, as the saying goes, I am my ancestors' wildest dreams. I rest, drink clean water, eat nourishing food, send love to my body, and read the work of women like Adiele to help heal them as me. Adiele's offerings, ever expanding, are balms to Black girls who know what it is to not feel like a friend to their body.

I continue to seek out Sharonda's healing touch and sage advice. Unlike my experience with doctors, when I'm with her I feel heard, cared for, supported, healed. I also feel those things with Adiele's writings. Although she does not claim the African American tradition as it is widely understood, her memoirs do the work that centuries of women of African descent have done through their writing. They tell their own stories as tools of liberation for themselves as inextricable from that of their communities.

PART TWO

BUDDHISM AND BLACK WOMEN

IN THE 1967 FILM *Guess Who's Coming to Dinner*, a set of white middle-class liberal parents' espoused values are put to the test when their daughter brings her Black boyfriend home to meet them.[1] In a delicious play on that title, the cultural critic Carol Cooper titled her 2001 essay "Guess Who's Coming to Dharma: Black Women Embrace Western Buddhism."[2] Cooper's title is fitting for several reasons: First, it brings attention to the fact that, contrary to common perception, Black Buddhists exist. Second, because of the way that Buddhism was brought to the United States, many sanghas and meditation societies are overwhelmingly white and affluent. Third, like the Christian church, the convert Buddhism that has taken hold in the United States has a race problem.[3] Finally, quiet as it's kept, Black people—Black women in particular—are forging their own unique paths, revolutionizing and democratizing the power structure of American convert Buddhism[4] and forcing white Buddhists, many of whom are middle- to upper-class liberals, to interrogate what they believe they believe.[5]

In fact, as Cooper asserts, Black women have unwittingly become the world's most spontaneous lay Buddhist preachers, testifying to their own liberation and alerting others to the possibility.[6] By doing so, they are changing the face *and* body, and hopefully also the heart, of Western convert Buddhism.

Thousands of Black women have found refuge in the Buddha's teachings. Most do so "quietly, without much visibility or commercial fanfare." They meditate daily, then take the insights they receive on the cushion into their lives as "mothers, mates, social activists, and career women."[7] There are also teachers and leaders like Marlene Jones, Roshi Merle Boyd, Konda Mason, Gina Sharpe, Sebene Selassie, Sister Peace, Kaira Jewel Lingo, JoAnna Hardy, and Leslie Booker, who point other seekers to the dharma and help guide their awakening. My project has focused on a few such teachers and leaders—Jan Willis, bell hooks, Osho Zenju Earthlyn Manuel, Rev. angel Kyodo williams, Spring Washam, and Faith Adiele. There are many more Black women scholars, teachers, and practitioners of Buddhism that I might add to this list, including Noliwe Alexander, Myokei Caine-Barrett, Valerie (Vimalasara) Mason-John, Ruth King, and Pamela Ayo Yetunde, to name a few. Although these and other such Black women Buddhist leaders deserve attention, I decided to focus on a smaller group so as to have space for sustained analysis of their lives and work. The project celebrates these self-identified Black women's commitment to attending to their embodiments, and it highlights their unique vocations as spiritual warriors dedicated to realizing their personal psychic and spiritual liberation as it is bound to that of the larger human family. Both the inward-looking world of awakening and the outward-directed social engagement find a home in them.

As we have seen in the preceding chapters, the work of these women in each case began with their individual encounters with hardship. When their work moved outward to challenge and transform unjust social structures,[8] they joined a long tradition of Black social activists. For example, Willis and Osho Zenju were involved in 1960s and '70s grassroots social activism movements; Willis in the civil rights movement and briefly the Black Panther Party, and Osho Zenju in the civil rights and Pan-Africanist movements. Rev. angel has started her own social justice movements, finding her activist niche in her collaborative Radical Dharma summer camps and open discussion forums around battling racism, as well as in the multifaceted work of the Liberated Life Network. She infuses her writing with her spiritual practice as an expression of social activism. Spring, in her own unique way, focuses on the work of liberation from the societal binds that keep us tied to illusions about the self that cause suffering. She combines her two paths as a teacher and healer in her work as the founder of Lotus Vine Journeys, where she blends indigenous healing practices with Buddhist wisdom. Faith Adiele, another elder, began her activist work among Asian immigrants while a university student and chose to continue her Buddhist path as an upasika, a lay Buddhist. bell hooks, best known for her feminist writings and her social activism, was also a lay Buddhist and Sufi practitioner who infused her writings with her practice. Those who marched and protested when they were younger continue their activism through their cultural production in the form of books, speaking engagements, interviews, blog posts, essays, films, and more. Those who have come after them stand on their shoulders, combining their spiritual practice with their social activism in an interrelated gesture of freedom.

While diverse and unique, the women whose work I discuss are connected in several key respects: they are African Americans in female-identified bodies whose commitment to their personal liberation is inextricable from that of the collective. They have also felt compelled to express in many venues and in different ways their experiences as spiritual seekers and the way that their suffering has laid the path to their awakening. Several of the women publicly engage with social justice issues not only as dharma practitioners but also from a worldview that extends beyond Buddhism, embracing other traditions that have helped them achieve personal and collective freedom. I propose that they do so in the tradition of their African and African diasporic ancestors, both named and unnamed, who also took up the call of spiritual warriorship and on whose shoulders they stand.

Black Women, Social Activism, and Engaged Buddhism

Black women in the US have a long and robust history of social and political activism. The call to activism stems from the history of oppression, exploitation, and violence that has circumscribed Black life from the moment African people landed on these shores. Time and again over the centuries, Black women have used their bodies, pens, and voices to protest injustice and advocate for equality.

Their commitment to the realization of Black liberation is embodied, for example, in Harriet Tubman's leading almost one hundred enslaved African American souls to freedom before the Civil War, then freeing another 250 at the Combahee River during the war. Or Sojourner Truth's leadership as an abolitionist and women's suffragist, insisting on having her voice heard at the (majority white) Women's Convention in 1851 in Akron, Ohio. Black women's commitment to collective liberation can also be seen in the narratives written by women such as Harriet Jacobs, who penned her autobiography with the goal of aiding the abolitionist movement, and in the work of Mary McLeod Bethune, a woman born to formerly enslaved people, who lived to become one of the most important Black educators, civil and women's rights leaders, and government officials of the twentieth century. It is also apparent in the anti-lynching campaigns waged by the journalist Ida B. Wells under constant threat of death. Black women's commitment to community uplift can likewise be found in the National Association of Colored Women's Clubs' 125-year-old motto "Lifting as We Climb" as well as in the 1970s Combahee River Collective's revolutionary collaborative work to dismantle capitalism and patriarchy. We find it in the lives and work of women such as Angela Davis, Assata Shakur, and Elaine Brown, who published their autobiographies as part of their commitment to Black collective liberation. And in the political career of Congresswoman Shirley Chisholm, who dedicated her life to giving a voice to the disenfranchised and marginalized and paved the way not only for Barack Obama's 2008 election to the US presidency but also Senator Kamala Harris's election to the vice presidency in 2020. It is also there in the example of Congresswoman Maxine Waters, who rose to fame in 1992 as one of the prosecutors in the case against the officers who beat the unarmed Rodney King. Despite regularly receiving death threats to this day from angry white conservative men who want to silence her, Waters has never ceased speaking truth to power.[9] In short, the list of Black women who have put their lives on the line in their commitment to humanity's collective freedom is vast.

The women I discuss in this project may also be seen as practicing what is known as engaged Buddhism, brought to the West when the Zen priest Thich Nhat Hanh was forced into exile from Vietnam in 1966. According to the scholar Christopher S. Queen, with Nhat Hanh came a "general pattern of belief and practice that . . . is unprecedented" in Buddhist history, and thus "tantamount to a new chapter in the history of the tradition."[10] Engaged Buddhism is marked by a commitment to "human rights, social justice, political activism, and due process that have evolved in the Western cultural tradition"[11] and its many influences. Both Nhat Hanh and the Dalai Lama, the spiritual leader of Tibet, have spoken and written about the need for religious people "to contribute all they can to solving the world's problems."[12] However, as the Buddhism scholar Rima Vesely-Flad points out in "Black Buddhists and the Body: New Approaches to Socially Engaged Buddhism," "Both leaders write from a social heritage that does not acknowledge oppression based on race, nor do they acknowledge social oppression based on gender and sexuality."[13]

Vesely-Flad notes that this lack of attention to race, gender, and sexuality can also be found in socially engaged "predominantly white, affluent Buddhist communities that have emerged in the West since the 1970s."[14] She attributes that lack in large part to such communities' understandings of the Buddhist teaching of "no self," or *anatta*.[15] She notes that most analyses of socially engaged Buddhism do not account for the way that racialized bodies have been constructed and degraded in the West. Dharma seekers of African descent, who in their daily lives as well as in majority white sanghas must confront the social constructs of the Black body that result in violence against it, push back against teachings that "deny differences and suffering that arise from racism."[16] In fact, as Vesely-Flad argues, "to describe 'No Self' to people who have been historically dehumanized is often received as dismissive of the weight of colonialism, genocide, slavery, and systemic racism that have been justified by interpretations of the body."[17] The denigration of the Black body lives on in the wake of these historical systems of oppression and exploitation.[18] As such, Black dharma teachers and practitioners call for an acknowledgment of the reality of the Black body and insist that the truth of "no self" be "deconstructed and contemplated."[19] (See chapter 8, "The African American Autobiographical Tradition and Its Legacy," for a more detailed consideration of how Black thinkers have considered selfhood throughout American history.)

For Black women, this need to acknowledge, deconstruct, and contemplate the body in light of the history of slavery and its legacy of continued denigration and devaluation of blackness is compounded by mainstream culture's continued denigration and devaluation of the feminine. Both aspects circumscribe Black women's lives inside and outside of their inherited and chosen communities. Given this history and contemporary reality, it is necessary to reflect on socially engaged Buddhism through a lens of Black womanhood.

Black Women's Revolutionary
Care Within *Then* Without

As the Buddhism scholar Ann Gleig indicates in *American Dharma: Buddhism Beyond Modernity*, people of color in the US are challenging certain aspects of what is known as "Buddhist modernism"—Buddhism as it has been configured in the West and to some extent in Asia by forces of modernity such as colonialism and science and by modern values such as individuality. One prominent case is the privileging of the individual meditator at the expense of the collective.[20] Indeed, as inheritors of the Black activist tradition, many Black dharma teachers speak, write, and teach about the inextricability of individual and collective liberation.[21] Black women are at the forefront of articulating a socially engaged Buddhism concerned with collective liberation. Yet they are simultaneously showing how such work can be done in a sustainable way from a place of wise self-care. This way of thinking about care is at odds with the way that Black women especially are socialized as caretakers for others, often at the expense of their own mental, physical, and spiritual health.

Sister Peace, an African American monastic in Nhat Hanh's Plum Village, explains engaged Buddhism as, first, taking care of ourselves. "Our practice is to come back to ourselves, to stop, to be aware of our breathing, to be conscious of it, and that right away helps us to calm down and get in touch with the things that we need to address within ourselves," she says. "And hopefully, the transformation process can begin. And once we've done that we then can turn to others and help them to do the same." Sister Peace continues: "So when we say 'engaged' it's not just with ourselves, but also with the entire community around us. . . . We are out there with our sangha, with our community which happens to be the world ultimately."[22]

Sister Peace's message echoes for me the words of human rights activist Angela Davis: "Anyone who is interested in making change in the world also has to learn to take care of himself, herself, theirselves."[23] Although Sister Peace is speaking on behalf of her sangha, I home in on her blackness and her womanness as the bearer of this message of self-care. As we have seen, the women who are the subjects of this project have all engaged with deep work of inner healing—of attending to their own wounds and traumas—that is a preliminary step and also ongoing. Like them, Sister Peace's embodiment as a Black woman helps other Black women who hear her words reflect on their own need for self-care.

On Interbeing and Blackness

These women's engagement with their "beloved communities," which include but extend well beyond traditional sanghas, speaks to their commitment to the foundational Buddhist teaching of the interconnectedness of all beings. They understand that their fate is inextricably entwined with the fate of other sentient beings. I propose that the existence of suffering in the world impels them to act. But it is also based in a Black worldview that is steeped in commitment to community.

We see this worldview coming through, for instance, in comments from DaRa Williams, a teacher in the Theravada Buddhist tradition. As a panelist on a forum on Black activism and community, she prefaced her remarks with the declaration that she has been Black a lot longer than she has been Buddhist. As such, her blackness serves as the way that she enters conversations about the intersections of Buddhism, community, and activism. She identified herself relationally, first as her mother and father's child, a descendant of people who made the journey from the South to the North, the Northwest, and the Midwest during the Great Migration. She went on to say that because of the history of terrorism against Black people in this country, there is no way that she could *not* be an activist and part of community. Even though she is an individual, "there is always the collective; always the community."[24] Williams concluded her remarks by stating that everything that she has undertaken has been undergirded by the question: "Does this venue, does this environment, does this set of circumstances serve me to move forward in contributing to the lessening of suffering for people?" She is concerned with people in general but adds, "I am particularly committed to [suffering] in the Black community . . . not at the expense of other communities, but that's where my intention—that's where my *attention*—is often."[25] As one of the teachers in Deep Time Liberation, a retreat experience founded by Insight Meditation teachers Noliwe Alexander and Devin Berry, she lives out that commitment.[26]

Although the Buddhist concept of interdependence has clearly been important to Black women teachers, they have pushed back against uses of the teaching that minimize the importance and social reality of embodiment. Osho Zenju remarks in *The Way of Tenderness: Awakening through Race, Sexuality, and Gender* that in spiritual settings, we often hear the statement, "We are not our bodies." Perhaps that view is drawn from the idea that in the context of interdependence and impermanence, attachment to the body is a cause for suffering. While such a statement may provide solace to certain dharma practitioners, Osho Zenju, who inhabits a Black, queer, and aging body, illustrates how little comfort such a statement provides to those who are traumatized through and because of their embodiments. As a way of pointing out the normative cultural perspective and privilege inherent in such a statement, she asks three rhetorical questions: Would this idea be useful to a child who is bullied at school because of their flat nose and thick lips? Would it be helpful to "a teen who is raped for wearing clothes of the 'wrong' gender?" Would we, as a society, "say to a white kid who is expected to gain entry to a prestigious school, but who was denied due to quotas based on race, 'You are not your body?'"[27] The simplicity of such questions makes real the impact of one's embodiment on their everyday existence. In asking them, Osho Zenju drives home the fact that being mindful of the body is sometimes an issue of life and death. Indeed, Black Buddhist practitioners have the imperative to account for their embodiment because the way that the Black body is perceived and treated in US society often carries over into largely white sanghas.

Having thus complicated the question of the interdependence of the body, Osho Zenju also cautions that while our experience may be different because of our embodiment, we should not lose sight of the fact that we are all connected. She draws on the *Sattipatthana Sutta*, the Buddha's famous Discourse on the Establishment of Mindfulness: "The body, it says, is comprised of the five *skandhas*, or aggregates: the physical body, feelings, perceptions, mental formations, and consciousness (the five senses and thought). We are our bodies from the perspective of these conditions."[28] Each of these aggregates depends on the others and is related to all things. Thus, "the meaning of the saying, 'We are not our bodies' is that we are not a single entity but an aggregate that exists in interrelationship. 'Not our bodies' means that our bodies are not ours alone, free from being conditioned by the existence of others. In fact, we are in a dynamic relationship with all that lives, with all bodies."[29] Or as Berry has explained, echoing Williams, when he thinks of anatta, he does so in relation to his ancestors.[30] In other words, we are not simply our individual selves; we are inextricable from the thread and the tapestry of our lineage. Rev. Zenju's, Berry's, and Williams's explanations of our interconnectedness are easily recognizable in the African philosophy of ubuntu, discussed in the introduction: "I am because we are" and "we are fostered in relation to other people."

Rev. Zenju's reading of the *Sattipatthana Sutta* connects the reality of the aggregate body to the concept of interrelatedness with other beings, or "interbeing," to use Thich Nhat Hanh's term. It takes us beyond the dualistic notion of being and nonbeing. Unlike *nonbeing*—a concept that can sound scary—*interbeing* allows us to see how everything is connected.[31] Nhat Hanh illustrated the concept of interbeing in very practical terms during a 1989 retreat that he led for Vietnam veterans. Reminding the attendees that their role in the violence perpetrated against the Vietnamese people during the war was inextricable from American society's propensity "to fight, destroy, kill, and die," he told them, "you were not the only one[s] responsible. . . . Our individual consciousness is a product of our society, ancestors, education, and many other factors. . . You have to look deeply to understand what really happened." This view toward interbeing not only helped illuminate the true source of the veterans' suffering but also opened a path toward healing and hope. The fact of interrelatedness meant that their healing—if allowed to flourish, like their violence against those who had been othered was allowed to flourish—had the potential to heal the larger society. Resonant with Sister Peace's sentiment discussed above, Nhat Hanh told them, "Your personal healing will be the healing of the whole nation, your children and their children."[32]

Guided by the concept of interbeing, Nhat Hanh identified with both the victim and the victimizer. He has also done so in speaking about injustices perpetrated against the marginalized Other in the United States. During that same gathering with the veterans, he referred to the police beating of Rodney King that was captured on video in 1991, calling on their sense of interbeing and appealing to their capacity for compassion:

People everywhere saw the Los Angeles policemen beating Rodney King. When I first saw that video on French TV, I felt I was the one being beaten, and I suffered a lot. I think you must have felt the same. All of us were beaten at the same time. We are all victims of violence, anger, misunderstanding, and the lack of respect for our human dignity. But as I looked more deeply, I saw that the policemen beating Rodney King were no different from myself. They were doing it because our society is filled with hatred and violence. Everything is like a bomb ready to explode, and we are all part of the bomb; we are all co-responsible. We are all the policemen and the victim.[33]

The first part of Nhat Hanh's statement is easily assimilable. The second part may be difficult to contend with for those of us who consider ourselves social activists. But it is the second part—to see ourselves not only in the victims but also in the perpetrators—that speaks to what a true adherence to interbeing asks of us. It demands that we understand that separation is a delusion that gave rise to the violence that unfolded in that blurry video and that has occurred across countless examples of race, gender-based, and sexual oppression over the course of our country's history.[34]

In being able to see himself as both victim and victimizer, Nhat Hanh enacts the kind of love ethic that spurred spiritual warriors such as Rev. Martin Luther King Jr., who placed such an ethic at the heart of his nonviolent movement. I believe that this love ethic also drives the work of the women whose work I focus on in this project. In line with the women on whose shoulders they stand, like Tubman and Truth, as well as the Buddhist teachings of social engagement, these women see how their individual liberation is inextricably tied to that of the larger collective. In this way, they demonstrate the truth of ubuntu and interbeing as well as the aptness of the oft-quoted truism, "The personal is political."

The Personal Is Political Is Spiritual: The Power of Testimony

The phrase "The personal is political" originated in an essay by Carol Hanisch, a member of New York Radical Women and a prominent figure in the 1970s women's liberation movement. "One of the first things we discover in these groups is that personal problems are political problems," Hanisch wrote. "There are no personal solutions at this time. There is only collective action for a collective solution."[35] Hanisch's essay was published in 1970 in *Notes from the Second Year: Women's Liberation*, and the editors titled it "The Personal Is Political." The phrase has figured heavily in Black feminist writings such as "A Black Feminist Statement," authored by the Combahee River Collective, Audre Lorde's essay "The Master's Tools Will Never Dismantle the Master's House," and the anthology *This Bridge Called My Back: Writings by Radical Women of Color*, edited by Gloria E. Anzaldúa and Cherríe Moraga. More broadly, as the civil rights lawyer and legal scholar Kimberlé Crenshaw observes, "This process of recognizing as social and systemic what was formerly perceived as isolated and individual has also characterized the identity politics of African Americans, other people of color, and gays and lesbians, among others."[36] As such, the individual circumstances that bear down on people in marginalized groups must be recognized as the result of larger political systems. The way to address them is by recognizing and attending to those systems that underpin the symptoms, not simply understanding suffering in what the law professor and rights activist john a. powell has called "individualistic and human terms."[37]

One way that Black women demonstrate the intersections between the personal and the political is in their tradition of testimony. The linguist Geneva Smitherman defines *testifying* as telling "the truth through story. . . . The content of testifying, then, is not plain and simple commentary but a dramatic narration and communal reenactment of one's feelings and experiences."[38] Testifying reaffirms one's humanity within the group and diminishes the testifier's sense of isolation.[39] The gender and race studies scholar DoVeanna S. Fulton has remarked that the act of testifying in its many forms also empowers Black women to resist objectification and injustice.[40]

The writer and critic Toni Morrison has written that a certain kind of work should have "something in it that enlightens; something in it that opens the door and points the way."[41] In a similar vein, the women whose work I discuss in this project document their own paths to liberation as a way of pointing the way to liberation for others. Their testifying about their personal and spiritual journeys sheds light on the way that their spiritual practice informs their lives and how their lives in turn inform their spiritual practice. The women demonstrate how both spheres share a deep concern with suffering, which is an animating force in their recursive relationship.[42]

Buddhism, Black Feminisms, and the Power and Politics of Love

In August 2002, Alice Walker delivered a dharma talk, "This Was Not an Area of Large Plantations: Suffering Too Insignificant for the Majority to See," at the first meditation retreat for African Americans at Spirit Rock Meditation Center. In it she highlighted the importance of honoring the feminine as an essential part of the African American struggle for dignity and freedom: "We have been strengthened by the rise of the Feminine, brought forward so brilliantly by women's insistence in our own time."[43] "The rise of the Feminine" that Walker invokes had been a long time coming by 2002. She had been integral to its emergence, having coined the term *womanism*, and supplied multiple definitions for it in her celebrated collection of essays, *In Search of Our Mothers' Gardens: Womanist Prose.*[44]

Walker's remark on "the Feminine" is immediately followed by a point about the collective struggles of African Americans for dignity and freedom. This sequence is indicative of the womanist commitment "to wholeness of entire people, male *and* female." In other words, as the feminist scholar Patricia Hill Collins reminds us, Black feminists, who clearly see "womanism as rooted in black women's concrete history in racial and gender oppression," also recognize that Black women's liberation is inextricably linked to Black collective liberation.[45] In 1977, the Combahee River Collective made a similar point when they stated that they understood that their "development [as black feminists] must also be tied to the contemporary economic and political position of Black people."[46] Indeed, Black feminism has traditionally distinguished itself from "feminism"—meaning white feminism—in part through its position on men. Unlike many white feminists of the 1970s who positioned themselves in opposition to men, Black feminists wished to work *alongside* Black men on a mutual path of liberating African American people. It is Black people working together, as Walker posits, who have "inspired the world."[47]

Another key element of Walker's definition of womanism is love. The definition itself comes from a place of love—for women, for men, for Black people in our many manifestations, iterations, and struggles, as well as a love for humanity. In fact, love is a thread that runs through each of Walker's multiple definitions of womanism. In her second definition, she states that a womanist is a "woman who loves other women, sexually and/or nonsexually. She appreciates and prefers women's culture, women's emotional flexibility (values tears as a natural counterbalance of laughter), and women's strength." She "sometimes loves individual men, sexually and/or nonsexually."[48] She also loves herself because while she is committed to wholeness and bringing people together, she does not do so at the expense of her own health. In this second definition we find echoes of Audre Lorde and Sister Peace in their words regarding the importance of self-care. We also hear the aforementioned Combahee River Collective's statement. Black women must prioritize ourselves. And because white supremacy is a worldwide disease and women of color are most deeply affected, the wellness of the global community is incumbent upon our health. World freedom is incumbent upon our realization of freedom.

Finally, in her third definition of womanism, Walker expands her sense of love beyond anthropocentrism to include music, dance, the moon, Spirit, food, and roundness. She "loves struggle. Loves the Folk." Again, she "loves herself. *Regardless*."[49] The love that Walker refers to transcends sentimentality to arrive at something akin to "Loving Your Enemies," the title and central proposal of one of Rev. King's most famous sermons. After all, while womanists may "love struggle," the work of moving society to a place of justice and healing often entails enduring personal violence and harm. We witness this fact, for example, in African American people being lynched during Reconstruction, and later in the Jim Crow era for daring to exercise their right to vote. Their hope of making it easier for those who would come after them cost them their lives. It is seen contemporarily in state-sanctioned violence against peaceful advocates of racial justice. Loving "the Folk" also means that Rev. King continued to love Izola Ware Curry, the Black woman who stabbed him in his chest in 1958, even though, of course, he did not *like* her actions. In a press release issued after the assault, Rev. King wrote that he hoped Curry, who suffered from mental illness, would get "the help she apparently needs if she is to become a free and constructive member of society."[50] The freedom that he wished for Curry may have been physical, but even more importantly, he meant freedom from the hatred that imprisoned her mentally and spiritually.

In "Loving Your Enemies," Rev. King explained that his understanding of love was "not to be confused with some sentimental outpouring" but was "something much deeper than emotional bosh."[51] He distinguished between three words for love from the Greek language: *eros* for aesthetic or romantic love; *philia* for "reciprocal love and the intimate affection and friendship between friends"; and *agape* for understanding and creative goodwill for all. As Rev. King maintained, "An overflowing love which seeks nothing in return, *agape* is the love of God operating in the human heart."[52] This was the version of love that inspired his civil rights work.

Agape has a parallel term in Buddhist Pali: *metta*, commonly translated as "lovingkindness." Because agape or metta transcends space and time, we are able to extend it to our distant ancestors as well as those who are present in our lives and those who are yet to arrive.

According to Walker, those global ancestors who had no idea who their descendants would be, nor what challenges they would face, nevertheless loved us so much that we are able to practice metta as a way to "embody peace and create a better world."[53] The women whose work I explore take up the mantle of love that their global ancestors passed down to them. Leaning into their embodiments as Black and woman, they testify, telling their stories as acts of love on behalf of those who lived in the past, are alive now, and also the not yet born.

THE AFRICAN AMERICAN AUTOBIOGRAPHICAL TRADITION AND ITS LEGACY

THE AFRICAN AMERICAN autobiographical tradition has performed individual and collective work for over two hundred years. Two of its most well-known autobiographies are *Narrative of the Life of Frederick Douglass: An American Slave* and *Incidents in the Life of a Slave Girl* by Harriet Jacobs. Douglass's and Jacobs's autobiographies tell of their personal journeys from slavery to freedom, and both served as effective testimonies to the horrors of slavery, compelling their white audiences to organize on the side of abolition. Their personal lives of relative freedom in a slave-holding nation were inextricably tied to those still in bondage. In the words of the immediatist abolitionist William Lloyd

Garrison, Douglass wrote his autobiography because of "his ever-abiding remembrance of those who are in bonds, as being bound with them!"[1] Or as Douglass said himself at the conclusion of his narrative, because although he was free, he saw himself as speaking out on behalf of the anti-slavery reform movement, "plead[ing] the cause of [his] brethren."[2]

We find this sentiment throughout the Black autobiographical tradition. Some one hundred years after Douglass's autobiography, for instance, Rev. King famously pronounced the words "No one is free until we are all free." In *Bearing Witness: Selections from African-American Autobiography in the Twentieth Century*, the scholar of African American studies Henry Louis Gates details the connections between autobiography and selfhood for Black writers. Contemporary African American memoir, he writes, "constructed upon an ironic foundation of autobiographical narratives written by ex-slaves . . . more clearly and directly than most, traces its lineage—in the act of declaring the existence of a surviving, enduring ethnic self—to this impulse of autobiography."[3] Indeed, autobiography is foundational to the contemporary African American writing tradition. In her essay "The Site of Memory," Toni Morrison makes a direct link between the two. As a writer and a Black person who has inherited the autobiographical tradition, Morrison saw it as her duty to "rip that veil drawn over 'proceedings too terrible to relate,'"[4] a common refrain of nineteenth-century writers who were compelled to shield their majority white readers from the horrors of slavery. For her, the charge is not a singular one but rather the responsibility of anyone who is Black or a member of a marginalized community. As such, though primarily a fiction writer, Morrison placed herself firmly in the milieu of the nineteenth-century writers who penned their autobiographies in the service of African Americans' collective freedom.

Morrison was also driven by a desire to tell "the truth" of the African American experience as distinct from "the fact" of it. While the "facts" about an event may not be remembered exactly, one is advised to remain loyal to the *feeling about* the event. This is how one is able to get at the truth of it. Indeed, as she posited, "Facts can exist without human intelligence, but truth cannot."[5] Her emphasis on "truth" raises the subjective and often capricious or unreliable nature of memory, which for Morrison was the source of truth. Sensitive to the way that the fullness of the Black experience has been traditionally discounted by hegemonic society and "History" that is written from the position of those in power, Morrison understood the need for subjected people to trust and rely on our innate knowledge if we are to reclaim and write our own "histories."[6] Because all too often she did not find her story in the annals of history, she needed to trust and rely on her own recollections as well as the recollections of others. As such, "memory" weighed heavily on what she wrote, in how she began, and in what she found to be significant.[7] She testified that the "memories within" were the subsoil of her work.[8]

As a fiction writer, Morrison was well aware that, like fiction, the genre of autobiography is a highly subjective form of writing that is heavily dependent upon one's ability to "remember" and "tell the truth," and that its truthfulness can be subjected to intense scrutiny. Scrutiny of autobiographies written by African Americans in the nineteenth century was such that each one had to have introductions provided by white abolitionists that attested to their veracity.[9] Contemporary African American writers of autobiography are ostensibly free from the need for approval by their white counterparts, beneficiaries, and patrons. They are also able to do something that their ancestors were not able to do: provide a window into their interior lives by taking up the space and time to fully explore their thoughts and feelings about the experiences that they detail in their narratives. Douglass, in one of his autobiographical narratives, begs the reader's indulgence while he spends half a page on the death of his grandmother, a woman who raised him after his mother was sent to a plantation eight miles away. Again, remember that the audience for Douglass and those like him was white readers who could support their fight for freedom. Very few people of African descent would have had access to the written word and even less power to influence the African American condition. By contrast, contemporary African American writers can now speak directly to people of African descent. They also are able to fully explore their experiences and their feelings about them. As such, while Douglass's narrative with its gaps and erasures would have provided a certain level of revelation and catharsis for the few Black people who could read him, contemporary writers are able to provide more nuanced sites for reflection on which to build their self-emancipation.

Much of contemporary African American autobiography carries on the tradition that began in the eighteenth century: to document, testify, and educate.[10] While the autobiography is the account of one person's life, it is also written on behalf of those who may not have the opportunity to tell their story. As such, as the scholar Stephen Butterfield writes in *Black Autobiography in America*, the "self" of Black autobiography is "conceived as a member of an oppressed social group, with ties and responsibilities to the other members."[11] It is a conscious political identity, drawing sustenance from the past experience of the group to pass the mantle to successive generations.[12] In short, "the autobiographical form is one of the ways that black Americans have asserted their right to live."[13]

Black Women's Spiritual Autobiography

In *Bearing Witness*, Gates documents the Black autobiography tradition. "Of the various genres that comprise the African-American literary tradition, none has played a role as central as black biography," he writes. "For hundreds of black authors, the most important written statement they could make seems to have been the publication of their life stories. . . . The ultimate form of protest, certainly, was to register in print the existence of a 'black self' that had transcended the limitations and restrictions that racism had placed on the personal development of the black individual."[14]

While much has changed from the time that early African Americans penned their autobiographies, much has remained the same. Racial terrorization of people of African descent has been fundamental to this country since Africans first stepped onto these shores enchained and stripped of personhood. It remained alive and well during Willis's, hooks's, and Rev. Zenju's childhoods, which were characterized by racial segregation legitimized through Jim Crow laws and enforced by the Ku Klux Klan. It continues contemporarily in reinvigorated attempts to disenfranchise African American voters, state-sanctioned violence in the rampant murdering of Black people by police, and a marked revitalization of white nationalist aggression. As such, the need for African Americans to protest our treatment and register our "Black selves" remains prescient. The women's autobiographies that I explore in this text, each unique, speak of larger truths. They are of vital importance to the continuing Black struggle for true liberation. They are illustrative of a sentiment expressed by James Baldwin in "Sonny's Blues": "While the tale of how we suffer, and how we are delighted, and how we may triumph is never new, it always must be heard," he writes. "There isn't any other to tell, it's the only light we've got in all this darkness. . . . And this tale, according to that face, that body, those strong hands on those strings, has another aspect in every country, and a new depth in every generation."[15] The women of this book write in this tradition, telling their stories so that others may read and benefit from the telling.

Gates dwells on the significance of the "self" in African American autobiography in the context of slavery, whereby Black people were denied access to the tools of formal memory: reading and writing. Without access to the written word, they could not access "ordered repetition or memory," which, in turn, foreclosed the possibility of history. Gates cites the memoir of a slave-era abolitionist to illustrate his point: when the abolitionist, upon encountering an enslaved worker, asked about the worker's "self," he responded, "'I ain't got no self.' Without hesitation, the abolitionist asked the black man, 'Slave are you?' 'That's what I is'"[16] came the response. Enslaved people of African descent were denied their selfhood and their humanity. In that context, autobiography countered the psychological and spiritual violence leveled against them. It was instrumental in their declaring for themselves and others their truth as autonomous, feeling, thinking human beings. "The connection among language, memory, and *the self* has been of signal importance to African-Americans," remarks Gates, "intent as they have had to be upon demonstrating both common humanity with whites and upon demonstrating that their 'selves' were, somehow as whole, integral, educable, and as noble as were those of any other American ethnic group."[17]

We see in this discussion how the issue of the self/no self has plagued the African American mind, body, and spirit for centuries, well before we were introduced to Buddhist concepts. This question must be acknowledged, contemplated, and addressed, as Black embodiment in a white supremacist nation remains an urgent issue. Similar to the way that formerly enslaved autobiographers wrote to agitate for an acknowledgment of their autonomous selves, the women whose work I study here seek to agitate. The difference—and it is a big difference— is that today's autobiographers can speak *directly* to those who remain in bondage, who perhaps have not as yet questioned their own personhood and those who are on the path.

The Particularities of Black Buddhist Women's Writing

While there is an impressive cadre of African American Buddhist men who have written about their experiences—among them Ralph Steele, Dr. Charles Johnson, Lama Choyin Rangdröl, Lama Rod Owens, Jarvis Jay Masters, and Calvin Malone[18]—I have chosen to focus on autobiographical writings by Black women for a number of reasons. One of the most obvious is that I see myself in the stories that they tell. My blackness and my womanness are inextricable from one another. But beyond those two identities, as Angela Davis argues, we are challenged with not only "understanding the complex ways race, class, gender, sexuality, nation, and ability are intertwined—but also how we move beyond these categories to understand the interrelationships of ideas and processes that seem to be separate and unrelated."[19] Separation— or rather, the illusion of separation from one's self, one's community, the environment, the Other, and Spirit—is how white supremacy works.

My identity as a Black cisgender heterosexual woman impacts how I experience the world on a daily basis.[20] It sometimes means that I am granted access to places that others who inhabit different bodies would not be welcome. Other times, often for reasons of safety, it means that places that I would like to venture are beyond my reach. I am a child of the US, born to parents of the diaspora and with siblings and a son of my own; this body that I inhabit helps shape my worldview, biases, acceptances, curiosities, inclinations, aversions, fears, and strengths. In addition, as someone who is a spiritual seeker, I, like these women, have found myself in many a "strange" setting. As someone who has experienced the transformative power of Buddhism, I am curious about the experience of others who look like me. As the Buddhist scholar Marianne Dresser notes in her introduction to *Buddhist Women on the Edge*, the number of books by women in the Buddhist tradition has increased substantially since she began studying.[21] Even so, a rich diversity of voices remains hidden behind the veil of tales "too terrible to relate."

In invoking tales "too terrible to relate," I uplift not only the Black autobiographical tradition but also the contemporary relevance of the phrase to describe the writings of the women I explore, several of which reveal experiences of not only race-based but also gender-related and sexual violence. It should not be glossed over that four of these six women include experiences of sexual assault in their narratives. While reading about the assaults was difficult, it also provided an opening for the surfacing of my own long-suppressed memories of sexual assaults, three by older males in my family and one by a religious leader. As these women's testimonies have given me the courage to face and embrace what were passed on to me as demons, I hope that this text will give those who read it the strength and courage to do the same in their own time.

Most importantly, I hope that my work honors the gift that these women are. I have undertaken it from what I believe is our shared position that, as the Combahee River Collective so eloquently asserted in their statement, "If Black women are free, it would mean that everyone else would have to be free since our freedom would necessitate the destruction of all the systems of oppression."[22]

Out of One, Many

In the tradition of those who have done so since the time of slavery, Black women who publish their autobiographies tell their stories not only to express their personal experience of suffering and triumph but also, and just as importantly, to help secure the freedom of those held in bondage. Although today we may not toil under the weight of physical chains, the vast majority of us feel imprisoned by our embodiments in a white-male-dominated society that is built on the illusion/delusion of separation. We struggle with the exploitation and oppression that is underpinned by implied and enacted violence. Consequently, as DaRa Williams observes, "Black folk continue to be enslaved in our minds." Her work, like that of the women in this project, is to "help free Black people from [the] chains."[23] The message of freedom no longer needs to be filtered through the editorial pens of well-meaning abolitionists. Helping secure the freedom of those of us held in bondage contemporarily means directly giving us the tools to wake up to our bondage. This is exactly what the women of this project do. Using their words and their bodies, they advocate for our collective freedom. We need only pick up the book and, as Rev. angel says, join the conversation. Part of these women's activism lies in insisting on taking account of and for their physical bodies. I see them as working from a place of fierce love for themselves and for others. I read their work through the lens of love as well as through a Black feminist/womanist sensibility and the African American autobiographical tradition. By doing so, I highlight the value of autobiography as a tool for personal and collective liberation.

CONCLUSION

The women whose work I have explored in this project were born at different times and hail from places all around the US: Jan Willis from Jim Crow Alabama, bell hooks from Jim Crow Kentucky, and Osho Zenju from California but with direct knowledge, through her family system, of Jim Crow Louisiana. Rev. angel comes from a working-class background in New York; Spring Washam is biracial from California; and Faith Adiele, biracial from rural Washington State. They are testaments to the truth of the myriad ways that Black people have sought to live free in a land that tries on a daily basis to have us, in Rev. angel's words, "small ourselves down," often under threat of death.[1] They are revolutionaries in their own right.

These women—and thousands of others like them, named and unnamed—are much more than part of the "new face" of Buddhism in the West, to reference a controversial 2016 cover headline from *Lion's Roar* magazine.[2] They are changing the entire body of Buddhism from the inside. They are fearlessly following the dharma path and the teachings of the Buddha, a social revolutionary, to interrogate the systems that keep us from becoming ourselves. Some of them do so by combining their traditional African American Christian heritage with that of their Buddhist practice. Others seek out indigenous wisdom teachings to help inform their application of the dharma to contemporary spiritual blockages. Their willingness to share their personal stories in the form of autobiography and memoir is at once an expression of their uniqueness and an outgrowth of the African American tradition of using autobiography to "lift as we climb."

As Buddhists from marginalized communities, they have all faced implicit and explicit challenges to their qualifications to teach. However, these women stand firm in their mastery of the Buddha's teachings, and they do what people of African descent have done for hundreds of years: they take the teachings that have come to them and use them, again in Rev. angel's words, to "express themselves differently and uniquely through their black bodies, minds, through black hearts, through black voices. . . . They're always going to speak into liberation."[3]

As several Buddhist scholars—Jan Willis and Charles Johnson, for example—and lay Buddhists, including Alice Walker, have noted, the Buddha's teachings offer a viable pathway to the end of the particular kinds of suffering that African Americans experience. Black women have an added layer of suffering that is rooted in slavery and its legacy. Rev. angel reminds us that

> we have been taught, especially as black women, to use anger
> as a decoy from the suffering we experience because it was too
> dangerous to feel our pain. There was too much of it. For so
> long having our babies taken away from us, having our hus-
> bands and children and sons and nephews and parents taken
> away from us. And so anger and stoicism became a proxy for
> our suffering because if someone saw you suffering they would
> take advantage of it.[4]

This, sadly, is still true.

But Black women's suffering is not our own, alone. Rather, it is shared by our communities. As contemporary Black women, the

authors of the works that I have explored operate from a deep awareness not only of this history but also of a time before it, which gives
them access to ancestrally rooted teachings. They bring an African
diasporic worldview to their approach to Buddhism, as well as a clarity
that their personal liberation is inextricable from that of the collective.

Buddhists of color are gaining traction in the wider Western Buddhist convert tradition. This is evidenced by the number of articles
and books that in the past six years have been published about their
presence in the sangha, both as practitioners and as teachers. It is also
evidenced by the swell of meditation retreats for people of color. Such
meditation retreats honor the African American Buddhist imperative
to speak into liberation personally and politically. In such spaces—sanctuaries, if you will—Black people are able to meditate on our suffering,
recognize and be willing to touch it. Having access to such sanctuaries,
Rev. angel says, "paradoxically incites black people's clarity of the right
and entitlement to liberation," a point most of us don't get to "because
we're trying to avoid our suffering." However, she counsels us, if we go
into our suffering, rest in the truth and knowledge of how consuming
it is, then we know that anything that gives us relief from that suffering is ours and we have to go for it.[5] This is the kind of liberation that
the different lineages of Buddhism and meditation offer to the African
American soul that is tender from living in a country where the Black
body is constantly under assault.

The face and body of Buddhism *is* changing, even if those in positions
of what we commonly think of as power[6] do not see it. It is glimpsed
in the way that, quiet as it's kept, Black Buddhists are sharing the
dharma through their particular lenses in the many online webinars
that, with the arrival of COVID-19, have begun leveling the access
field. This includes the African American Wisdom Summit and more
recently The Afrikan Wisdom Summit. It is in the way that Black
Buddhists have brought a different spiritual perspective to the Black

Lives Matter movement. It is in the arrival of two BIPOC-centered meditation apps: *Shine*, which is founded and run by women of color, and *Liberate*. In these ways and many more, Black Buddhists are spreading the revolution one breath at a time.

Black women are leading the way. Consider, for example, that the 2019 gathering of Black Buddhists at Spirit Rock, and which featured a dharma talk by Angela Davis, was organized by four Black women: Noliwe Alexander, Myokei Caine-Barrett, Konda Mason, and Rev. angel. Also consider that the first collection of writings of Black Buddhists, *Black and Buddhist*, was edited by Pamela Ayo Yetunde and Cheryl Giles, two prominent Buddhist scholars. They also organized, in collaboration with Shambhala Publications and the Awake Network, the Black and Buddhist Summit, which brought several of the contributors together in conversation. Consider also that several of the most recent additions to the corpus of publications on Buddhism and the Black experience have been written or edited by Black women. As their numbers grow, we can be certain that many more autobiographies and memoirs will be added to the store of wisdom and inspiration from which we can draw on our own paths to awakening.

As I finished up an early draft of this manuscript, Tina Turner, a foremother in the Black Buddhist tradition as a Soka Gakkai adherent, published her own memoir, *Happiness Becomes You: A Guide to Changing Your Life for Good*, centered on her coming to the dharma. Like several of the women whose work I discuss in this project, Turner's memoir weaves together her personal story with dharma principles and lessons to act as a guide to others who are suffering. As such, echoing the advice of the Buddha, *Ehi passiko* (See for yourself), she frequently addresses the reader directly, encouraging them to try chanting for themselves. Turner could be said to be the one who started it all, inspiring thousands of African American people to take up chanting after they saw how it helped her free herself from an abusive relationship that was on course to lead her to an early grave. She lived to be over eighty years old after her second husband gifted her one of his kidneys!

This text is an offering—an invitation to join in the liberatory work that these women have undertaken. They are the inheritors not only of countless other African diasporic spiritual warriors but also of the Buddha as a social revolutionary. In the tradition of these women, there is a new generation taking root, changing and transforming Buddhism to meet the needs of our times—which, as Thich Nhat Hanh counseled, is necessary if the Buddha's teachings are to stay healthy and vibrant.[7]

Suggested Further Reading

In addition to the works that I have explored in these pages, there exists a wide range of offerings from Black Buddhists. They include nonfiction works (and, in the case of Charles Johnson, a mixture of nonfiction and fiction works) that either delineate the author's Buddhist path or utilize a Buddhist lens through which to explore their chosen subject. Sometimes they do both. Below is a selection of a few I have spent some time with. I beg the reader's forgiveness for any harm caused by inadvertent omissions.

Ferguson, Gaylon. *Natural Wakefulness: Discovering the Wisdom We Were Born With*. Boulder: Shambhala Publications, 2009.

——. *Natural Bravery: Fear and Fearlessness as a Direct Path of Awakening*. Boulder: Shambhala Publications, 2016.

Johnson, Charles—nonfiction:

——. *Being and Race: Black Writing Since 1970*. Bloomington: Indiana University Press, 1988.

——. *Taming the Ox: Buddhist Stories and Reflections on Politics, Race, Culture, and Spiritual Practice*. Boston: Shambhala Publications, 2014.

——. *Turning the Wheel: Essays on Buddhism and Writing*. New York: Scribner, 2007.

Johnson, Charles—fiction:

Johnson, Charles, and Steven Barnes. *The Eightfold Path.* New York: Abrams ComicArts, 2022.

Johnson, Charles. *All Your Racial Problems Will Soon End: Cartoons of Charles Johnson.* New York: New York Review Comics, 2022.

——. *Dr. King's Refrigerator and Other Bedtime Stories.* New York: Scribner, 2005.

——. *Faith and the Good Thing.* New York: Scribner, 2001

——. *Middle Passage.* New York: Scribner, 1998.

——. *Nighthawks: Stories.* New York: Scribner, 2019.

——. *Oxherding Tale.* New York: Scribner, 2005.

Kakuyo, Alex. *Perfectly Ordinary: Buddhist Teachings for Everyday Life.* Independently Published, 2020.

King, Ruth. *Healing Rage: Women Making Inner Peace Possible.* New York: Gotham Books, 2007.

——. *Mindful of Race: Transforming Racism from the Inside Out.* Boulder: Sounds True, 2018.

Lingo, Kaira Jewel. *We Were Made for These Times: Ten Lessons for Moving Through Change, Loss, and Disruption.* Berkeley: Parallax Press, 2021.

Magee, Rhonda. *The Inner Work of Racial Justice: Healing Ourselves and Transforming Our Communities Through Mindfulness.* New York: TarcherPerigee, 2019.

Mason-John, Valerie, ed. *Afrikan Wisdom: New Voices Talk Black Liberation, Buddhism, and Beyond.* Berkeley: North Atlantic Books, 2021.

——. *Detox Your Heart: Meditation for Healing Emotional Trauma.* Somerville, MA: Wisdom Publications, 2017.

——. *Eight Step Recovery: Using the Buddha's Teachings to Overcome Addiction.* Somerville, MA: Wisdom Publications, 2014.

Masters, Jay Jarvis. *Finding Freedom: How Death Row Broke and Opened My Heart.* Boulder: Shambhala Publications, 2020.

——. *Finding Freedom: Writings from Death Row.* Junction City, CA: Padma Publishing, 1997.

——. *That Bird Has My Wings: The Autobiography of an Innocent Man on Death Row.* New York: HarperOne, 2009.

Mumford, George. *Unlocked: Embrace Your Greatness, Find the Flow, Discover Success.* New York: HarperOne, 2023.

Owens, Lama Rod. *Love and Rage: The Path of Liberation through Anger.* Berkeley: North Atlantic Books, 2020.

Rangdröl, Lama Choyin. *Black Buddha: Changing the Face of American Buddhism.* San Rafael, CA: Rainbowdharma, 2006.

Selassie, Sebene. *You Belong: A Call for Connection.* New York: HarperOne, 2020.

Steele, Ralph. *Tending the Fire: Through War and the Path of Meditation.* Honolulu: Sacred Life Publishers, 2004.

Thurman, Howard. *Meditations of the Heart.* New York: Beacon Press, 1999.

Turner, Tina. *Happiness Becomes You: A Guide to Changing Your Life for Good.* New York: Atria Books, 2020.

Vesely-Flad, Rima. *Black Buddhists and the Black Radical Tradition: The Practice of Stillness in the Movement for Liberation.* New York: New York University Press, 2022

Walker, Alice. *The Cushion in the Road: Meditation and Wandering as the Whole World Awakens to Being in Harm's Way.* New York: The New Press, 2014.

Ward, Larry. *America's Racial Karma: An Invitation to Heal.* Berkeley: Parallax Press, 2020.

Yetunde, Pamela Ayo. *Buddhist-Christian Dialogue, U.S. Law, and Womanist Theology for Transgender Spiritual Care.* Cham, Switzerland: Palgrave Pivot, MacMillan, 2020.

———. *Casting Indra's Net: Fostering Spiritual Kinship and Community—Wisdom from Buddhism, Christianity, Judaism, Hinduism, and More.* Boulder: Shambhala, 2023.

———. *Object Relations, Buddhism, and Relationality in Womanist Practical Theology.* Cham, Switzerland: Palgrave Pivot, MacMillan, 2018.

Yetunde, Pamela Ayo, and Cheryl Giles, eds. *Black and Buddhist: What Buddhism Can Teach Us about Race, Resilience, Transformation, and Freedom.* Boulder: Shambhala Publications, 2020.

Notes

Preface

1. A sampling of stories similar to mine include Spring Washam's in *A Fierce Heart: Finding Strength, Courage, and Wisdom in Any Moment* (Carlsbad, CA: Hay House, 2019); Rev. angel Kyodo williams's that she recounts in *Being Black: Zen and the Art of Living with Fearlessness and Grace* (New York: Viking Compass, 2000) and in her interview with Rima Vesely-Flad in "Racism and Anatta: Black Buddhists, Embodiment, and Interpretations of Non-Self," in *Buddhism and Whiteness: Critical Reflections*, ed. George Yancy and Emily McRae (Lanham, MD: Lexington Books, 2019), 80. Rev. Zenju Earthlyn Manuel also discusses her experience in predominantly white sanghas in *The Way of Tenderness: Awakening through Race, Sexuality, and Gender* (Somerville, MA: Wisdom Publications, 2015), 7; and Ann Gleig recounts the traumatic experience of Travis Spencer, who visited one of Tara Brach's popular classes at Insight Meditation Center of Washington, DC. Gleig's writing also attends to the work that is being done to transform the community after Spencer reached out to Brach. See: *American Dharma: Buddhism Beyond Modernity* (New Haven, CT: Yale University Press, 2019), 142–52.
2. There very well may have been other BIPOC practitioners who felt the way I did, but in the few conversations I had with those who would make eye contact, I did not get the sense that that was true.
3. "5 Responses to the Awkwardly Titled 'New Face of Buddhism,'" *Buddhist Peace Fellowship*, January 27, 2016, https://www.bpf.org/blog/5-responses-to-the-new-face-of-buddhism.

4. I am aware of the esoteric forms of Buddhism in which dreadlocks are worn.

Introduction: How We Do

1. J. Sunara Sasser, "Why Are There So Many Black Buddhists?" *Tricycle: The Buddhist Review*, October 16, 2018, https://tricycle.org/article /black-buddhists.
2. Sasser, "Why Are There So Many Black Buddhists?"
3. Rev. Zenju Earthlyn Manuel, *Tell Me Something about Buddhism: Questions and Answers for the Curious Beginner* (Charlottesville, NC: Hampton Roads, 2011), 27.
4. Manuel, *Tell Me Something about Buddhism*, 27.
5. Manuel, *Tell Me Something about Buddhism*, 28.
6. Manuel, *Tell Me Something about Buddhism*, 28.
7. Lilly Greenblatt, "The Absolute Beauty of Blackness: Konda Mason on The Gathering II," *Lion's Roar*, November 19, 2019, lionsroar.com /the-absolute-beauty-of-blackness-konda-mason-on-the-gathering-ii.
8. The word *ubuntu* seems to have originated among the Zimbabwean people and spread to South Africa, the country with which it is often associated. Steve Paulson, "'I Am Because We Are': The African Philosophy of Ubuntu," To the Best of Our Knowledge, September 30, 2020, ttbook.org/interview/i-am-because-we-are-african-philosophy-ubuntu.
9. Quoted in Paulson, "'I Am Because We Are.'"
10. I am grateful to Konda Mason, who made this important connection during her dharma talk at the Spirit Rock online BIPOC sangha gathering on July 12, 2020.

Chapter One: Jan Willis—Carrying On the Tradition

1. Dis/comfort because, although familiar, she experiences an uneasiness that pushes her out of that familiarity.
2. Emily Cohen, "Interview with Jan Willis," *Journal of Feminist Studies in Religion* 33, no. 2 (Fall 2017): 128.
3. Cohen, "Interview with Jan Willis," 129.
4. Courtney Potts, "Tibetan Buddhist Scholar Jan Willis Grew Up Baptist

in the U.S. South but Began Her Spiritual Journey at Cornell," *Cornell Chronicle*, January 6, 2006, https://news.cornell.edu/stories/2006/01/tibetan-buddhist-scholar-jan-willis-began-spiritual-journey-cornell.

5. Jan Willis, *Dreaming Me: Black, Baptist, and Buddhist—One Woman's Spiritual Journey* (Somerville, MA: Wisdom Publications, 2008), 42.

6. Willis italicizes "children" in her text to bring attention to the early indoctrination of white supremacy that took place in her community. Willis, *Dreaming Me*, 76.

7. Willis, *Dreaming Me*, 77.

8. Potts, "Tibetan Buddhist Scholar Jan Willis."

9. Willis, *Dreaming Me*, 105.

10. Willis, *Dreaming Me*, 115, 116.

11. Willis, *Dreaming Me*, 141.

12. Willis, *Dreaming Me*, 221.

13. I am grateful to Pam Kingsbury, who organized Willis's biography for *Encyclopedia of Alabama*: http://encyclopediaofalabama.org/article/h-3488.

14. Willis, *Dreaming Me*, 11.

15. Willis, *Dreaming Me*, 7–8.

16. William David Hart, *Black Religion: Malcolm X, Julius Lester, and Jan Willis* (New York: Palgrave Macmillan, 2008), 156.

17. Willis, *Dreaming Me*, 8.

18. Combahee River Collective, in *How We Get Free: Black Feminism and the* Combahee River Collective, ed. Keeanga-Yamahtta Taylor (Chicago: Haymarket Books, 2017), 19. Danielle L. McGuire does an excellent job of exploring the use of rape as a weapon of political oppression in *At the Dark End of the Street: Black Women, Rape, and Resistance—a New History of the Civil Rights Movement from Rosa Parks to the Rise of Black Power* (New York: Vintage Books, 2010).

19. See, for example, Olga Khazan, "Inherited Trauma Shapes Your Health," *The Atlantic*, October 16, 2018, https://www.theatlantic.com/health/archive/2018/10/trauma-inherited-generations/573055/; and Olga Khazan, "Being Black in America Can be Hazardous to Your Health," *The Atlantic*, July/August 2018, https://www.theatlantic.com/magazine/archive/2018/07/being-black-in-america-can-be-hazardous-to-your-health/561740.

20. Ruth King, *Mindful of Race: Transforming Racism from the Inside Out* (Boulder, CO: Sounds True, 2018), 24.

21. I'm alluding here to Bessel van der Kolk, *The Body Keeps the Score: Brain, Mind, and Body in the Healing of Trauma* (New York: Penguin, 2014).

22. Willis, *Dreaming Me*, 13.

23. Willis, *Dreaming Me*, 13–14, emphasis added.

24. Willis, *Dreaming Me*, 14.

25. Cohen, "Interview with Jan Willis," 130.

26. Hart, *Black Religion*, 168.

27. Willis, *Dreaming Me*, 20.

28. J. Brooks Bouson, *Quiet As It's Kept: Shame, Trauma, and Race in the Novels of Toni Morrison* (Albany: State University of New York Press, 2000), 4.

29. Willis, *Dreaming Me*, 20.

30. Willis, *Dreaming Me*, 59.

31. Willis, *Dreaming Me*, 61.

32. Willis, *Dreaming Me*, 61.

33. See Sarah A. Suh, "'We Interrupt Your Regularly Scheduled Programming to Bring You This Very Important Public Service Announcement . . .' aka Buddhism as Usual in the Academy," in *Buddhism and Whiteness: Critical Reflections*, ed. George Yancy and Emily McRae (Lanham, MD: Lexington Books, 2019), 13; Melissa Harris-Perry, *Sister Citizen: Shame, Stereotypes, and Black Women in America* (New Haven, CT: Yale University Press, 2011).

34. Suh, "'We Interrupt Your Regularly Scheduled Programming,'" 12.

35. Willis, *Dreaming Me*, 35.

36. Willis, *Dreaming Me*, 41.

37. Willis, *Dreaming Me*, 41.

38. Willis, *Dreaming Me*, 41.

39. Willis, *Dreaming Me*, 56.

40. Willis, *Dreaming Me*, 57.

41. Willis, *Dreaming Me*, 45–46.

42. *Sèvitè* are Vodou practitioners. Sèvitè do not say they practice Vodou. Rather, they say they "serve the *lwa*," spirits in the Vodou pantheon. Lwa are said to be riding their horses when they possess their sèvitè.

43. Willis, *Dreaming Me*, 187.
44. Willis, *Dreaming Me*, 296–97.
45. Willis, *Dreaming Me*, 297.
46. Willis, *Dreaming Me*, 301.
47. Willis, *Dreaming Me*, 255.
48. Willis, *Dreaming Me*, 33.
49. Potts, "Tibetan Buddhist Scholar Jan Willis."
50. Frederick Douglass, *Narrative of the Life of Frederick Douglass* (Mineola, NY: Dover Publication, 1995), 19.
51. Willis, *Dreaming Me*, 255.
52. Douglass, *Narrative of the Life of Frederick Douglass*, 22.
53. Meta Y. Harris, "Black Women Writing Autobiography: Autobiography in Multicultural Education," in *Narrative and Experience in Multicultural Education*, ed. Joan Phillion, Ming Fang He, and F. Michael Connelly (New York: Sage Publications, 2005), 36.
54. Willis, *Dreaming Me*, 103.
55. Willis, *Dreaming Me*, 108–9.
56. Willis, *Dreaming Me*, 108.
57. Jan Willis, "We Cry Out for Justice" *Lion's Roar*, May 29, 2020.
58. Willis, "We Cry Out for Justice."
59. Willis, "We Cry Out for Justice."
60. Willis, *Dreaming Me*, 154.
61. "A Joint Biography of Lama Yeshe and Lama Zopa Rinpoche," FPMT, accessed December 1, 2022, https://fpmt.org/teachers/yeshe/jointbio/.
62. Willis, *Dreaming Me*, 165.
63. Willis, *Dreaming Me*, 163.
64. Willis, *Dreaming Me*, 174.
65. Willis, *Dreaming Me*, 176.
66. Willis, *Dreaming Me*, 176.
67. Willis, *Dreaming Me*, 240.
68. Willis, *Dreaming Me*, 248.
69. Willis, *Dreaming Me*, 254.
70. Willis, *Dreaming Me*, 265.
71. Willis, *Dreaming Me*, 12; emphasis in original.
72. Willis, *Dreaming Me*, 275.

73. Willis, *Dreaming Me*, 275. I, too, know what it feels like to be misread. In my younger years I was often asked if I was "part white," was called "*blan*" when I traveled in Haiti and "*obruni*" the whole time I was in Ghana. Each of these labels was like a thousand cuts to my soul.

74. Martin King Luther King Jr., "Loving Your Enemies," in *Strength to Love* (New York: Harper and Row Publishers, 1963), 38.

75. Willis, *Dreaming Me*, 279.

76. Willis emphasizes "confidence" in the essay. Jan Willis, "Buddhism and Race: An African-American Baptist-Buddhist Perspective," in *Buddhist Women on the Edge: Contemporary Perspectives from the Western Frontier*, ed. Marianne Dresser (Berkeley, CA: North Atlantic Books, 1996), 86.

77. Willis, *Dreaming Me*, 61.

78. Willis, *Dreaming Me*, 307.

79. Willis, *Dreaming Me*, 308.

80. Willis, *Dreaming Me*, 321.

81. Willis, *Dreaming Me*, 322.

82. Willis, *Dreaming Me*, 323–24.

83. Willis, *Dreaming Me*, 344–45.

84. Willis, *Dreaming Me*, 345.

85. Willis's text was originally published by Riverhead Press in 2001 as *Dreaming Me: An African American Woman's Spiritual Journey*. It was reissued under its current title by Wisdom Publications in 2008. We may note that the new title is much more descriptive, setting Willis apart from earlier examples of African American women's spiritual autobiography, which were usually focused on Christian awakening.

86. Kazuaki Tanahashi, ed., *Treasury of the True Dharma Eye: Zen Master Dogen's Shobo Genzo* (Boulder: Shambhala Publications, 2010), 30.

87. Zenju Earthlyn Manuel, *The Way of Tenderness: Awakening through Race, Sexuality, and Gender* (Somerville, MA: Wisdom Publications, 2015), 18.

88. Stephen Butterfield, *Black Autobiography in America* (Amherst: University of Massachusetts Press, 1974), 1.

89. Bettina Aptheker, afterword to *Dreaming Me: Black, Baptist, and*

Buddhist—One Woman's Spiritual Journey, by Jan Willis (Somerville, MA: Wisdom Publications, 2008), 250.

90. Willis, *Dreaming Me*, 323.

Chapter Two: bell hooks—Being Love, Finding Home

1. bell hooks, *Belonging: A Culture of Place* (New York: Routledge, 2009), 6.
2. bell hooks, *All about Love: New Visions* (New York: William Morrow, 2001), 4.
3. bell hooks, "Divine Inspiration: Writing and Spirituality," in *Remembered Rapture: The Writer at Work* (New York: Henry Holt, 1999), 125.
4. Roshi Merle Kodo Boyd, "A Child of the South in Long Black Robes," in *Dharma, Color, and Culture*, ed. Hilda Gutiérez Baldoquin (Berkeley, CA: Parallax Press, 2004), 101–2.
5. bell hooks, "A Life in the Spirit: Faith, Writing, and Intellectual Work," in *Remembered Rapture: The Writer at Work* (New York: Henry Holt, 1999), 122.
6. hooks, "A Life in the Spirit: Faith, Writing, and Intellectual Work," 122.
7. See George Yancy and bell hooks, "bell hooks: Buddhism, the Beats, and Loving Blackness," *New York Times*, December 10, 2015, https:// opinionator.blogs.nytimes.com/2015/12/10/bell-hooks-buddhism -the-beats-and-loving-blackness.
8. Carol J. Moeller, "'bell hooks Made Me a Buddhist': Liberatory Cross-Cultural Learning—or Is This Just Another Case of How White People Steal Everything," in *Buddhism and Whiteness: Critical Reflections* (2019): 185.
9. Pamela Ayo Yetunde, "Bowing to and for Professor bell hooks," in "Yes, She Was a Powerful Woman! A Dedication to bell hooks," *Lion's Roar*, December 24, 2021, https://www.lionsroar.com/yes-she-was -a-powerful-woman-a-dedication-to-bell-hooks.
10. hooks, *Belonging*, 6.
11. bell hooks, *Teaching to Transgress: Education as the Practice of Freedom* (New York: Routledge, 1994), 2.
12. hooks, *Belonging*, 7.
13. I am aware of the irony of beginning a discussion of the writings of

someone who wanted to foreground their work rather than their personal story with her personal story. However, I do so as a way of orienting the reader and providing a context for the liberatory work that hooks was committed to.

14. "Remembering bell hooks and Her Critique of 'Imperialist White Supremacist Heteropatriarchy'" *Democracy Now!* YouTube video, 16:01, December 17, 2021, https://www.youtube.com/watch ?v=DkJKJZU7xXU.

15. See her interview with Sharon Salzberg, "Real Love Series: bell hooks," episode 54, *Metta Hour Podcast*, 43:07, May 22, 2017, https://www.sharonsalzberg.com/metta-hour-podcast-episode-54-real-love-series-bell-hooks.

16. "Get to Know bell hooks," Berea College, accessed July 11, 2022, https://www.berea.edu/bhc/about-bell.

17. bell hooks, "Writing Autobiography," in *Women, Autobiography, Theory: A Reader*, ed. Sidonie Smith and Julia Watson (Madison: University of Wisconsin Press, 1998), 431.

18. bell hooks, foreword to *Bone Black: Memories of Girlhood* (New York: Henry Holt, 1996), xiv.

19. hooks, "Writing Autobiography," 430.

20. hooks, *Belonging*, 18.

21. hooks, *Belonging*, 18.

22. hooks, *Bone Black*, 15.

23. hooks, *Bone Black*, 101.

24. hooks, *Bone Black*, 102.

25. bell hooks, *Feminism Is for Everybody: Passionate Politics* (Boston: South End Press, 2000), 73.

26. hooks, *Feminism Is for Everybody*, 77.

27. "BioMyth," accessed April 12, 2023, biomyth.wordpress.com/about.

28. hooks, "Writing Autobiography," 432.

29. hooks, "Writing Autobiography," 432.

30. hooks, "Writing Autobiography," 429.

31. hooks, "Writing Autobiography," 429.

32. hooks, "Writing Autobiography," 432.

33. See, for example, "Morrison White Gaze," YouTube video, 3:05, October 6, 2016, https://www.youtube.com/watch?v=SHHHL31bFPA.

34. hooks, *Bone Black*, 32.
35. hooks, *Belonging*, 70.
36. hooks, *Belonging*, 71.
37. hooks, *Bone Black*, 165.
38. hooks, *Belonging*, 71.
39. Toni Morrison, "The Site of Memory," in *Inventing the Truth: The Art und Craft of Memoir*, 2nd ed., ed. William Zinsser (Boston: Houghton Mifflin, 1995), 91.
40. Morrison's fiction, though distinct from autobiographical writing, embraces certain autobiographical strategies. See Toni Morrison, "The Site of Memory," 85–102.
41. Morrison, "Site of Memory," 92.
42. hooks, "Writing Autobiography," 430.
43. hooks, "Writing Autobiography," 431.
44. hooks, "Writing Autobiography," 430.
45. hooks, *Belonging*, 107.
46. hooks, *Bone Black*, 21.
47. hooks, *Bone Black*, 19–21.
48. hooks, *Bone Black*, 21.
49. hooks, *Belonging*, 145.
50. hooks, *Belonging*, 145.
51. Jeanne Braham, *Crucial Conversations: Interpreting Contemporary Literary Autobiographies by Women* (New York: Teachers College Press, 1995), 37–38.
52. hooks, "Writing Autobiography," 432.
53. hooks, *All about Love*, xxiii.
54. hooks, *All about Love*, xxiii, xxiv.
55. hooks, *All about Love*, xxiv.
56. hooks, *All about Love*, ix.
57. hooks, *All about Love*, x.
58. hooks, *Belonging*, 215.
59. hooks, "Real Love Series: bell hooks."
60. In fact, it is not only Buddhism that informs her writing. She has come to theorize about love through her spiritual practices that include Christianity, Sufism, and Buddhism, all of which inform her worldview. She has also stated that Lorraine Hansberry's asking

whether Black people are loving people or are we too damaged, too traumatized, got her to start thinking critically about Black people and love. See "Black Female Voices: Who Is Listening: A Public Dialogue Between bell hooks and Melissa Harris-Perry," November 8, 2013, Amara.org, video, 1:36:19, https://amara.org/videos/Pcjj1Z3UDATx /en/606709.

61. hooks, "Real Love Series: bell hooks."
62. hooks, *All about Love*, xxviii–xxvix.
63. hooks, "Waking Up to Racism: Dharma, Diversity, and Race," *Tricycle: The Buddhist Review* (Fall 1994): 43.
64. hooks, "Waking Up to Racism," 42.
65. hooks, "Waking Up to Racism," 42.
66. hooks, "Waking Up to Racism," 42.
67. hooks, "Waking Up to Racism," 42.
68. Jan Willis, "Yes, We're Buddhists Too!" *Buddhist-Christian Studies* 32 (2012): 40.
69. hooks, "Waking Up to Racism," 42. Lama Choyin Rangdröl makes a similar point in *Black Buddha*, saying, "In the West, African Americans in Buddhism have not organically emerged." He discusses a 2000 report about a prominent African American pastor in San Francisco stating that those who leave the Black Church to explore Eastern spirituality are traitors. He remarks that the pastor's remarks are not unique; rather "African Americans often view black Buddhists as defectors." *Black Buddha: Changing the Face of American Buddhism* (San Rafael, CA: Rainbowdharma, 2006), 14–15. One can also see this sentiment in the YouTube channel *Black People Don't Practice Buddhism*, which has several episodes featuring Black people refuting this misconception.
70. hooks, "Waking Up to Racism," 42.
71. hooks, "Waking Up to Racism," 42.
72. Willis, "Buddhism and Race: An African-American Baptist-Buddhist Perspective," in *Buddhist Women on the Edge: Contemporary Perspectives from the Western Frontier*, ed. Marianne Dresser (Berkeley, CA: North Atlantic Books, 1996), 85. Emphasis in original.
73. Willis, "Yes, We're Buddhists Too!" 41.

74. Willis, "Buddhism and Race," 85. Lama Rangdröl also makes a case for African Americans' embrace of Buddhism beginning with the fact that, unlike Christianity, "no African American in the history of our nation can say that they were raped, beaten, whipped, sold, lynched or enslaved by a Buddhist." *Black Buddha*, 7–8. He also points to several revered people in the Black community, like Rev. King, Malcolm X, and John Coltrane—and we may add, Alice Coltrane—who embraced Eastern traditions and used those teachings to "make tremendous contributions to America and humanity." *Black Buddha*, 8.

75. hooks, "Contemplation and Transformation," in *Buddhist Women on the Edge: Contemporary Perspectives from the Western Frontier*, ed. Marianne Dresser (Berkeley, CA: North Atlantic Books, 1996), 291.

76. This is a point that Resmaa Menakem makes in *My Grandmother's Hands: Racialized Trauma and the Pathway to Mending Our Hearts and Bodies* (Las Vegas: Central Recovery Press, 2017), and elsewhere. He posits that white people are also traumatized and suffer from low self-esteem because of not only the trauma their ancestors experienced before they made their way to the "New World" but also because of the trauma that they inflict on others through white supremacy.

77. hooks, "Waking Up to Racism," 44.

78. hooks, "Waking Up to Racism," 44.

79. hooks is quoting from the biblical Book of Psalms, "Waking Up to Racism," 45.

80. hooks, "Waking Up to Racism," 45.

81. hooks, "Waking Up to Racism," 42.

82. Gesshin Greenwood, "Will the Real Buddhist Please Stand Up?" *That's So Zen* blog, August 25, 2015. Rev. Greenwood has since taken the blog down. Email communication, 3/20/2023.

83. Greenwood, "Will the Real Buddhist Please Stand Up?"

84. Greenwood, "Will the Real Buddhist Please Stand Up?"

85. hooks, "Waking Up to Racism," 42.

86. hooks, *Belonging*, 6.

87. hooks, *Belonging*, 117.

Chapter Three: Osho Zenju Earthlyn Manuel— Embodying the Self, Walking with the Ancestors

1. Osho is the same honorific as Reverend, Sensei, Roshi. It means "teacher." I use "Rev. Zenju" and "Osho" interchangeably in the text.
2. See "Breaths," https://www.flashlyrics.com/lyrics/sweet-honey-in-the-rock/breaths-70.
3. "About," Zenju Earthlyn Manuel, accessed July 11, 2022, http://zenju.org/about.
4. Zenju Earthlyn Manuel, *Sanctuary: A Meditation on Home, Homelessness, and Belonging* (Somerville, MA: Wisdom Publications, 2018), 82.
5. She adds parenthetically that everything else for her is of a worldly nature. Zenju Earthlyn Manuel (website), accessed June 16, 2022, https://zenju.org.
6. Interviewed on a Mind and Life Institute podcast, she stated, "Social justice is spirituality and spirituality is social justice." "Zenju Earthlyn Manuel—Identity as Path," *Mind & Life*, November 5, 2021, 36:15, https://podcast.mindandlife.org/zenju-earthlyn-manuel.
7. Zenju Earthlyn Marselean Manuel, "Bearing Up in the Wild Winds," in *Dharma, Color, and Culture: New Voices in Western Buddhism*, ed. Hilda Gutiérrez Baldoquín (Berkeley, CA: Parallax Press, 2004), 42.
8. "About," Zenju Earthlyn Manuel (website), accessed July 15, 2020, http://zenju.org/about/.
9. She has participated in the Lakota sun dance for twenty years and in African traditions for about twenty years (more than the Dahomey ceremonies). Email communication Nov. 29, 2020.
10. They stopped the practice in 1989.
11. Zenju Earthlyn Manuel, *The Way of Tenderness: Awakening through Race, Sexuality, and Gender* (Somerville, MA: Wisdom Publications, 2015), 3.
12. "Zenju Earthlyn Manuel—Identity as Path."
13. Manuel, "Bearing Up in the Wild Winds," 39–40.
14. Manuel, "Bearing Up in the Wild Winds," 42.
15. I say "seeming" because I have no way of knowing what the therapist's experience with Rev. Zenju's story was.
16. Manuel, "Bearing Up in the Wild Winds," 40.

17. Manuel, "Bearing Up in the Wild Winds," 40.
18. Manuel, "Bearing Up in the Wild Winds," 41.
19. Manuel, "Bearing Up in the Wild Winds," 41.
20. Manuel, "Bearing Up in the Wild Winds," 42.
21. Resmaa Menakem, *My Grandmother's Hands: Racialized Trauma and the Pathway to Mending Our Hearts and Bodies* (Las Vegas: Central Recovery Press, 2017), 20.
22. Manuel, "Bearing Up in the Wild Winds," 39. Emphasis added.
23. Manuel, "Bearing Up in the Wild Winds," 41.
24. "Black Angel Cards: 36 Oracles and Messages for Divining Your Life," Zenju Earthlyn Manuel (website), June 27, 2020, http://zenju.org/black-angels-cards.
25. "*Zenju's Path* Trailer," YouTube video, 6:34, July 14, 2014, https://www.youtube.com/watch?v=0TSSenvjSIw.
26. "*Zenju's Path* Trailer."
27. "Black Angel Cards."
28. "*Zenju's Path* Trailer."
29. It was 2016 when I had my session. The oracle cards have been out of print since April 20, 2020.
30. Charles Johnson, foreword to *The Way of Tenderness: Awakening through Race, Sexuality, and Gender* (Somerville, MA: Wisdom Publications, 2015), x.
31. Johnson, foreword to *The Way of Tenderness*, x.
32. John S. Mbiti, *African Religions and Philosophy* (Boston: Heinemann, 1990), 88.
33. Mbiti, *African Religions and Philosophy*, 88.
34. Mbiti, *African Religions and Philosophy*, 88.
35. Manuel, *Black Angel Cards* booklet, n.p.
36. Manuel, *Black Angel Cards* booklet, n.p.
37. Manuel, *Black Angel Cards* booklet, n.p.
38. Manuel, *Black Angel Cards* booklet, n.p.
39. Manuel, "Bearing Up in the Wild Winds," 40.
40. Zenju Earthlyn Manuel, *Tell Me Something about Buddhism: Questions and Answers for the Curious Beginner* (Newburyport, MA: Hampton Roads, 2011), ix.
41. Manuel, *Tell Me Something about Buddhism*, 12.

42. Manuel, *Sanctuary*, 71.

43. Manuel, *Sanctuary*, 71.

44. Lama Choyin Rangdröl, *Black Buddha: Changing the Face of American Buddhism* (San Rafael, CA: Rainbowdharma, 2007), 1.

45. *Sakyadhita* means "Buddha's daughter" in Pali. Email communication with Osho Zenju, January 26, 2023.

46. Manuel, *Sanctuary*, 91.

47. I say "awakeness" rather than "awareness" to stress the centrality of being fully present to the sources and experience of suffering; not trying to dull, deflect, or dance around it.

48. Manuel, "What Does Buddhism Have to Do with Black People?" Zenju Earthlyn Manuel (website), accessed June 19, 2019, http://zenju.org/what-does-buddhism-have-to-do-with-black-people.

49. Toni Morrison, "Rootedness: The Ancestor as Foundation," in *Black Women Writers 1950–1980: A Critical Evaluation*, ed. Mari Evans (New York: Anchor Books, 1984), 342.

50. Tracy Jan and Jose A. Delreal, "Carson Compares Slaves to Immigrants Coming to a 'Land of Dreams and Opportunities,'" *Washington Post*, March 6, 2017, https://www.washingtonpost.com/news/wonk/wp/2017/03/06/carson-compares-slaves-to-immigrants-coming-to-a-land-of-dreams-and-opportunity/?utm_term=.479cb958acc5.

51. Manuel, *Sanctuary*, 5.

52. Johnson, foreword to *Way of Tenderness*, xii.

53. Manuel, *Way of Tenderness*, 6.

54. Manuel, *Way of Tenderness*, 8.

55. Manuel, *Way of Tenderness*, 7.

56. Manuel, *Way of Tenderness*, 7.

57. Manuel, *Way of Tenderness*, 25.

58. Manuel, *Way of Tenderness*, 17.

59. Manuel, *Way of Tenderness*, 16. Emphasis added.

60. Manuel, *Way of Tenderness*, 17. Emphasis added.

61. Manuel, *Sanctuary*, 58.

62. Manuel, *Sanctuary*, 58.

63. Manuel, *Way of Tenderness*, 26.

64. Manuel, *Way of Tenderness*, 28.

65. Zenju Earthlyn Manuel, "Sweeping My Heart," *Lion's Roar*, June 15, 2021, https://www.lionsroar.com/sweeping-my-heart.

66. Manuel, "Sweeping My Heart."

67. Manuel, "Sweeping My Heart."

68. Manuel, "Sweeping My Heart."

69. Manuel, "Sweeping My Heart."

70. Marian Wright Edelman, *The Measure of Our Success: A Letter to My Children and Yours* (Boston: Beacon Press, 2013), 15.

71. Manuel, "Sweeping My Heart."

72. Manuel, *Sanctuary*, 10.

73. Elizabeth J. West, *African Spirituality in Black Women's Fiction: Threaded Visions of Memory, Community, Nature, and Being* (Lanham, MD: Lexington Books, 2011), 1.

74. West, *African Spirituality in Black Women's Fiction*, 1.

75. Manuel, *Sanctuary*, 10.

76. A sangoma is a highly respected healer among the Zulu people of South Africa who diagnoses, prescribes, and often performs the rituals to heal a person physically, mentally, emotionally, or spiritually. *Encyclopaedia Britannica Online*, s.v. "sangoma," accessed December 15, 2022, https://www.britannica.com/science/sangoma.

77. Manuel, *Sanctuary*, 60. Manuel clarified several points about the vision quest in her email communication with me (November 29, 2020), saying, "I led the drum and songs and that is the tradition that the dancers gift their shawls to the lead drummer and singer. Homeland was Africa, not Lakota. My Native American background is the Opelousas Indians of Louisiana as my father was born there."

78. Kimberly Winston, "Black, Bisexual, Buddhist and Not Afraid to Embrace Who She Is." *Sojourners*, Religion News Service, August 4, 2015. https://sojo.net/articles/black-bisexual-buddhist-and-not-afraid-embrace-who-she.

79. West, *African Spirituality in Black Women's Fiction*, 1.

80. Winston, "Black, Bisexual, Buddhist and Not Afraid to Embrace Who She Is."

81. Winston, "Black, Bisexual, Buddhist and Not Afraid to Embrace Who She Is."

82. Manuel, *Way of Tenderness*, 17.

83. West, *African Spirituality in Black Women's Fiction*, 11.

84. West, *African Spirituality in Black Women's Fiction*, 11.

85. "Difference and Harmony: An Interview with Zenju Earthlyn Manuel," *Tricycle: The Buddhist Review*, November 8, 2011.

86. "Difference and Harmony."

87. "Difference and Harmony."

88. Zenju Earthlyn Manuel, "The Zen Mirror of Tokeiji," in *The Hidden Lamp: Stories from Twenty-Five Centuries of Awakened Women*, ed. Zenshin Florence Caplow and Reigetsu Susan Moon (Somerville, MA: Wisdom Publications, 2013), 129.

89. Manuel, "Zen Mirror of Tokeiji," 129.

90. Osho Zenju is one of the women Buddhist practitioners featured in the collection *The Hidden Lamp*. In her contribution, she offers insight into not only zazen (sitting meditation) but also the trial and potential triumph that the body represents. The koan is about nuns from the convent of Tokeiji who, while sitting zazen in front of a mirror, concentrate on the question, "Where is the single feeling, a single thought, in the mirror image at which I gaze?" The koan ends with a verse that was composed by one of the abbesses: "Heart unclouded, heart clouded; standing or falling, it is still the same body." "The Zen Mirror of Tokeiji," 128–30.

91. Manuel, *Tell Me Something about Buddhism*, 51.

92. Manuel, *Tell Me Something about Buddhism*, 52.

93. Manuel, *Tell Me Something about Buddhism*, 54.

94. Manuel, "Zen Mirror of Tokeiji," 130.

95. Thanks to Osho for the clarification of this point.

Chapter Four: Rev. angel Kyodo williams— Waking Up, Staying Woke

1. If you visit the White Plum Asanga website, you'll see, for example, in the "About" tab, a link to their "Bearing Witness Council for George Floyd and All Those Who Have Suffered from Racial Injustice," "a living statement to the world on racial injustice"; https://whiteplum .org/bearing-witness-to-george-floyd-and-all-who-suffer-from-racial -injustice.

2. "Meet the Founder," Transformative Change, accessed June 15, 2019, https://transformativechange.org/founder.

3. See "Meet the Founder"; and John Demont, "The Radical Buddhism of Reverend angel Kyodo williams," *Lion's Roar*, March 8, 2019, https://www.lionsroar.com/love-and-justice-the-radical-buddhism-of-rev-angel-kyodo-williams.

4. "BBC's Bookstand," BBC Television, YouTube, November 13, 2018, httpo://www.youtube.com/watch?v=MuyInnpbAxo; originally aired April 16, 1963.

5. "angel Kyodo williams: The World Is Our Field of Practice," *On Being with Krista Tippett*, April 19, 2018, podcast, 50:55, https://onbeing.org/programs/the-world-is-our-field-of-practice-apr2018.

6. "What We Do," Transformative Change, accessed June 15, 2019, https://transformativechange.org/about-us/what-we-do.

7. See "Remarks by the President Upon Arrival": "Our nation was horrified, but it's not going to be terrorized. We're a great nation. We're a nation of resolve. We're a nation that can't be cowed by evildoers." South Lawn, White House, Washington, DC, September 16, 2021, 3:23 EDT, https://georgewbush-whitehouse.archives.gov/news/releases/2001/09/20010916-2.html.

8. angel Kyodo williams, *Being Black: Zen and the Art of Living with Fearlessness and Grace* (New York; Viking Compass, 2000), 169.

9. williams, *Being Black*, 173.

10. Claudia Rankine, "The Condition of Black Life Is One of Mourning," in *The Fire This Time: A New Generation Speaks about Race*, ed. Jesmyn Ward (New York; Scribner, 2016), 150.

11. Jasmine Syedullah, *Radical Dharma: Talking Race, Love, and Liberation* (Berkeley, CA: North Atlantic Books, 2016), 19.

12. williams, *Being Black*, 75. *Oryoki*, which translates as "just enough," synchronizes mind and body through bringing awareness to how we eat. See John Kain, "Eating Just the Right Amount," Fall 2003, *Tricycle: The Buddhist Review*, https://tricycle.org/magazine/eating-just-right-amount.

13. williams, *Radical Dharma*, 27.

14. williams, *Radical Dharma*, 28.

15. williams, *Radical Dharma*, 29.

16. williams, *Being Black*, 3–4.

17. williams, *Radical Dharma*, 29.

18. williams, *Radical Dharma*, 32.

19. williams, *Radical Dharma*, 32.

20. williams, *Being Black*, 29–30.

21. williams, *Radical Dharma*, 33.

22. williams, *Being Black*, 45.

23. williams, *Being Black*, 45.

24. Tracy Curtis, "Born Into This Body: Black Women's Use of Buddhism in Autobiographical Narratives," in *New Media in Black Women's Autobiography* (New York: Palgrave Macmillan, 2015), 189.

25. Curtis, "Born Into This Body," 189.

26. Curtis, Born Into this Body," 196.

27. williams, *Being Black*, 176.

28. williams, *Being Black*, 176.

29. "angel Kyodo williams: The World Is Our Field of Practice."

30. bell hooks, "A Public Dialogue between bell hooks and Cornel West," New School for Liberal Arts, October 10, 2014, YouTube video, 1:27:01, https://www.youtube.com/watch?v=_LLok6_pPKw&t=2107s.

31. Toni Morrison, *Beloved* (New York: Alfred Knopf, 2019), 88–89.

32. williams, *Being Black*, 167.

33. James Baldwin, "Who Is the Nigger?" from *Take This Hammer*, directed by Richard O. Moore (New York: National Education Television, 1964); excerpt, April 24, 2010, YouTube video, 3:02, https://www.youtube.com/watch?v=LoL5fciA6AU.

34. Baldwin, "Who Is the Nigger?"

35. williams, *Being Black*, 167.

36. "James Baldwin and Nikki Giovanni: A Conversation," SOUL! And shoutfactorytv, London, November 1971, YouTube video, 1:56:41, September 9, 2022, https://www.youtube.com/watch?v=y4OPYp4sotc.

37. Cornel West, "A Public Dialogue between bell hooks and Cornel West," New School for Liberal Arts, October 10, 2014, YouTube video, 1:27:01, https://www.youtube.com/watch?v=_LLok6_pPKw&t=2107s. bell hooks, who is standing beside him when he makes the remark, counters his assessment saying that she would call it "colonized."

38. "angel Kyodo williams: The World Is Our Field of Practice."

39. williams, *Being Black*, 167; Curtis, "Born Into This Body," 195.

40. williams, *Being Black*, 167–68; Curtis, "Born Into This Body," 195.

41. "Buddhism in Black America Charles Johnson and Lama Rangdröl," April 10, 2018, YouTube video, 1:31:08, https://www.youtube.com /watch?v=wWDsgpmiq2o.

42. "James Baldwin and Nikki Giovanni: A Conversation."

43. williams, *Being Black*, 64.

44. williams, *Being Black*, 65.

45. williams, *Being Black*, 65.

46. williams, *Being Black*, 66. As a term this is closely related to what Gloria Anzaldúa calls "spiritual activism" but from within an African American experience, given the association of African American people and men, especially, with a warrior spirit that favors aggression over peace-seeking. See Gloria E. Anzaldúa, *Interviews/Entrevistas*, ed. AnaLouise Keating (New York: Routledge, 2000), 38, 178.

47. williams, *Being Black*, 66.

48. Quoted in Christopher S. Queen, ed. *Engaged Buddhism in the West* (Somerville, MA: Wisdom Publications, 2000), 6.

49. Born enslaved in 1766 Toussaint earned his freedom and became a noted philanthropist to the poor people of New York City. He is venerable in the Catholic tradition.

50. williams, *Being Black*, 83.

51. Adeana McNicholl, "Being Buddha, Staying Woke: Racial Formation in Black Buddhist Writing," *Journal of the American Academy of Religion* 86, no. 4 (December 2018): 907.

52. bell hooks did something similar in *Belonging*. See chapter 3.

53. bell hooks, *All about Love: New Visions* (New York: William Morrow, 2000), 14.

54. "angel Kyodo williams: The World Is Our Field of Practice."

55. "angel Kyodo williams: The World Is Our Field of Practice."

56. williams, *Being Black*, 143.

57. williams, *Being Black*, 145.

58. "Rev. angel Kyodo williams," *Metta Hour Podcast*, episode 42, October 10, 2016, https://www.sharonsalzberg.com/metta-hour-podcast -episode-42-rev-angel-kyodo-williams.

59. williams, *Being Black*, 145–47.

60. "Why Meditation Is Not Enough: Rev. angel Kyodo Williams," *CTZN-WELL Podcast with Kerri Kelly*, accessed June 16, 2019, https://www.ctznwell.org/ctznpodcast/angel-kyodo-williams.

61. "Why Meditation Is Not Enough: Rev. angel Kyodo williams."

62. "Why Meditation Is Not Enough: Rev. angel Kyodo williams."

63. Aisha, "Radical Dharma: Talking Race, Love and Liberation Is the Book for Right Now" Autostraddle, November 15, 2016, https://www.autostraddle.com/radical-dharma-talking-race-love-and-liberation-is-the-book-for-right-now-357012.

64. Dr. Rima Vesely-Flad and I are on the same wavelength in thinking about Rev. angel's work. Although she goes much further than I do in her excellent treatment of several Black Buddhists' orientations in her book *Black Buddhists and the Black Radical Tradition: The Practice of Stillness in the Movement for Liberation* (New York: New York University Press, 2022).

65. Kehinde Andrews, *Back to Black: Retelling Black Radicalism for the 21st Century* (London: Zed Books, 2018), xxii.

66. C. L. Griffin and Angela Y. Davis in *Afro-American Orators: A Bio-Critical Sourcebook*, ed. Richard W. Leeman (Westport, CT: Greenwood Press, 1996).

67. Angela Y. Davis, *Freedom Is a Constant Struggle: Ferguson, Palestine, and the Foundations of a Movement* (Chicago: Haymarket Books, 2016), 7.

68. Andrews, *Back to Black*, xvii.

69. williams, *Radical Dharma*, xxiii.

70. "How You Can Transform Race in Your Circles, Centers, Communities, Congregations (with a Framework That Works for You Not Against You) and Even Have Fun," March 28, 2019, https://programs.revangel.com/register-rd-summer-2019. This is the registration page for a webinar to introduce a Radical Dharma camp that was to be held that summer.

71. williams, *Radical Dharma*, xxiii.

72. williams, *Radical Dharma*, 107.

73. williams, *Radical Dharma*, 108.

74. Jasmine Syedullah, "How You Can Transform Race in Your Circles, Centers, Communities, Congregations (with a Framework That

Works for You Not Against You) and Even Have Fun." Dr. Syedullah made this statement during the webinar.

75. williams, *Radical Dharma*, xii.

76. williams, *Radical Dharma*, v.

77. Khaleda Rahman, "Full List of 229 Black People Killed by Police Since George Floyd's Murder," *Newsweek*, May 25, 2021, https://www.newsweek.com/full-list-229-black-people-killed-police-since-george-floyds-murder 1594477.

78. Alana Wise, "It's Been Two Years Since George Floyd Was Murdered by Police in Minneapolis," *Morning Edition*, NPR, May 25, 2022, https://www.npr.org/2022/05/25/1101141297/its-been-2-years-since-george-floyd-was-murdered-by-police-in-minneapolis.

79. John Demont, "The Radical Buddhism of Rev. angel Kyodo williams," *Lion's Roar*, March 8, 2019, https://www.lionsroar.com/love-and-justice-the-radical-buddhism-of-rev-angel-kyodo-williams.

80. angel Kyodo williams, "Where Will You Stand?" *Lion's Roar*, November 10, 2017, https://www.lionsroar.com/where-will-you-stand. See also "There Is No Neutral," *Radical Dharma*, xxiv–xxvi.

81. williams, "Where Will You Stand?"

82. williams, *Being Black*, 1.

83. williams, "Where Will You Stand?"

84. Stokely Carmichael, *Stokely Speaks: From Black Power to Pan-Africanism* (New York: Vintage Books, 1971), 206.

85. See "Reparations for Slavery Reading," Constitutional Rights Foundation, accessed December 11, 2022, https://www.crf-usa.org/brown-v-board-50th-anniversary/reparations-for-slavery-reading.html.

86. williams, "How You Can Transform Race in Your Circles, Centers, Communities, Congregations." Some repetition has been edited out to facilitate the flow of Rev. angel's words.

87. williams, "How You Can Transform Race in Your Circles, Centers, Communities, Congregations."

88. The Radical Dharma Five are contemplative approach, embodied practice, liberatory path, prophetic praxis, and collective process.

89. See, for example, "Letter from Rev. angel: LIB5 Challenge," Rev. angel Kyodo Williams (website), accessed December 11, 2022, https://angelkyodowilliams.com/letter-from-rev-angel-lib5-challenge.

90. Quoted in McNicholl, "Being Buddha, Staying Woke," 885.
91. McNicholl, "Being Buddha, Staying Woke," 885.
92. McNicholl, "Being Buddha, Staying Woke," 885.
93. McNicholl, "Being Buddha, Staying Woke," 885.
94. williams, "How You Can Transform Race in Your Circles, Centers, Communities, Congregations."
95. williams, "How You Can Transform Race in Your Circles, Centers, Communities, Congregations."
96. williams, "How You Can Transform Race in Your Circles, Centers, Communities, Congregations."
97. "Rev. angel Kyodo williams."
98. "Rev. angel Kyodo williams," 42:30–44:30.
99. "Rev. angel Kyodo williams," 45:17–45:30.
100. "Rev. angel Kyodo williams," 54:00–55:09
101. Demont, "Radical Buddhism of Reverend angel Kyodo williams."
102. Demont, "Radical Buddhism of Reverend angel Kyodo williams."
103. Demont, "Radical Buddhism of Reverend angel Kyodo williams."

Chapter Five: Spring Washam—A Lotus in the Mud

1. Spring Washam, *A Fierce Heart: Finding Strength, Courage and Wisdom in Any Moment* (Berkeley, CA: Parallax Press, 2017), 5.
2. Thich Nhat Hanh, *No Mud, No Lotus: The Art of Transforming Suffering* (Berkeley, CA: Parallax Press, 2014), 13.
3. I don't know of a nongendered word for *hero/heroine*, but if I did, I'd include that as well. From this point in my discussion of the personal experiences Spring relates in her text, however, I will refer to them simply as part of the heroine's journey since Spring identifies herself as a woman.
4. Washam, *Fierce Heart*, 2.
5. Washam, *Fierce Heart*, 2.
6. Washam, *Fierce Heart*, 1.
7. Washam, *Fierce Heart*, 2.
8. Washam, *Fierce Heart*, 107.
9. Washam, *Fierce Heart*, 101.
10. DaRa Williams, Deep Time Liberation Retreat, May 13–16, 2021.

Accessed online via Zoom. Williams remarks came during a whole participant session.

11. Washam, *Fierce Heart*, 101.

12. Washam, *Fierce Heart*, 107.

13. Washam, *Fierce Heart*, 116.

14. Spring Washam, *The Spirit of Harriet Tubman: Awakening from the Underground* (Carlsbad, CA: Hay House, 2023), 19.

15. In 2014 I also read Paramahansa Yogananda's autobiography during a summer of traveling around Haiti and was transformed.

16. Washam, *Fierce Heart*, 13.

17. Washam, *Fierce Heart*, 140.

18. "Radical Inclusivity Practices," East Bay Meditation Center (website), accessed July 11, 2020, https://eastbaymeditation.org/about/radical -inclusivity/radical-inclusivity-practices.

19. Washam, *Fierce Heart*, 141.

20. Washam, *Fierce Heart*, 146.

21. Sharpe not only identifies him as a civil rights leader but as a person of color who was a social radical. See "The Buddha Was a Person of Color: An Interview with Gina Sharpe," *Tricycle: The Buddhist Review*, August 20, 2012.

22. Washam, *Fierce Heart*, 147.

23. Washam, *Fierce Heart*, 150.

24. Washam, *Fierce Heart*, 150.

25. Jack Kornfield, *Buddha's Little Instruction Book* (New York: Bantam Books, 1994), 77.

26. Arnold van Gennep, *The Rites of Passage* (Chicago: University of Chicago Press, 1966), 21.

27. Joseph Campbell, *The Hero with a Thousand Faces* (Novato, CA: New World Library, 2008), 6.

28. Washam, *Fierce Heart*, 95.

29. Washam, *Fierce Heart*, 95–96.

30. Joseph Goldstein, "The Example of the Buddha: Relating the Life of the Buddha to Our Own," *Tricycle: The Buddhist Review*, accessed March 19, 2023, https://tricycle.org/magazine/the-example-of-the -buddha.

31. Washam, *Fierce Heart*, 163.

32. Washam, *Fierce Heart*, 163.

33. Washam, *Fierce Heart*, 165.

34. angel Kyodo williams, *Being Black: Zen and the Art of Living with Fearlessness and Grace* (New York: Penguin Compass, 2000), 83–84.

35. Washam, *Fierce Heart*, 163.

36. Washam, *Fierce Heart*, 164.

37. Washam, *Fierce Heart*, 165.

38. Alice Walker, "This Was Not an Area of Large Plantations," in *We Are the Ones We Have Been Waiting For: Inner Light in a Time of Darkness—Meditations* (New York: New Press, 2006), 99. Emphasis in original.

39. Walker, "This Was Not an Area of Large Plantations," 50.

40. Washam, *Fierce Heart*, 84.

41. Washam, *Fierce Heart*, 84.

42. Washam, *Fierce Heart*, 86.

43. Washam, *Fierce Heart*, 86–87.

44. Thich Nhat Hanh, *Love Letter to the Earth* (Berkeley, CA: Parallax Press, 2013), 8.

45. Washam, *Spirit of Harriet Tubman*, 20.

46. Washam, *Spirit of Harriet Tubman*, 21.

47. Washam, *Fierce Heart*, 87.

48. "The Dharma of Harriet Tubman—Spring Washam," *Ten Percent Happier with Dan Harris*, episode 257, June 17, 2020, https://podcasts.apple .com/bs/podcast/the-dharma-of-harriett-tubman-spring-washam /id1087147821?i=1000478303714.

49. "Dharma of Harriet Tubman—Spring Washam."

50. https://www.springwasham.com/events/2020/7/19/the-church-of -harriet-tubman-amp-the-underground-railroad-crew, accessed May 29, 2021. The website has since been replaced by Spring's updated website. See https://www.springwasham.com/harriet-tubman.

51. Warren Crichlow, "Baldwin's Rendezvous with the Twenty-First Century: *I Am Not Your Negro*," *Film Quarterly* 70, no. 4 (Summer 2017): 9.

Chapter Six: Faith Adiele—Finding Faith

1. Hereafter referred to as *The Nigerian-Nordic*.

2. Leah Samuel, "Finding Faith," *Harvard Magazine*, November–

December 2004, https://www.harvardmagazine.com/2004/11/
finding-faith.html.

3. "Meet the Writer Behind the Sleep Story: Faith Adiele," Calm, February 17, 2021, https://blog.calm.com/blog/meet-the-writer-behind-the
-sleep-story-faith-adiele.

4. I use the two women's first names in this opening section to distinguish between mother and daughter. I use Adiele's last name once I
begin my discussion of her teenage years and beyond.

5 Faith Adiele, "Civilization," *Literal Latte* (December 1999/January
2000): 12.

6 Adiele, "Civilization," 12.

7. Faith Adiele, "Locating Biafra: The Words We Wouldn't Say," in
Names We Call Home: Autobiography on Racial Identity, ed. Becky
Thompson and Sangeeta Tyagi (New York: Routledge, 1996), 76.

8. Adiele, "Locating Biafra," 81.

9. Faith Adiele, *Meeting Faith: The Forest Journals of a Black Buddhist
Nun* (New York: W. W. Norton, 2004), 109.

10. Adiele, *Meeting Faith*, 109.

11. Adiele, *Meeting Faith*, 112.

12. Adiele, *Meeting Faith*, 112.

13. Adiele, *Meeting Faith*, 112.

14. Adiele, *Meeting Faith*, 102.

15. Adiele, *Meeting Faith*, 113.

16. Adiele, *Meeting Faith*, 98.

17. Adiele, *Meeting Faith*, 110.

18. This is a painfully brief summary of a very long history. For more
reading on this topic, see Tameka Ellington and Joseph L. Under-
wood, *Textures: The History and Art of Black Hair* (Munich: Hirmer,
2020).

19. Adiele, *Meeting Faith*, 98.

20. Adiele, *Meeting Faith*, 110.

21. Samuel, "Finding Faith."

22. Samuel, "Finding Faith."

23. Samuel, "Finding Faith."

24. Adiele, *Meeting Faith*, 13.

25. Adiele, *Meeting Faith*, 14.

26. *My Journey Home: Faith's Story*, written by Faith Adiele, directed by Renee Tajima-Pena (Washington, DC: WETA-TV, 2004).

27. The insight meditation tradition in the US, of which several leading Black Buddhists are a part, is a heavily Westernized adaptation of the Southeast Asian Theravada that Adiele trained in.

28. Adiele, *Meeting Faith*, 88.

29. *Bhikkhuni* means "she who has received higher ordination, alms-woman, female monk." A *bhikkhu* is a monk. Adiele, *Meeting Faith*, 90.

30. Adiele, *Meeting Faith*, 123.

31. Adiele, *Meeting Faith*, 93–94.

32. Adiele, *Meeting Faith*, 94.

33. Adiele, *Meeting Faith*, 94.

34. Adiele, *Meeting Faith*, 97.

35. Adiele, *Meeting Faith*, 97.

36. Adiele, *Meeting Faith*, 97.

37. Adiele, *Meeting Faith*, 98.

38. Adiele, *Meeting Faith*, 98–99.

39. Adiele, *Meeting Faith*, 99.

40. Adiele, *Meeting Faith*, 102.

41. Adiele, *Meeting Faith*, 103.

42. Adiele, *Meeting Faith*, 111.

43. Adiele, *Meeting Faith*, 113.

44. Curtis, "Born Into This Body," 189–90.

45. Adiele, *Meeting Faith*, 274.

46. Adiele, *Meeting Faith*, 280.

47. This is the way advice is written in Adiele's text, which I see as commentary on the off-handed way with which fibroids are treated by medical staff.

48. Black women are up to five times more likely to suffer with fibroids. Faith Adiele, *The Nigerian-Nordic Girl's Guide to Lady Problems* (Bronx, NY: Shebooks, 2013), Kindle, loc. 99.

49. Dollar cabs are wonderful examples of Black ingenuity and creativity. A person, usually a man, with a van, picks people up from bus stops and for a fraction of the cost of bus fare, takes commuters along the bus route to their destinations. In a Ghanaian context, they're called *tro tros*. In a Haitian context, *tap taps*.

50. Fibroids can grow very large, with the largest recorded one weighing in at 140 pounds. Adiele, *Nigerian-Nordic Girl's Guide to Lady Problems*, loc. 31.
51. Adiele, *Nigerian-Nordic Girl's Guide to Lady Problems*, loc. 20.
52. Adiele, *Nigerian-Nordic Girl's Guide to Lady Problems*, loc. 24.
53. Adiele, *Nigerian-Nordic Girl's Guide to Lady Problems*, loc. 20–24.
54. Adiele, *Nigerian-Nordic Girl's Guide to Lady Problems*, loc. 195.
55. Adiele, *Nigerian-Nordic Girl's Guide to Lady Problems*, loc. 172.
56. Adiele, *Nigerian-Nordic Girl's Guide to Lady Problems*, loc. 241.
57. There are, of course, other reasons. A full discussion of those reasons are outside the purview of this project. For its impact on Black women, in particular, see Nandita Rose, "Roe v Wade Ruling Disproportionately Hurts Black Women, Experts Say," Reuters, July 27, 2022, https://www.reuters.com/world/us/roe-v-wade-ruling-disproportionately -hurts-black-women-experts-say-2022-06-27; or Michelle Goodwin, "The Racist History of Abortion and Midwifery Bans," ACLU, July 1, 2020, https://www.aclu.org/news/racial-justice/the-racist-history -of-abortion-and-midwifery-bans.
58. Adiele, *Nigerian-Nordic Girl's Guide to Lady* Problems, loc. 394.
59. See Diedre Copper Owens, *Medical Bondage: Race, Gender and the Origins of American Gynecology* (Athens: University of Georgia Press, 2017); and Rachel Zellars, "Black Subjectivity and the Origins of American Gynecology," Black Perspectives, May 31, 2018, https://www.aaihs.org/black-subjectivity-and-the-origins-of-american -gynecology/.
60. Adiele, *Nigerian-Nordic Girl's Guide to Lady* Problems, loc. 376.
61. Adiele, *Nigerian-Nordic Girl's Guide to Lady Problems*, loc. 380.
62. Adiele, *Nigerian-Nordic Girl's Guide to Lady Problems*, loc. 387.
63. Adiele, *Nigerian-Nordic Girl's Guide to Lady Problems*, loc. 399.
64. Audre Lorde, *A Burst of Light and Other Essays* (Mineola, NY: Ixia Press, 1988), 130.

Chapter Seven: Buddhism and Black Women

1. The film starred Spencer Tracy as the father, Katharine Hepburn as the mother, Katharine Houghton as the daughter, and Sidney Poitier

as the fiancé. *Guess Who's Coming to Dinner*, directed by Stanley Kramer (Culver City, CA: Columbia Pictures, 1967).

2. Carol Cooper, "Guess Who's Coming to Dharma: Black Women Embrace Western Buddhism," *Village Voice*, July 3, 2001.

3. I use "Western convert Buddhism" to be expedient here, but more information about the ongoing debates around who and what constitutes "Western convert Buddhism" can be found in Ann Gleig's study, *American Dharma: Buddhism Beyond Modernity* (New Haven, CT: Yale University Press, 2019), 35–36. Some leading scholars who have weighed in are Charles S. Prebish, Kenneth Tanaka, Duncan Ryuken Williams, Richard Hughes Seager, and Christopher S. Queen. Although there are concerns about the distinction that Jan Nattier makes between what she calls "import, export, and baggage Buddhism" with regard to the way that racism and white privilege have operated under the distinctions she makes, she moved beyond the dichotomy of Buddhism as either "heritage Buddhism" associated with Asian American Buddhists and that associated with elite Euro-American Buddhists. She also tried to account for the fact that convert Buddhists can also be African American, Latinx, and Asian Americans who came from other religious or secular backgrounds.

4. hooks remarks that she believes that people are disturbed "not by a black presence, but rather by a black presence that seeks to revolutionize and democratize." Cooper, "Guess Who's Coming to Dharma."

5. Yes, that phrase should be doubled. It comments on the reflective act that is so important to inner exploration through meditation.

6. Cooper, "Guess Who's Coming to Dharma."

7. Cooper, "Guess Who's Coming to Dharma."

8. Analouise Keating, ed., "Shifting Perspectives: Spiritual Activism, Social Transformation, and the Politics of Spirit," in *Entre Mundos / Among Worlds: New Perspectives on Gloria Anzaldúa* (New York: Palgrave Macmillan, 2005), 244.

9. Doreen McCallister, "Report: Death Threat Forces Rep. Maxine Waters to Cancel Events in Texas and Alabama," NPR, https://www.npr.org/2018/06/29/624558078/report-death-threat-forces-rep-maxine-waters-to-cancel-events-in-texas-and-alaba, June 29, 2018.

10. Christopher S. Queen, *Engaged Buddhism in the West* (Somerville,

MA: Wisdom Publications, 2000), 1. Indeed, in Donald S. Lopez Jr.'s reading of the bodhisattva vow, he notes, "It does not portray the bodhisattva as a political organizer. And . . . we do not find significant evidence in the premodern period of acts of charity performed by Buddhist monastics. Where real giving, in the real world, becomes important in Buddhism, it is not giving to the lay community; it is giving to the monastic community." See Donald S. Lopez Jr., "Buddhism and the Real World," *Tricycle. The Buddhist Review* (Summer 2021) https://tricycle.org/magazine/history-of-buddhism-and-activism.

11. Queen, *Engaged Buddhism in the West*, 2.

12. Rima Vesely-Flad, "Black Buddhists and the Body: New Approaches to Socially Engaged Buddhism," *Religions* 8, no. 11 (October 2017), 239.

13. Vesely-Flad, "Black Buddhists and the Body," 239.

14. Vesely-Flad, "Black Buddhists and the Body," 239.

15. Rima Vesely-Flad, "Racism and Anatta: Black Buddhists, Embodiment, and Interpretations of Non-Self," in *Buddhism and Whiteness: Critical Reflections*, ed. George Yancy and Emily McRae (Lanham, MD: Lexington Books, 2019), 79–97.

16. Vesely-Flad, "Black Buddhists and the Body," 239.

17. Vesely-Flad, "Black Buddhists and the Body," 239.

18. I am drawing from the many meanings of the word *wake* that Christina Sharpe explores in *In the Wake: On Blackness and Being* (Durham, NC: Duke University Press, 2016), two being "the aftermath" and as the ritual that is part of the work of laying a loved one to rest.

19. Vesely-Flad, "Black Buddhists and the Body," 239.

20. Gleig, *American Dharma*, 3, 175.

21. I have heard this sentiment expressed by several dharma teachers of color that I have meditated under.

22. "Interview with Sister Peace, Plum Village Monastic," in *Walk with Me*, written and directed by Marc J. Francis and Max Pugh (London: Speakit Films, 2017), extras.

23. "Radical Self-Care: Angela Davis," AfroPunk, December 17, 2018, YouTube, 4:27, https://www.youtube.com/watch?v=Q1cHoL4vaBs&list=WL&index=162&t=122s.

24. DaRa Williams, Kamilah Majied, and Willie Mukei Smith, "Black American Buddhists on Activism and Community" (panel discussion, Rubin Museum of Art, New York, NY, July 24, 2019).
25. Williams, "Black American Buddhists on Activism and Community.'"
26. According to the website, "Deep Time Liberation delves into the exploration of how our ancestral legacy and historical beliefs influence our present lives. Once we understand the need for committing to our individual and collective healing, the pathway to healing appears. We can then recognize and acknowledge the experiences and history clouding our perceptions causing us to continually cause harm to ourselves and others because of our reactions. Identifying the genesis of our suffering comes in part from the intergenerational and vicarious traumas known or unknown, past or present. The attachments, the delusion and the aversion that we've experienced blocks the portal to healing and the way out is through the recognition and honoring of our historical harm. Deep Time Liberation will engage you in rituals, story-telling, drumming and discovery through the lens of Insight Meditation practices." "About," Deep Time Liberation (website), accessed July 27, 2022, https://www.deeptimelib.org /about. I was scheduled to attend a retreat in May 2020 when the pandemic hit. Through the magic of Zoom, I very gratefully participated in one of the retreats in winter 2020. Although we participated from a distance, the organizers were able to create an intimate experience, going so far as to mail retreaters materials to build a sacred space in our own homes.
27. Zenju Earthlyn Manuel, *The Way of Tenderness: Awakening through Race, Sexuality, and Gender* (Somerville, MA: Wisdom Publications, 2015), 106–7.
28. Manuel, *Way of Tenderness*, 107.
29. Manuel, *Way of Tenderness*, 107. As Bhikkhu Bodhi explains, the Buddha teaches that the enduring self, the self-subsistent entity, independently existing, is a delusion. When we investigate our own experience using the tools of mindfulness and investigative wisdom, we cannot find that self-subsistent ego entity. Rather, we find a constant process of ever-changing events which can be the bodily events or physical process which we call the body and then the

mental process which can be dissected into different components of feeling, perception, acts of volition, and then the awareness of this or consciousness. It's a constellation of different constituents of experience that are always arising and passing away and which all exist in dependence on conditions. Seeing this knocks away the underlying premise or assumption or grasping that we have a self-subsistence ego entity, the underlying root of suffering, the basis for craving. "The Words of the Buddha," *Ten Percent Happier with Dan Harris*, podcast, episode 302, 01:11:38, Nov. 23, 2020, https://www.tenpercent.com /podcast-episode/bhikkhu-bodhi-302.

30. Devin Berry, personal communication, May 16, 2021.
31. Thich Nhat Hanh, *The Other Shore: A New Translation of the Heart Sutra with Commentaries* (Berkeley, CA: Palm Leaves Press, 2017), 27–29. In his article "'There Is No Self': 'Nope, Never Said That Either'—The Buddha," Thanissaro Bhikkhu explains that "'there is no self' is the granddaddy of fake Buddhist quotes, which has survived so long because of its superficial resemblance to *anatta*, or not-self, which was one of the Buddha's tools for putting an end to clinging." *Tricycle: The Buddhist Review*, Spring 2014, https://tricycle.org /magazine/there-no-self.
32. Patricia Hunt-Perry and Lyn Fine, "All Buddhism Is Engaged," in *Engaged Buddhism in the West*, ed. Christopher Queen (Somerville, MA: Wisdom Publications, 2000), 47.
33. Hunt-Perry and Fine, "All Buddhism Is Engaged," 47–48.
34. While the beating of King was one of the first to be captured on camera and circulated worldwide, we can easily summon the past four hundred years of this country's founding and development based in genocide and the forced labor and oppression of the nonwhite body.
35. Carol Hanisch, "The Personal Is Political: The Women's Liberation Classic with a New Explanatory Introduction," February 1969, http:// www.carolhanisch.org/CHwritings/PIP.html.
36. Kimberlé Williams Crenshaw, "Mapping the Margins: Intersectionality, Identity, and Violence Against Women of Color," in *The Public Nature of Private Violence*, ed. Martha Albertson Fineman and Roxanne Mykitiuk (New York: Routledge, 1994), 93–118; https://www .racialequitytools.org/resourcefiles/mapping-margins.pdf.

37. john a. powell, *Racing to Justice: Transforming Our Conceptions of Self and Other to Build an Inclusive Society* (Bloomington: University of Indiana Press, 2012), 198.

38. Geneva Smitherman, *Talkin and Testifyin: The Language of Black America* (Detroit, MI: Wayne State University Press, 1986), 151.

39. Smitherman, *Talkin and Testifyin*, 151.

40. DoVeanna S. Fulton, *Speaking Power: Black Feminist Orality in Women's Narratives* (Albany: SUNY Press, 2006), xi.

41. Toni Morrison, "Rootedness: The Ancestor as Foundation," in *Black Women Writers 1950–1980: A Critical Evaluation*, ed. Mari Evans (New York: Anchor Books, 1984), 341.

42. powell, *Racing to Justice*, 197.

43. Alice Walker, "This Was Not an Area of Large Plantations: Suffering Too Insignificant for the Majority to See," in *We Are the Ones We Have Been Waiting For: Inner Light in a Time of Darkness* (New York: New Press, 2006), 93. A talk by the same name, published in *Lion's Roar*, is a variation of that in her collection. The article in *Lion's Roar* is titled "Suffering Too Insignificant for the Majority to See," May 1, 2007, https://www.lionsroar.com/suffering-too-insignificant-for-the -majority-to-see. "Feminism" is capitalized in the original.

44. Although this was not the first time that Walker had used the term *womanist*, it first appeared in her 1979 short story "Coming Apart," in *In Search of Our Mothers' Gardens* (Orlando, FL: Harvest, 1983), where she defined the term and introduced it to the general public.

45. See Patricia Hill Collins, "Sisters and Brothers: Black Feminists on Womanism," in *The Womanist Reader*, ed. Layli Phillips (New York: Routledge, 2006), 59.

46. "Combahee River Collective Statement" in Keeanga-Yamahtta Taylor, ed., *How We Get Free: Black Feminism and the Combahee River Collective* (Chicago: Haymarket Books, 2017), 18. It is outside the purview of this text to explore the similarities and differences between "womanism" and "black feminism." Layli Phillips, in her excellent introduction to *The Womanist Reader*, does a thorough delineation of the "womanist" concept as well as its relationship to "black feminism."

47. Walker, "This Was Not an Area of Large Plantations," 94.

48. Alice Walker, "Womanist," in *The Womanist Reader*, ed. Layli Phillips (New York: Routledge, 2006), 19.

49. Walker, "Womanist." 19.

50. Curry reportedly suffered from paranoid schizophrenia at the time. In fact, illustrating his deep commitment to love, from his hospital bed as he recovered from surgery to remove the letter opener blade that she had plunged into his chest, King issued a press release in which he reaffirmed his belief in "the redemptive power of nonviolence," stating, "I felt no ill will toward Mrs. Izola Currey [sic] and know that thoughtful people will do all in their power to see that she gets the help she apparently needs if she is to become a free and constructive member of society." See "MLK: A Close Call in Harlem," The Smoking Gun, accessed April 27, 2019, http://www.thesmokinggun.com/file/mlk-close-call-harlem?page=0.

51. Martin Luther King, Jr., "Loving Your Enemies," in *Strength to Love* (Philadelphia: Fortress Press, 1963), 36.

52. King, "Loving Your Enemies," 36–37.

53. Walker, "This Was Not an Area of Large Plantations," 106.

Chapter Eight: The African American Autobiographical Tradition and Its Legacy

1. William Lloyd Garrison, preface to *Narrative of the Life of Frederick Douglass* (New York: Dover Publications, Inc., 1995), vii.

2. Douglass, *Narrative of the Life of Frederick Douglass*, 69.

3. Henry Louis Gates, ed., introduction to *Bearing Witness: Selections from African-American Autobiography in the Twentieth Century* (New York: Pantheon, 1991), 4.

4. Toni Morrison, "The Site of Memory," https://blogs.umass.edu/brusert/files/2013/03/Morrison_Site-of-Memory.pdf, 91.

5. Morrison, "Site of Memory," 93.

6. I make a distinction here between "History" as an example of a master narrative, authoritative and in the service of hegemony, and "histories," more inclusive and respectful of different, equally valid perspectives and a tool of liberation of marginalized groups.

7. Morrison, "Site of Memory," 91–92.

8. Morrison, "Site of Memory," 92.
9. Indeed, the fickle nature of memory is witnessed in the sometimes conflicting accounts of his life that Frederick Douglass provided in his three autobiographies.
10. One of the earliest was by Briton Hammon. See https://docsouth.unc.edu/neh/hammon/hammon.html.
11. Stephen Butterfield, *Black Autobiography in America* (Amherst: University of Massachusetts, 1974), 2.
12. Butterfield, *Black Autobiography in America*, 2.
13. Butterfield, *Black Autobiography*, 2.
14. Gates, *Bearing Witness*, 3.
15. James Baldwin, "Sonny's Blues," in *The Jazz Fiction Anthology*, ed. Sascha Feinstein and David Rife (Bloomington: Indiana University Press, 2009), 47.
16. Gates, *Bearing Witness*, 7.
17. Gates, *Bearing Witness*, 7. Emphasis added.
18. See, for example, Jay Jarvis Masters, *That Bird Has My Wings: The Autobiography of an Innocent Man on Death Row* (New York: HarperOne, 2009); Calvin Malone, *Razor-Wire Dharma: A Buddhist Life in Prison* (Somerville, MA: Wisdom Publications, 2008); Lama Choyin Rangdröl, *Black Buddha: Changing the Face of American Buddhism* (San Rafael, CA: Rainbowdharma, 2007); Ralph Steele, *Tending the Fire: Through War and the Path of Meditation* (Los Gatos, CA: Smashwords, 2014); Charles Johnson, *Taming the Ox: Buddhist Stories and Reflections on Politics, Race, Culture, and Spiritual Practice* (Boston: Shambhala Publications, 2014) and *Turning the Wheel: Essays on Buddhism and Writing* (New York: Scribner, 2003); and Lama Rod Owens, *Love and Rage: The Path of Liberation through Anger* (Berkeley, CA: North Atlantic Books, 2020).
19. Angela Y. Davis, *Freedom Is a Constant Struggle: Ferguson, Palestine, and the Foundations of a Movement* (Chicago: Haymarket Books, 2016), 4.
20. These are, of course, just a few aspects of my identity.
21. Marianne Dresser, *Buddhist Women on the Edge: Contemporary Perspectives from the Western Frontier* (Berkeley, CA: North Atlantic Books, 1996), xv.

22. "The Combahee River Statement," in *How We Get Free: Black Feminism and the Combahee River Collective*, ed. Keeanga-Yamahtta Taylor (Chicago: Haymarket Books, 2017), 22–23.

23. DaRa Williams, Kamilah Majied, and Willie Mukei Smith, "Black American Buddhists on Activism and Community" (panel discussion, Rubin Museum of Art, New York, NY, July 24, 2019).

Conclusion

1. "Loving, Living, Learning: A Liberated Life Talk with Rev. angel Kyodo williams," *Black Girl in Om*, episode 44, podcast, 01:08:00, accessed March 20, 2023, https://www.blackgirlinom.com/podcast-blog/2019/6/loving-living-learning-a-liberated-life-talk-with-rev-angel-kyodo-williams.

2. In March 2016, the premier issue of *Lion's Roar* magazine (formerly *Shambhala Sun*) featured fourteen Buddhist teachers on its three-panel cover, under the heading "The New Face of Buddhism." Among those pictured were three black women: Rev. angel Kyodo williams, Kate Johnson, and Gina Sharpe. Based on the Buddha's teaching that the proclamation of the dharma is as fearless as a lion's roar, the teachers were asked to respond to the question: "What is the most important truth to proclaim in today's troubled world?" While the magazine publisher's intention was to be more inclusive in featuring a relatively diverse array of teachers, several members of the Buddhist community, led by the Buddhist Peace Fellowship (BPF), saw the need to unpack the issue's title and the selection of the featured teachers. See "5 Responses to the Awkwardly Titled 'New Face of Buddhism,'" *Buddhist Peace Fellowship*, January 27, 2016, bpf.org/blog/5-responses-to-the-new-face-of-buddhism.

3. "Loving, Living, Learning: A Liberated Life Talk with Rev. angel Kyodo williams."

4. "Loving, Living, Learning: A Liberated Life Talk with Rev. angel Kyodo williams."

5. "Loving, Living, Learning: A Liberated Life Talk with Rev. angel Kyodo williams."

6. I have phrased it this way in order to bring attention to the different

forms of power that exist, internally and externally. I think it is important to rethink what constitutes power in a way that accounts for both individual and collective power in seen and unseen worlds.

7. Thich Nhat Hanh, foreword to *Tell Me Something about Buddhism: Questions and Answers for the Curious Beginner*, by Zenju Earthlyn Manuel (Charlottesville, NC: Hampton Roads, 2011), xiii.

Index

Index